PRAISE FOR
BAMBOO SECRETS

Patricia Dove Miller writes with a lyrical pen, an open heart, and a deep connection to the natural world. *Bamboo Secrets* interlaces the beauty of Japanese art, music, and ceremony with the story of a personal journey through the shadows that can disrupt a woman's life and threaten her marriage.

— Judy Reeves, author of *Wild Women, Wild Voices*
and *A Writer's Book of Days*

Some people go to Japan seeking enlightenment, some the beauty of traditional disciplines. In *Bamboo Secrets*, Patricia Dove Miller chronicles her experience of these quests as they become entangled in the Japanese legal bureaucracy as a result of a drug bust. Unable to leave Japan, she sees her aesthetic dream turn into a nightmare, which she endures by engaging even more deeply with Japanese culture. This is a painfully honest and harrowing tale of personal and cultural awakening.

— Liza Dalby, anthropologist and author of *Geisha, Kimono, The Tale of Murasaki*, and *Hidden Buddhas*

Patricia Dove Miller has woven for us a tapestry as shaded with nuance as the Japanese culture itself. Propelled by bright moments of transcendence lyrically rendered, a gut-punching reversal of fortune, and a battle of wits with Kafkaesque bureaucracy, *Bamboo Secrets* draws us through a surprising saga that is, ultimately, as spiritually enriching as it is d   ls an important tale, and does so

In the Unlikely Event of a W

f
f

Bamboo Secrets precisely captures a common contradiction for foreigners in Japan: the traditional arts instill awe and insight, while the arcane bureaucracy and social conventions stymie and frustrate. Patricia Dove Miller accompanies her husband to Japan, thinking she will immerse herself in the noble, meditative traditions of the *shakuhachi* and ikebana. Instead, she suddenly finds herself thrust into a murky legal nightmare when her husband is detained on drug charges. Most expats in such a situation turn bitter and direct their negativity toward Japan. Not so for Miller, who, as a middle-aged artist struggling with career and marriage, transforms this excruciating experience into a path for personal growth. In her own words, she learns "to distinguish between the public legal face of Japan and the private artistic face." One she resents, the other she loves, but both form the framework for her salvation.

— Christopher Yohmei Blasdel, *shakuhachi* performer and teacher;
Artistic Director, International House of Japan, 1987–2013
(U.S.–Japan Creative Artists Program);
author of *The Shakuhachi: A Manual for Learning* and
The Single Tone: A Personal Journey into Shakuhachi Music

When I read *Bamboo Secrets*, I feel as if Patricia Dove Miller were born Japanese in a past life, to be able to recognize and appreciate so many aspects of Japanese culture. And yet, she also has to be an outsider to notice them. For me, her many evocative scenes bring back fond memories of growing up in Japan, when I smelled, saw, and felt these sensations. The scent of wet wool, on the long bus ride to her flute lesson, as she wipes off the foggy window, searching for the correct street signs; the eager innocence of the young women in the ikebana class; her *shakuhachi* sensei instructing her to use her heart as she listens and plays, instead of taking notes. Miller describes the healing power of art as she journeys full circle from her childhood, when her teacher tears up her drawings, to later in Japan when she discovers her own art forms. I recommend this memoir to anyone who wants to learn about Japanese culture and about finding one's own true heart.

— Takayo Miyazaki Harriman

BAMBOO SECRETS

ONE WOMAN'S QUEST

THROUGH THE

SHADOWS OF JAPAN

Patri. Dove

PATRICIA DOVE MILLER

Illuminated Owl Press
Nevada City, California

ISBN: 978-0-9972539-0-0
Library of Congress Control Number: 2016903202

COVER DESIGN: Shubin Design & Dovetail Publishing Services
COVER ART: *Bamboo and Plum Tree*, Ogata Kōrin, Edo period/ 18th century, two-fold screen, color on gold-leafed paper. Courtesy of Tokyo National Museum.
INTERIOR DESIGN: Joan Keyes, Dovetail Publishing Services

Printed in the United States of America

First Edition

Published by Illuminated Owl Press
Nevada City, California
IlluminatedOwlPress@oro.net
PatriciaDoveMiller.com

CONTENTS

For my mother, Virginia Elizabeth Dove Miller Russell,
who always believed in me.
(1906–2002)

AUTHOR'S NOTE

I have changed names and, in some cases, altered identifying characteristics or locations in order to protect each individual's privacy. I believe memory and truth are subjective. I have told this story as honestly as I am able, the best that I can remember it. Others may have their own versions.

The wet bamboo clacking in the night rain
crying in the darkness whimpering softly
as the hollow columns touch and slide
along each other swaying with the empty
air these are sounds from before there were voices
gestures older than grief from before there was
pain as we know it the impossibly tall
stems are reaching out groping and waving
before longing as we think of it or loss
as we are acquainted with it or feelings
able to recognize the syllables
that might be their own calling out to them
like names in the dark telling them nothing
about loss or about longing nothing
ever about all that has yet to answer.

— "Chorus" by W. S. Merwin

OVERTURE
The *Bunraku* Storyteller Chants a Bittersweet Tale

One muggy day in early May of 1992, I sat behind my huge desk, sweat dripping down my shoulder blades, arms folded across my chest, as I scowled at the chaos of the twenty-five second graders shouting and jumping in and out of their seats. I tried to stare them into silence, as my Aunt Bea, a longtime schoolteacher, had counseled me, but it wasn't working. From the other end of the room, my assistant glared at me in disdain, refusing to help, daring me to bring order. I was a brand-new teacher, having worked my way up from assistant-teacher, trying out yet another career at age fifty-one.

And yet I already knew I didn't belong—in this job, in this school. But what was I going to do instead? And how and when would I ever figure it out? Maybe during my upcoming year in Japan I'd find answers.

My husband Steven had already left two weeks earlier, to begin his anthropology research at the university in Kyoto. Only thirty more long days and I would be free to join him for another adventure abroad. *Whose* adventure, though? For me, this would be yet another escape from a dead-end job. Once again, quitting to follow my husband on *his* journey.

True, it had gradually become *our* journey, during the last three years, while we had carefully planned and prepared to make it happen. But this trip would be different. I was determined to make it *my* journey. I was embarking on a personal quest. While Steven immersed himself in his work, I would try on a new life, a new Pat, to see who I could become, to finally discover what I really wanted.

In Kyoto, I hoped to teach English as a Second Language—something I'd never done before. My stepson, who had taught ESL in Kyoto a few years earlier, had advised me which workbook to buy and where to post ads to find students. I dreamed of studying the bamboo flute—if only I could find a teacher who would agree to work with me. The only lead I had was a scrap of paper my daughter had given me, with the phone number of her friend's teacher.

My life until now had been lucky. Nine years earlier, in 1983, I had found the man of my dreams. We now lived in a rambling home in a wild, narrow canyon west of Los Angeles. My two grown children were following their own paths in distant cities.

But at age fifty-one, something was still missing. I had tried a string of jobs over the last twenty-four years: seven years as a teacher in four different schools; seventeen years in university research, in a series of different disciplines and positions. I could never find the right fit. Nothing sparked a passion. Now, it was my turn to discover my path in life.

Japan had enchanted me ever since our first trip there in 1986, when Steven and I traveled for a month in the rural countryside of the remote north coast of Honshu with only our backpacks, a Japanese dictionary, and a slim paperback of *The Narrow Road to the Deep North*, Bashō's classic book of haiku. We vowed to return. Over the next three years, we made three more trips, exploring the country's various islands.

For me, Japan held a kind of beauty that spoke to my soul. The aesthetics of understated simplicity, balance, and asymmetry all captivated me. The values of privacy, solitude, silence, and reverence for nature and antiquity all sang to me.

The people, shrines, temples, gardens, processions, festivals, forests, mountains all looked as if they had just jumped off the four-hundred-year-old scrolls and screens in the museums and temples: The lone fisherman standing on the rock offshore in the stormy sea, silhouetted against the sky like a cormorant in a *sumi-e* painting. The kerchiefed old woman bending over in the middle of the stream in the public garden, washing each round pebble clean of moss. The workers wading in the Kamo River, washing out long streamers of newly dyed *yūzen* cloth, the hues of red, orange, and yellow flowing into the water and drifting downstream. Each guest writing a poem at the ikebana festival and tying it on a *hagi* bush to blow in the breeze. The *bunraku* storyteller chanting a high-pitched, rhythmic song, accompanied by the haunting music of the *shamisen*, while the three puppeteers, dressed in black robes and black translucent hoods, stand behind the half-life-sized puppets, moving their heads and limbs to animate the story.

As I boarded the plane that June, eager to see Steven after six weeks apart, I mused about our life together. So far, for me, our wedding, our marriage, and our years together had felt like a fairy tale. I first met Steven when I was forty. Exactly two years later, we went out on our first date. After knowing him for only three months, I followed him to Australia, to travel together for six weeks. He'd gone ahead a few weeks earlier to Canberra to finish writing his book on anthropology. As I'd disembarked down the plane's long outside staircase, my hands had trembled as they'd clutched the railing. What was I doing here? I hardly knew this man. Was I crazy? But I always had a contingency plan. If it didn't work out, I'd fly to New Zealand to visit my cousin Carol. Or I'd take the train to the Australian outback to my friend's sheep ranch.

Steven had greeted me at the Sydney gate with a bouquet of red roses and had led me to a romantic luxury hotel overlooking the harbor. He introduced me to my first opera, *La bohème*, at the new opera house with its billowy white sails flying as if ready to soar. And to Aboriginal art with its rough red bark, and the stylized spine and heart of the kangaroo exposed like in an X-ray. In New Zealand, when I caught strep throat after a long cold boat ride on one of the fjords of the South Island, he spoon-fed me tiny sips of soup and hot tea until I was well. When he came down with the same cold, I did the same for him. Strolling the windy beach off the northwest coast of the North Island, we gathered seashells and driftwood sculptures. Once home, Steven created a seascape collage from them, for my first Christmas gift.

On April Fools' Day in 1989, six years after our first date, we finally married. We stood on the cliffs of Malibu, creating an eclectic ceremony that blended Thai animism and Japanese Buddhism. Thai banners streamed in the wind above our heads. Below us, a meadow of wild spring grasses, monkey flowers, and lupine blossomed—green and gold and lavender all interlaced. Our families gathered around us—my two children, his three children, his sister, and my mother, in a circle of blessing.

Now, I was embarking on our next big adventure. Our life together had been a series of them—the travels in Australia and New Zealand; the six months living and working in a tiny, isolated, and impoverished rice-farming village in Northern Thailand; the three short trips to Japan; and then the one summer living in Kyoto. I thought this next year in Kyoto would be another one of our exciting journeys. And yet, I hoped it would also be something more. A special time together: immersed in the daily life of Japanese culture, exploring its arts and festivals, studying Japanese at a language school, and meditating at the local temples and shrines.

After twenty-four hours alone with my thoughts, I finally deplaned in Osaka. I rushed into Steven's welcoming arms, no doubt looking as wilted as the bouquet of daisies he handed me. Holding him tight for an extended hug, I felt a tingle up and down my spine, a mixture of excitement and anxiety. I was ready to begin our year in Kyoto, whatever it would bring.

I didn't know that seven months later, my love for Steven and my love for Japan would collide. That I would discover the dark side of Steven. And the dark side of this culture.

I didn't know that our dream and my personal quest would all smash into a thousand shards, like a dropped teapot.

PART I

Shūgakuin International House: Kyoto

BAMBOO FLUTE
A Prelude of Music

Such a river flows
yesterday to today
a flute plays
a wand on the riverbank
tomorrow's moon fills my cup.

— KATH ABELA WILSON

Stone foxes scamper
shakuhachi floats on the wind
long climb to the shrine.

— PATRICIA DOVE MILLER

At four a.m. ghostly sounds echoed through the pine forest as I struggled awake. It was 1989, at Zen Mountain Center, California, my first weekend *sesshin*, a meditation retreat. What was that sound? The rough-hewn notes matched the bark of the pine, the angled modulations swept with the wind and the stream. It must be a *shakuhachi*, the Japanese bamboo flute! Who was playing it? I couldn't see through the dark. The music came closer and closer, passed my cabin, then gradually faded as the flute player walked down the path back to the *zendō*. I supposed it was our wake-up call for five a.m. *zazen*, the musician walking the forest paths with a flute instead of someone ringing the usual bell. It was as if the bamboo grew out of the forest, out of the wind, and into this person's mouth as he or she blew the Zen pipe.

I had heard of *suizen*: to blow Zen, to blow meditation or concentration; to make music your practice; to breathe in and out, becoming the flute and the song. But I had never heard the *shakuhachi* played live, only on a tape that my husband Steven's Zen teacher had given him. It was nothing like the golden silver tones of the Western flute that I had played since junior high school. This was new, magical. I knew at that moment I must learn to play the *shakuhachi*.

Three years later, I was living in Kyoto, Japan, and ready for my first *shakuhachi* lesson. On this day, I would learn if Kuroda sensei, the teacher, would take me on as a student. The rain poured down, gray and fast, pooling on our balcony. I watched through the blurry window, wishing the rain would turn to snow, but that wouldn't happen until December. And yet I loved the rain too, how thick and straight it streamed down as if the bright white sky were emptying its soul and refreshing its spirit. For me rain had always been a good omen.

I walked the short block to the familiar tram, my umbrella held low against the wind, my feet snug in my new black boots as I waded through the puddles. The one-car tram, headed south toward the center of Kyoto, clanged to a stop, and I boarded. As we chugged downtown, I watched the shimmering streets, the lit-up storefronts and signs, and the spongy dark green squares of backyards of houses.

The tram soon pulled into Demachiyanagi station. I rushed through the wet street to the subway and down the steep escalator, trying to read the overhead signs, not wanting to miss this crucial connection. Just in time, I jumped onto the right train.

I sunk back into the seat for the long ride to the southern edge of the city, where I had never been before. I checked my map, adding up the number of stops before I got off, since I wouldn't be able to understand the conductor announcing each station. Commuters bustled back and forth on the platform, stale air rushed in, and the doors clanged open and shut. Then the train plunged through the darkness of the tunnel, lights flashing against the dark blank window next to me, illuminating the reflection of my face. I closed my eyes and meditated, following my breath, trying to let go of my anxiety about the journey and the teacher.

Light from the sky poured through the wet train window, onto my closed eyelids. The subway had come up above ground. My station was next. I gathered my things and dashed off the train. My fellow passengers dispersed immediately. I hunched under the meager roof and pulled out my map and Kuroda sensei's directions, puzzling out north, south, east, and west. I was surrounded by only steel track, rain, busy city streets. There was no one to ask. The train was gone, the ticket window empty.

I faced the track I had just traveled on, turned right, and trudged down the stairs. More rights and lefts, past small shops and under the train's overpass, out onto a big street, up a long hill, and finally to a bus stop. The way felt long and complex, but I followed Kuroda sensei's directions exactly. It was like a treasure hunt with the invisible sensei at my side.

I sat on the bench at the windy bus stop, huddling under the shelter. Would I spot the correct bus? Would the driver understand me? I wouldn't be able to read the *kanji* on the front of the bus. Buses didn't use our Western alphabet for Japanese words. I peered down the long street, filled with people and cars, but no one approached my stop. Suddenly, I didn't want to learn the *shakuhachi*. Kuroda sensei probably wouldn't speak good enough English, or he would refuse to take me on. Why not retrace my path and go home?

I pulled my coat tighter around my chest, my hood close around my face. Finally, a bus arrived with the right number on it. I climbed tentatively aboard.

"Rakuyo?" I spoke the word for the bus stop that Kuroda sensei had told me to say.

The driver nodded. "*Hai.*"

I dropped into my seat. The bus gradually warmed me up, but cold air whistled through the doors each time they opened. People came and went, crowded the seats, but never sat next to me. The smell of wet wool and stale cooking mixed with sweat and bus exhaust. I wiped off the foggy window with my glove and peered out. Would I be able to find my stop? The rain smeared the streets and smudged the *kanji* writing on the shop signs.

The bus groaned past endless small shops, some wooden and traditional, but most new and nondescript metal and plaster. I watched for each of Kuroda sensei's markers as we went. The driver spoke too fast, words slurred together, so I couldn't identify the words I was supposed to listen for. Suddenly, Renge-ji, the ancient wooden temple, loomed up on my right, many-layered, beautiful, mysterious. I was getting close. I inched my way forward and sat behind the driver.

"Rakuyo?" I said, again parroting Kuroda sensei's meaningless word.

The driver nodded and smiled, pointing up ahead. "*Hai.*"

Had he really understood me? Finally, after two more stops, he pulled the bus over to the curb.

He leaned back, gestured to the right, and repeated slowly, "Rakuyo."

"*Dōmo arigatō.*" I hurried off the bus. It was still raining, and the sky had darkened. I pulled back the cuff of my mitten to glance at my watch. It had only taken an hour, exactly as Kuroda sensei had said. It felt like I'd been traveling all day. I walked ahead two shops and located the fruit and vegetable stand on my left, with a bright green square pay phone in front. I slipped my coin in and dialed his number.

"*Moshi moshi,*" a voice answered, which I recognized from our phone conversation last week.

"*Moshi moshi.*" I sighed with relief. "This is Patricia Dove. I am at the fruit stand."

"Stay there. I come. Bye."

Once again I huddled under my umbrella beneath the eave of the shop. How would I recognize him? But suddenly, there he was, striding toward me. Tall for a Japanese man, solidly built with broad shoulders, wearing a tan double-breasted belted trench coat, holding an umbrella. Of course he knew who I was, the only *gaijin* in sight, tall and blonde. He walked up to me and bowed formally from the waist with his whole body, his hands at his sides, his face closed and sedate. Straightening up, he looked me in the eye, reached out, and shook my hand firmly, his face sparkling with a wide smile. "I am Kuroda. I am pleased to meet you."

My whole body relaxed as I returned his firm handshake and smile. "I am Patricia Dove. I am very happy to meet you." My head dipped in a small nod, still unsure of the various gradations of proper bowing.

He turned to walk up the street at a brisk pace, holding his umbrella high. "Come. We use mine." Our heads, close under the umbrella, were about the same height.

I couldn't tell his age: he was younger than I, but mature, maybe in his forties. It was hard to see his face in the rain, but his eyes glimmered through thick round glasses. He was silent except for the occasional directions.

As we walked the several blocks to his house, turning right, left, right, he pointed out the landmarks of café, wooden fence, empty lot, tree. "You must learn very well. You come yourself next time."

This was my only chance to learn the way. But I couldn't write it down. There were no street signs, and the shops and houses all looked alike. I frantically tried to focus on each corner, each landmark, feeling the right turn in my body, drawing the curves of the *kanji* from the café sign with invisible fingers in my pocket.

"This one, my street."

We turned up a small residential lane, lined with ancient wooden houses on both sides. He spread both arms wide. "This called Karoda section."

He stopped by a low picket fence of faded wood. "This one, my house. Before, my father's house." He creaked open the gate.

We weren't that far from the big old temple. This part of southern Kyoto must have once been farmland with only the huge temple and its own scattering of support houses like this one. Kuroda sensei's garden grew in a carefree tangle of beautiful plants on both sides of the path. Two trees, small bushes, and random flowers danced in the wind. It was not like the manicured gardens of so many homes here.

I followed him up the two stairs to the enclosed side porch that served as an entryway.

"There, umbrella. Over there, coat. Here, boots."

In my stocking feet I entered the living room, which was crowded with chairs and sofas, upholstered in gaudy old-fashioned floral prints. The rug, also with a large floral design, felt thick and rough.

Sliding into his own slippers, he pointed to those for guests, lined up by the door, with toes all facing toward the inside of the room. "Please, slippers. Sit down."

"Thank you," I said, as he disappeared into a back room.

I sat on the edge of the overstuffed Western couch that was stiff and hard to sink into, wondering what was next. I could hear no sound from the back. The room smelled musty and stuffy, with no windows.

I stood up and paced around. On one wall hung a beautiful black-and-white calligraphy scroll. On a chest stood a graceful ceramic pot glazed in blue and green. Snug against the far wall, steep narrow stairs with no railing rose toward the ceiling. Below the stairs, I detected a thin door, looked around over my shoulder, opened it a crack, and peeked inside. A toilet room the size of a closet. I used it hurriedly, not wanting him to find me there, then returned to my pacing, gradually warming up in the toasty room. A dish rattled behind the door where he had disappeared, then a teakettle gurgled. I waited. Soon I heard footsteps. I rushed to sit down as the door swung open.

Kuroda sensei appeared with a smile, holding a small square tea tray loaded with a pot, two cups, two plates, and one tangerine.

"Please, come." He led the way up the steep stairs.

As we entered his attic studio, we both removed our slippers before walking onto the golden sweet-smelling tatami mats that stretched from one end of the room to the other. Silvery light streamed through the huge windows on three sides, the sky lightening even as the rain kept falling. He gestured toward two large square cushions set on the tatami.

Setting the tea tray on a small wooden table between us, he sat opposite me, cross-legged. He wore loose khaki pants and a baggy wool sweater. His handsome face was sober and strict. I sat *seiza*, kneeling on the flat cushion, with my feet and legs tucked under me, the proper way for a woman to sit.

He bowed. "Welcome."

I bowed back, wondering whether to use English or to try to practice my Japanese. I decided to use both. "Thank you very much. *Dōmo arigatō gozaimasu.*"

As he poured the green tea into our cups, the rain pattered on the roof close above our heads, trickling down from the eaves onto a flat porch. Tiled rooftops, electric wires, and muted gray sky stretched out below and beyond. He peeled the tangerine, one neat section at a time. Pulling it apart into two halves, he handed me one, saying, "*Dōzo.*"

I bowed again. "*Dōmo.*"

His face softened and opened up. The brown skin contrasted sharply with the white smile and the thick black hair with streaks of iron gray running through. His hair fell neatly to his collar in back, with one straight shock hanging down over one eyebrow. An artist's haircut, not a businessman's.

We sipped our tea in silence, chewing the tangerine segments, the rain now drifting more gently on the roof, the sky brightening even more as it illuminated the room. I sank into the plush cushion, relaxed and at home. Taking off my sweater, I folded it next to me on the tatami, and shifted my legs into a cross-legged position.

After tea, Kuroda sensei asked the usual questions I heard when meeting new Japanese people: "How long have you been here?" "How long will you stay?" "What does your husband do?" "Do you like Japan?" And always, "Your Japanese is very good," even if I could only speak two words.

I had rehearsed my own list of questions on the bus and wondered when to ask them.

Finally, he set the tea tray to one side on the floor, straightened his shoulders, and closed his face into impassive seriousness. "Have you tried *shakuhachi*?"

"No. I have played the Western silver flute off and on since I was twelve. I have listened to *shakuhachi* on tapes. Once I heard it live."

He reached behind his cushion where wooden flutes of various lengths were lined up in a row along the wall. He slid one of them out of its peacock blue silk case. It was made out of a single piece of bamboo, using the actual root of the bamboo so it flared out and curved up at the end.

"I play for you." He paused. "First, I tell you story. This piece, 'Kyorei.' Means empty bell, empty spirit. Oldest *shakuhachi* piece. There is Japanese legend about famous Chinese priest. He chanted and rang beautiful bell. Disciple loved sound, had no bell. He took bamboo stalk, cut it here and here, blew into it. Made this song. Was thirteen hundred year ago. Really, this piece about four hundred year. Melody come first, then title and legend."

He put the flute to his lips, his long strong fingers holding it vertically and out from his body at a forty-five-degree angle. He closed his eyes and began to play. The rich deep tones drifted in and out of the room, blending with the soft wind and rain. I was transported back to that Zen forest in California, among the pines and streams. An incantation of sound reverberated around me: mournful, low, and mellow; rough and breathy; then a rapid change to smooth and sweet; then powerful, resonant, and loud. The warbling trill of a bubbling mountain stream; the fluttering ring of a temple bell; the melancholy whisper of the wind; the rushing force of a waterfall. No melody, only emotion; off-key to Western ears, but not to mine. Once again, I vowed to learn to play this magical flute.

I watched his face and hands. Each slight movement of his head, mouth, finger, each tilt of the flute seemed to produce a new subtle modulation. His body swayed, eyes stayed closed. He became the flute, the music, the breath, the meditation.

He finished the piece, laid the flute in his lap, and bowed. "*Dōmo.*"

Why was he thanking me? I bowed back, breathless. "Thank you very much. *Dōmo arigatō.*"

"When play 'Kyorei,' almost fall asleep. Deep meditation, inside each note, breathing. Must focus to stay awake."

"It was beautiful."

"Do you want to learn?"

"Very much."

He held up the same flute. "I teach you its name, *shakuhachi.* In old Japan, we had old measurements, not feet and inches. My parents only knew old way—I learned both. *Shaku* was one measure, about twelve inches." He straightened his back and shoulders. "I am almost six *shaku* tall. One *shaku* has ten *sun.* Length of flute is one *shaku* plus eight *sun.* Number eight is *hachi* in Japanese. So, this is a one *shaku* and *hachi sun* flute. Or *shakuhachi.*" He held the flute out to me.

I let out a big breath, shifting my legs back to *seiza* position, and smiled. "What do I do?"

BAMBOO SECRETS

He demonstrated each procedure: how he held the flute, shaped his lips, placed them against the mouthpiece, and blew the air stream. He handed it to me. "Please try."

Holding the *shakuhachi* in my lap, I slid both my hands up and down the smooth warm wood of the bamboo, my eyes savoring the swirling shapes within the grain and the color modulations from rich dark brown to pale golden tan. As I put the flute to my mouth, he reached across the table to gently adjust my fingers, the angle of the flute against my lips, and its position below my lower lip.

I blew. No sound. I blew again.

He made more adjustments, offered more advice about the angle of air stream and the shape of lips. "Relax: lips, shoulders, breath. Big breath, from diaphragm. Forget silver flute. Breathe, deep, into flute."

I blew again. A sound! I couldn't believe it. Maybe I'd really be able to learn. Maybe he would agree to take me on as his student. Most teachers wouldn't teach *gaijin*, especially a woman. I blew again. Another sound!

He gave a slight smile, a slight nod, his face smooth. "Very good."

Winded from the effort, I beamed at him. "I would like very much to take lessons with you."

"Of course." He nodded again, pulled out a sheet of music, and laid it flat on the table, facing me. "'Kyorei.'"

Exactly what I had hoped for. My first piece would be the beautiful and meditative one he had played. I studied the complex blur of squiggles and curves, lines and spaces, in dismay. The sheet music was a mass of black calligraphy, uneven and artistic, written with a brush, probably by some ancient master. I looked up at him, puzzled.

18

虚鈴　普大寺　所傳、古典本曲、(虚吹)

"Kyorei" — "Empty Bell"

He gave a short laugh from his belly. "It's easy. Read it top to bottom, right to left." He pulled out a fingering chart. "Only five characters, for five holes of flute."

I was delighted: I already knew and used these characters! They were from the *katakana* syllabary of forty-six syllables, one of the three Japanese writing systems. On this chart they were large, square, and stylized. I would have to learn to translate them into the rough, hand-stroked calligraphy version on the sheet music. I could do it.

Kuroda sensei taught me how to play each of the five notes. We played them together over and over; sometimes I made a breathless note, sometimes a noisy breath. I reached for my new lavender notebook.

He stopped me. "Don't write. You must learn with your body and mind." I put away the notebook, although taking notes was how I learned everything.

He told me where and how to buy a *shakuhachi* for my next lesson, and he drew me a detailed map of how to find the store. He told me how to practice in front of a candle to make sure I was blowing correctly. If the flame went out, it was wrong; if it didn't move, it was wrong; if it wavered slightly, that was precisely right.

"Don't worry if no sound. Breath sound, okay. Just practice five notes. Relax. Breathe in and out." He brought out a large hand-drawn calendar and placed it on the table between us. "Please, write name when you want to come next week."

"Sensei, how much do you charge?" Not that I cared what he'd say.

"Eight thousand yen each month. Come as often as you like. Lessons are one hour."

"I will come once a week." I reached for my purse.

"Pay next time. Today, no charge."

I rested my fingertips on the edge of the table, bowing low from my waist. "*Dōmo arigatō gozaimazu.*" He bowed back, not as deep, from his shoulders.

Once out the door, I put up my umbrella and glided down the street, feeling as if I could click my heels, raise my umbrella high, and float up into the sky. The silky rain misted around me, glistening on the tile roofs. Lustrous sky and cloud reflected in the wide puddles, and as I passed the tree at his corner, a round drop of rain shone from the tip of each pine needle. Climbing aboard the bus for the long trek home, I could still hear the magic he had played in that attic room. With a twinge of guilt, I pulled out my lavender notebook. As the bus bounced toward the train station, I scribbled down everything I could remember: his detailed instructions about how to play and practice; the legend about "Kyorei"; the five *katakana* notations; the tangerine and green tea. I couldn't wait until next Thursday. I couldn't wait to tell Steven that I had made a sound. I would practice every day until I could do it every time.

Glancing out the steamy window of the bus, I saw we were climbing the hill to my stop. I stepped off and sauntered the few blocks to the train, gazing in each shop window, admiring every bold artistic *kanji* shop sign. Each black stroke of the brush soared with clarity across the dark wood of the sign, flowing down, then up, and finally ending in a whisper.

MEN IN BLACK

Three times filled with green tea
flying through the murky air
wet leaves splatter bowed heads

smashing in a thousand shards
will it ever be whole again?

— Patricia Dove Miller

My turn to make tea this morning. The alarm rings at seven thirty, as usual. I push snooze for another five minutes and press my body against Steven's back, soaking up his heat while sinking into the thick cotton of our handmade quilt and futon, all plump and tufted. I love this futon, with its horizon-blue background and design of miniature overlapping red and green fans dancing over the cloth like the wings of herons soaring across the sky. And this maroon quilt, with its profusion of meandering blue and white flowers, as if down the side of a hand-painted kimono.

I think back to our struggles to buy this precious bedding seven months ago, a few weeks after we arrived in Kyoto to spend the academic year. First to convince the apartment manager to remove the narrow, lumpy twin beds. Next to convince the shopkeeper downstairs to special order both the futon and quilt—she with no English, we with only a Japanese dictionary, and Steven on the floor acting out the difference between what you sleep on and what you sleep under, since in Japanese both are called *futon*. There were none ready-made—we pondered and selected the fabric, the design, the size, the thickness of the cotton stuffing. When we finally burrowed into the firm

23

softness, floating between these two layers of billowy clouds, I began to feel at home in this strange new country.

The alarm blasts again. After tucking the quilt around Steven's shoulders, I slip into my winter robe and put on the kettle to boil. I prepare the tea, carry the burnished-gray teapot back to the futon, and pour the *genmai-cha* into our matching *chawan*. The toasty brown rice fragrance floats up, and the low round cup warms my palm as I cradle it. Under the quilt, Steven's hip and thigh nestle against mine. I sip my tea and curl my toes over his.

Sliding deeper under the covers, I nuzzle my nose into his soft skin, with my arm encircling his waist. Part of me wants to linger here with him forever, treasuring the closeness, the dreamy state of just-awake mind, our slow lazy talk or easy communal silence. We're most open to each other in these early mornings, before we go our separate ways for the day.

I shift onto my back, staring up at the squares on the ceiling. The other part of me wants to rise and begin my day. I'm pulled in two directions: toward him and away. Maybe I shouldn't rush off. Maybe we've become too separate during our time in Kyoto. Yet I'm eager to meander through my morning: write in my journal, read the Japanese art history book, play my two flutes and the piano in the downstairs lobby. I'm on a quest here in Kyoto, although I still don't know exactly what I'm looking for.

A sudden pounding on the front door breaks into my reverie.

"Who can that be?" I say. We never have visitors.

Steven pulls the quilt up to his chin while I walk to the door. Why am I doing this? He's the social one. I'm the hider. But I'm already up for the tea. And I seem to serve as his buffer here, as I did in Thailand seven years ago.

I open the door a crack to find two Japanese men in black suits. "Mr. Steven Solomon, please," one of them says in English.

I hold the door firmly half-closed, puzzled that he doesn't bow, or say, "*Ohayō gozaimasu*," the morning greeting, or "*Sumimasen*," the ubiquitous "excuse me."

"He is still in bed. Could you come back later?" I enunciate slowly, unsure how much English he understands.

They stand stiff and unbudging, hands at their sides, black hair neatly cropped, faces pale. The shorter of the two, unsmiling, sticks his foot in the doorway.

"It has to be now." He holds out a small card.

I cannot read the Japanese *kanji*. These men look official, but they wear no uniforms, no badges. I'm perplexed. Who are they? What do they want? I wonder if the man really speaks good unaccented English, or if these are his only phrases. With my stomach wedged against the edge of the door, one arm taut against the doorjamb, I wait for an explanation.

They gaze back, unblinking. "Mr. Steven Solomon, please," the headman repeats.

"Just a minute, I'll get him." I try to close the door, but they push in after me, stepping inside the matchbook-size entry hall and stumbling over the clutter of shoes, slippers, and umbrellas. Startled, I step backward into the kitchen. Japanese people never behave so intrusively.

They bend over and slip out of their shoes. It seems that even intruders remove their shoes. I rush into the bedroom. Steven sprawls under the quilt, his face dreamy. "Some men are demanding to see you," I say. "You better get up." He looks up at me, stretching and yawning. After taking one more sip of tea, he sets the cup down on the tray. Slipping into his thin cotton *yukata*, he knots the blue and white *obi* across his round belly and saunters into the kitchen.

Hovering behind Steven, I strain to hear their words. He stands at the edge of the kitchen, the two men facing him from the entry hall. The shorter man with good English questions him in a fast, low voice, and Steven answers in a slow murmur, his back angled to block me out.

Standing on tiptoes, I try to peer over his shoulders. What's this about? Why is Steven mumbling? A third man in a neat black suit appears at the open front door. He's followed by two more men, who are tall and heavy, with squinched eyes and clenched jaws. They wear dark work clothes, and their hair hangs long and loose over their thick necks to their collars. Tough and strong, they look like retired sumo wrestlers. They seem to be bodyguards.

Fully awake now, Steven squares his shoulders, his head high. "Won't you all please come in and have some tea?" He sweeps his arm toward the kitchen/living room, stepping aside to let the three suited men enter. I press my hips against the sink to let them pass. Out of respect, Steven bends his knees slightly as he glides past them, leading them onward to the office/bedroom. "Please, let's sit down in here. There's more room."

He glances at me and points toward the teakettle, raising one black bushy eyebrow. I turn on the flame and wait in the kitchen for the water to boil. The two huge men loiter in the front hallway.

Steven sits down on the stiff rug, ignoring our unmade unrolled-up futon, and moves our morning tea tray aside, with its two half-empty cups. The shorter man who seems to be in charge joins him on the rug, near our desk. His face is puffy, with thin lips and a sharp chin. They sit opposite each other, both cross-legged, backs straight, hands resting in their laps. The other two men flank the headman.

The headman's gaze bores straight at Steven. "Professor, will you please tell me, did you receive a manila envelope in the mail with marijuana in it?"

Steven bows his head. "Yes, sir, I did."

Oh my god, what in the world has Steven done? I step into our bedroom and stoop to pick up the teapot and cups, trying to keep the ceramics from rattling on the tray.

The man's face is impassive, as is Steven's. He sits in his morning meditation pose, breathing in and out, his eyes on the floor.

I can't read Steven's face or posture, whether it's curious or surprised, nervous or resigned, any more than I can peer into the depths of these strange men. I'm shut out, alone in this room. My dreams and our adventure are exploding in front of me like a dropped teapot.

I carry the rattling pot and cups back to the kitchen. Forgetting to breathe, I watch and listen from the open kitchen doorway.

The headman keeps his eyes on Steven's face. "Professor, would you mind telling me please: When did you receive it? And where did it arrive?"

His English is good, much better than my advanced students' or Steven's Japanese colleagues'. He doesn't pause to search for words; he can pronounce the *l*s, the *r*s, the *th*s. He must have studied in America; there's no British accent.

Steven sits very still, his head up, his eyes lowered. I can barely hear his answers. "I am very sorry, sir." He pauses. "I do not remember when. It arrived at my university office." He's matching the headman's speech pattern of extra politeness and serious formality, an old and useful anthropologist's habit, enunciating slowly to be sure he's understood. But he also seems scared, as he begins to squirm and wince, his voice a pinched monotone.

After pouring fresh boiling water onto our morning batch of *genmai* leaves, I return with the teapot and three mismatched cups. I set down the tea tray between them and fill the headman's cup. He places it on the rug in front of him.

When I pour fresh tea in Steven's cup, he glances up at me, his eyes flashing warmth, even though his face remains stony. I try to send him a message of love and serenity. Cradling the pot of green tea in my lap, I sit back on my heels, Japanese-woman style, with my legs folded under me. This is no time for anger.

But maybe the anger can't wait. I want to throw this teapot. And scream. At the police—or whatever exactly they are. At Steven. I can't yell at him—he's already beaten down. Nor at these men—I'm afraid of them. I want to grab my clothes, go out for a walk. But I must stay and find out what's happening. I forget to meditate, to match Steven's breath in and out. I don't breathe into the rigid pain in my clenched shoulders. I don't allow the fear and anger to rise up, to float through me and beyond, my practice too new for that.

Returning to the kitchen, I find the two strongmen pacing back and forth like caged bears. I hold up the teapot. "Would you like some tea?" They scowl, shaking their heads. Their eyes dart back and forth, first to the men in the next room and then out through the kitchen window, where the clouds hang dark, threatening rain.

Tugging my robe firmly around me, I pour myself a cup and move silently to the kitchen table. I don't want them to notice me. Or kick me out. I'm playing the Japanese wife, pouring tea and passivity. I want to sit in the corner and listen, invisible, like a cat with one eye open.

The headman takes one polite sip of tea. He leans slightly forward. "Please, Professor, if you could tell me, how often do you smoke marijuana?"

Steven almost whispers, his back still ramrod straight. "Umm . . . I do not know, sir . . . I am not sure . . . about once or twice a day, I guess."

What! Twice a day? I stride to the sink and bend way over, my eyes burning.

At home in the States, he didn't smoke that much. Or did he? Has he been smoking more in Japan for some reason? I wonder when and where. When we first lived together, I feared secrets more than marijuana. I didn't want him to smoke but was afraid he wouldn't love me if I said no. I told him, go ahead, but tell me when you smoke. But he didn't tell me, so I let it go. I didn't insist on what I really wanted. I don't like that side of Steven, so I've avoided it, let it be his private thing. I never realized it was so important to him.

I step to the table and clear away our dishes from last night's nightcap: two empty beer glasses, the elegant red lacquered plate Steven bought me for my birthday, crumbs from our cheese and crackers, and empty bean husks from our steamed *edamame*. At the sink, I turn on the hot water and scrub furiously.

We've traveled so much—to New Zealand, Australia, Thailand, and three earlier trips to Japan. Did he manage to smoke during those trips without me noticing? I know he smoked a bit with a friend in Thailand, but that was different—the two men on a rare trek up to a Hmong village in order to buy marijuana and smoke. I ignored it. He certainly didn't smoke in our Thai village, where we worked so closely together day and night. Or did he? Maybe I've presumed too much—that he'd be wise, that he'd know the rules in Japan were stricter than in the States.

I set the kettle to boil again. The apartment is as silent as a tea ceremony room, the only sounds the gurgle of the kettle as it heats up and the murmur of Steven and the headman in the next room. I can't hear their words, only muted monotones, as polite as if they were discussing a fine ceramic tea bowl. While I dry the dishes, I keep a watch on the two strongmen who lounge at the kitchen table, their legs stretched out, filling the room. I wonder what Steven wants me to do, what the headman expects of me.

I return to the office/bedroom, filling the teapot one last time. My Japanese friends have taught me to always make three potfuls: the first pot's too strong, the second one just right, the last one too weak. Kneeling on the rug next to Steven, as close as I can get without touching him, I pour him a cup, hand it to him, and search his face. As he accepts the tea, his hand cups mine with a quick caress. His eyes gleam at me, not with the usual sparkle of mischief, but with shifting emotion. Warm gratitude in his brown pupils shines like sunlight pouring through a stream, highlighting one round pebble. Then his eyes cloud over with a tight black fear. Both looks are for me alone.

I squeeze his hand, trying to transfer my strength into his. But, inside, I'm quaking. When Steven turns back to the interrogator, his eyes mask over, polite and distant. He casts them down at the floor like a submissive dog.

I pour a cup for myself and sit back on my heels again, next to Steven.

The headman's cup remains half full. He asks, "I would appreciate it if you would tell me, do you smoke with your students at the university?" Steven's university is one of the most prestigious in Japan, like Harvard or Yale.

Steven takes a small sip of tea, then sets his cup down. "No, sir, never."

"Do you give them marijuana or sell it to them?"

"No, sir, never."

The room has grown hot and stuffy. I push myself up off the floor, carrying my cup with me. I want to stay seated close to Steven, lending him my silent support, but I can't keep still. Pacing back and forth from kitchen to bedroom, I force myself to slowly inhale, exhale. I don't want to listen. But my fears are growing. Will they put him in prison? What about me?

The headman leans toward Steven. "Professor, do you have any here?"

I pause in the doorway. Steven's head sags to his chest and his voice drops to an obedient whisper. "Yes." He points toward the desk next to them.

"Please, if you would be so kind, take it out for me."

Steven unwinds one leg at a time, rising stiffly from the floor. In one step, he reaches the desk and bends down toward the bottom drawer. It rumbles open. He pulls out a thin manila envelope. It looks like a business envelope, nine by twelve inches. He holds it out to the man with two hands, using the Japanese respectful gesture for giving. Then he sits back down with his forehead in his palms.

My hands grip both edges of the doorjamb. That's his pipe and tobacco drawer. No reason for me to ever look in there. I prepare my ESL lessons at that desk every day. Six drawers: I use two; he uses two; the others we share. He's always respected my space, and I his.

I peer at the envelope in the man's hands. It's the color of tarnished gold. On the front, I can barely make out Steven's last name and a Kyoto address scribbled. I can't imagine who's sent it, or when, or how long it's been sitting in that drawer. I stare through the window up at the blank morning sky, then back to the four white walls of this tiny room. We've lived in such close quarters here, been together day and night. After nine years of living together, suddenly I feel as if I barely know him.

The headman takes the package and sets it down. He does not open it. "Thank you very much. Now, may we please search the apartment, if you wouldn't mind?" His voice is gentle, as if we have a choice.

I look over at Steven but can't speak. Certainly, search warrants must be required. We still aren't sure who these men really are. And yet if we refuse the search, maybe they will call in those two strongmen lurking in the kitchen.

Steven nods up at the headman.

The two assistants in black suits put on smooth white cotton gloves and begin their search. White gloves are not unusual in Japan; even the taxi drivers wear them. The men start with the desk.

My head is light from hunger, but I don't dare go into the other room to eat breakfast. I've no idea how long these men have been here. I can't brush past them to check my watch or my appointment book. I probably have students this afternoon, or a *shakuhachi* or ikebana lesson. I can no longer remember. The calendar on the wall above the desk, adorned with one of Hokusai's *Thirty-six Views of Mount Fuji*, says Friday, January 29, 1993. Today's date will be chiseled into my mind forever.

Steven remains on the floor in his flannel pajamas, answering each of the headman's questions in a subdued monotone. I can't look at him.

I plant myself between the two rooms, arms folded across my chest, keeping one eye on the two men in suits who are quietly investigating the desk and bedroom, the other on the strongman who searches the kitchen by banging the cupboards open and shut. The second strongman works on the bathroom, returning repeatedly to the ceramic tray on the back of the toilet that's filled with incense, incense holder, matches, and ash. He sniffs, pokes, and sifts the ash suspiciously. In Japan incense is only burned in temples or in front of the family altar. He doesn't know we use it for bathroom fragrance. Then he closes himself in the bathroom for the rest of the long morning. Not a sound comes from inside. I watch the door. He's never going to come out. Maybe he's sick, or has smuggled in a *manga* comic book under his coat to read.

In the office/bedroom, one man opens the drawers of the desk. First, Steven's pipe drawer. He pulls out several pipes, a tobacco pouch that he opens and sniffs, pipe cleaners, matches, lighters, and that funny little spoon Steven uses to clean out the ash. Next, the man tries the one locked drawer, the one we share. He glances at me for the first time. I reach for the key on its hook inside the kitchen cupboard and hand it to him. Inside the drawer are huge stacks of Japanese yen. He flips through them slowly, rummaging around in back for more. Steven's salary is paid in unusually large amounts of cash, the equivalent of thousands of dollars at a time. No pay check, no automatic bank deposit. Bank cards, credit cards, checking accounts are all still fairly new in 1993 Japan. Cash is used for most transactions.

The man closes the drawer and turns next to mine. He picks up my journal, thumbs through the pages, stops to study one page. I wonder if he can even read English. He scours my appointment book, my address book. Then he seizes my letters, shuffles through the ones from friends back home and the carbons of others I've written. He must be looking for contacts, thinking I'm implicated too. Will he confiscate my things? In the States, I'd immediately be under suspicion merely because I lived in the same house as Steven.

He pounces on my stack of books, leafs through them, scrutinizing each title. Why would it matter what type of book I read?

Meanwhile, the other suited man slides open my side of the bedroom closet. I yank my attention there. He attacks my neat piles of folded clothes. There are no hangers, no dresser, only this deep wide closet, meant for futon storage. He holds up my stack of nylon underpants, sifts them through his fingers, shakes them out. I feel nauseous and cover my face with my hands. I can't watch, yet I steal glimpses as he fingers my cotton camisoles and paws through my silk blouses. What's running through his mind? Perhaps he thinks the gloves keep him immune, separate, professional. He leaves my clothes in a jumble, making it appear as if the place has been burglarized. Slamming the door shut, he swivels to Steven's part of the closet.

I swallow hard, tucking the edges of my nightgown more securely inside my robe.

Steven and the men are all rising. "Professor Solomon, you will come with us now, please. We will search your university office and then take you to the police station."

"May I please get dressed, sir?" Steven's arms hang limply at his sides, his eyes still cast down.

"Yes, but my assistant must stay with you."

While the rest of the men wait in the kitchen, the assistant and I watch Steven rummage through his ransacked closet for a shirt and trousers, and then hurry to dress. I want to run forward and help him. Or to put my arms around him and press him to me, but I stay frozen.

I squint at my wristwatch on the desktop. Twelve noon. Steven walks to the kitchen, his eyes avoiding mine as he passes. I follow close behind, shivering, as I collapse into the chair nearest to the front door.

"I am ready, sir," Steven says, focusing on the headman.

The headman nods and leads the way out, each man pausing to bend down and slip on his shoes. From the door, Steven turns back toward me, his face stoic and surprisingly calm, as if he's resigned to what's happening.

"Call Takeda at the office, say we're on our way. Call Tom at home, he'll know what to do." Takeda is Steven's boss, Tom our friend and neighbor.

The door shuts behind Steven without a sound.

I stare at the closed silent door, then at the phone on its kitchen stand. Hugging myself with both arms, I try to stop the shivering, force myself to breathe deeply. I'm stunned, unable to move. But no, I must rush—they'll be at Takeda's soon. I drag myself from my seat, dial his number, and quickly tell him what's happened.

A long silence.

"Thanks, Pat, I'll meet them downstairs."

I call Tom. He is a friend of Steven's son, Robert, and a long-term expatriate married to a Japanese woman. Here in Kyoto, he's become a good friend of ours, too.

"I'm so sorry, Pat. I'll see what I can find out. You better call the consulate right away. I'll send Keiko over this afternoon to check on you."

Walking over to the chilled window, I watch the black stains from the rain creep down the gray wall of the square office building across the street. For this next call, I'd better sit down. Grabbing a sweater from the rumpled closet, I struggle into its sleeves, then force myself to dial the U.S. consulate in Osaka, a huge city over an hour away by tram, train, and bus.

The woman's voice is thin, businesslike. "Well, there's really nothing I can do, my dear, until he's actually in prison. I could give you the name of an American lawyer here, but he's very expensive. I know he's too busy right now, anyway. Here, we only monitor prison conditions—they can be pretty bad. Sometimes they force you to stand in silent meditation for hours. Or they put you in solitary confinement." Her voice rises, shrill, scolding me like a hungry Steller's Jay, then breaks off with an embarrassed laugh. "You don't want him to go there. It could be up to ten years. And once you're in prison, they often hold you incommunicado—you won't be able to contact him for a long time."

Each word, each punishment bores deeper into my numb brain, as if I'm trapped in a dentist's chair, the dentist drilling without enough novocaine. "But, what can I do?"

"Nothing, my dear. Call me back once he's in prison—we'll see what we can do then."

She laughs again, softening her tone a bit. "Now, don't you worry, honey. And do come by our office for a cup of tea—anytime. You know how to get here, dear, don't you?"

I don't answer. I slide the phone down my cheek and set it quietly in its cradle.

DOUBLE HAPPINESS
An Interlude of Romance

Even when a river of tears
courses through
this body,
the flame of love
cannot be quenched.

— IZUMI SHIKIBU (tr. Jane Hirshfield & Mariko Aratani)

I first met my true love at a funeral, when I was forty years old.

I arrived breathless at the synagogue in San Diego, right when the service was starting. I sat down quickly at the back. At the front giving the eulogy stood a distant figure, a yarmulke firmly atop his head. His black curls bounced as he strode back and forth. His bass voice resonated through the long narrow room like a mournful cello, full of tenderness and grief. Its rich tones soared up and down in melodious rhythms. I barely heard the words, though I sensed their eloquence, and this man's profound love and respect for his deceased brother-in-law. So this was the brother of Martha, my dear friend and colleague. I knew immediately. All year long, as her husband Jeff lay dying of cancer, she had told me stories about her beloved brother who traveled from Los Angeles every weekend to care for her and her three small children.

When I walked into Martha's house for the wake, I found a party in full swing. I had expected something black and somber. But here was a celebration of Jeff's life. His friends milled in and out of the house, to the sunny wooden deck where long tables overflowed with gourmet cheeses, French wines, chilled shrimp, and pita with eggplant dip. The spring air radiated with laughter, real conversation, not superficial chat, and constant tributes and memories.

Martha clasped my arm. "I want you to meet my brother." Eyes the color of chocolate, exactly like his sister's, sparkled with both a fierce intensity and a mischievous gleam. A neatly trimmed salt-and-pepper beard, with a thick black moustache, framed his darkly tanned face. With an old-fashioned courtly air, he bowed toward me, as if to kiss my hand, then shook it firmly instead. His hand felt warm and soft, his fingers slender and delicate, but strong. He focused all his attention on me, as if I were the only person there. "How do you do?" he said. Even up close his voice boomed. He stood with his shoulders thrown back, his chest out, a slender build but a commanding, almost theatrical, presence. A man sure of himself, I thought.

Red bougainvillea blazed around us as we plunged into conversation, he drawing me out about my upcoming trip to Scotland, my first solo trip at the age of forty. "You must go to Iona," he said, with insistent enthusiasm, like a professor describing his passion to his student. "You feel the spirits in every blade of grass. And the abbey—it's magnificent. From the thirteenth century. You must hear a mass there—or the Gregorian chants at vespers." His black bushy eyebrows danced up and down while both hands gestured broadly. "And the swallows flying in and out of the open windows, and the bells ringing through the gloaming."

I gave him a quizzical look. I didn't know what *gloaming* meant but was already enchanted by his poetic words. "That's the long summer twilight, at that latitude—it goes on and on till late at night."

Inspired by his enthusiasm, I tucked the name *Iona* away, promising myself that I'd go there.

A few weeks after the funeral, Martha told me Steven had asked for my phone number. So he had felt something, too.

"But he just left for Australia," she added. "He'll be gone for a year."

Okay, I'll wait for him, I told myself.

I would carry his voice, his name, and Iona close to my heart for the next two years, hidden away for I wasn't sure what. Something had captured me. Was it Martha's stories about her perfect brother, who had helped raise her, ever since she was one and he eleven, when their father died? This idealized myth of a brother who could do no wrong? Was it the magic of his voice, and his story of Iona? Or was it this exotic, exuberant Jew with his bounce and enthusiasm? I had never met anyone like him. The exact opposite of me.

I did travel to the island of Iona and took my dreams of Steven with me. I fantasized about a future with him as I basked in the sonorous chants at vespers and in the glowing pale golden light of the gloaming. I followed the double curves of the swallow's blue-black wings as they swooped in and out of the open stone archways. At dawn I wandered the green hillocks sprinkled with mounds of white sheep. I felt the magic Steven had spoken of, and yes, the spirit of that special place, as if elves or saints were hiding behind each rock or flower.

Over the next two years Martha and I plotted our moves. She was determined to get Steven and me together. So was I.

When I returned from my travels, I checked in with her, eager for any bits of news about her brother. He loved Australia, was traveling all over the country giving lectures, was writing an academic book, and had a new Australian girlfriend. That didn't discourage me. I tucked him away again, as if in my pocket. I knew I could wait. I had unfinished business with a couple of old boyfriends. I wasn't ready for Steven yet.

A year and a half after the funeral, Martha invited me to her family Thanksgiving party. "He's home from Australia, but that girlfriend's with him. Do you still want to come?"

"Yes." I wanted to glimpse him again, to see if the fire still burned. I didn't mind the girlfriend. Not yet.

When I walked into Martha's kitchen for Thanksgiving, the room bubbled over with the laughter of her extended family and closest friends, with tables piled high with platters of food. Steven stood in the middle of a circle of people, telling stories, more charming than ever. The curls were even wilder, the brown eyes even more shining than I remembered. His embroidered vest flowed, its bright red color like the blossom of an Indian Paintbrush. He rushed toward me as if we were old friends. I extended my hand, but instead he pulled me into a loose hug, Italian style, kissing me on both cheeks. That did it. I was in love. I'd never been kissed like that.

"I went to Iona," I said, with unusual bravado, not sure he would remember me or our conversation.

"How was it?" He stepped back, gazed into my eyes with that same curious intensity I remembered, and listened to my story. I was enchanted.

"Please meet Amy," he said. He drew her forward, a beautiful young blonde with short curly hair and a charming Australian accent. Too shy to stay near Steven, I retreated to a corner with Amy, asking her all about Australia. Maybe by getting to know her, I could get to know Steven.

Two months later, Martha reported that Steven had split up with Amy. But I shouldn't call him. He was heartbroken. Finally in April of 1983, two years after the funeral, Martha said, "He's recovered from Amy. Call him. Now. He's between girlfriends."

For the first time in my life, I called the man, instead of waiting for him to call me. He remembered me. Our phone conversation was warm and long. I felt instantly at ease with him, all my usual shyness evaporating. I don't remember what we talked about, but I remember huddling in my university office behind the closed door, oblivious to the work I should have been doing.

We set a date for a few weeks off, when I would be in Los Angeles visiting my mother. But he called back the next day. "Let's get together sooner," he said. He'd be in San Diego the following weekend with a family emergency.

He showed up three hours late, after two phone calls of apology, saying his mother had just been admitted to a psychiatric hospital. When he arrived, he took off his leather boots at the door and strode to the old easy chair by my antique ebony piano. He sat cross-legged, settling into the faded blue-and-brown-striped upholstery. His long slender fingers formed a steeple as he talked on and on about his mother, with husky sadness in his voice, his elastic face showing every emotion, from despair to joy. She had collapsed from drinking and depression. They suspected she had been a secret drinker ever since her husband's death forty years earlier.

At sunset I led him down the hill to the beach, showed him the final green flash of the sun as it disappeared into the sea—his first time to ever see it. Together we watched the lavender-gray that washed over the sky. We searched for somewhere to eat, but all the places I had hoped for were full on a Saturday night in my popular beach town. Finally we settled on the only one left, a Chinese restaurant called Double Happiness, a bare lunchroom place, with large gaudy vases.

Over dinner, I told him about my dreams of the Peace Corps. I had passed the first screening process; each of my teeth had been x-rayed and inventoried for later identification in case I ran into trouble; I was being considered for Africa because I had studied French and weaving. He told me about his travels all over Asia, his years living in Thailand, his anthropology research there. And his love of Asian cooking. I realized what a mistake this mediocre restaurant was. I had noticed how expertly he ordered, without hesitation, complementary dishes of spicy tofu with black bean sauce and bland steamed mustard greens. Later I would learn he was a gourmet cook of all types of Asian food. And how particular he was about the quality of everything he ate, whether at home or out. On that first date, he never said a word about the meal, scooping up the rice and vegetables with his chopsticks, eating with gusto and no complaint.

He called me the next morning. "I'd like to see you again before I drive home to L.A. How about dinner tonight?" I wasn't used to such passionate pursuit.

After dinner at a Mexican restaurant, we returned to my patio and sat side by side in my striped red and orange Colombian hammock. We rocked back and forth, sipping chamomile tea, while from the top of a pine a mockingbird cascaded song after song into the mild April evening, with what seemed like heartfelt intensity. The ocean surf hummed and the scent of night jasmine enveloped us. Again and again, Steven delayed his departure for home. He snuggled closer, drinking cup after cup of tea. Later I would discover he didn't even like chamomile.

At my doorstep he pulled me into a strong bear hug. I snuggled into the coziness of his soft wool sweater, which was the same brown as his eyes. The fragrance of pipe tobacco sweetened his clothes and the skin of his cheek. He caressed my lips with a quick light kiss and was gone.

The following weekend I made my first trip to his home in Topanga Canyon, outside of Los Angeles. Just to be safe, I combined it with a trip to visit my mother. We were both cautious. My difficult twelve-year marriage had ended, followed by two long-term boyfriends. His two marriages had ended, followed by a continuous string of girlfriends.

I'll never forget that first scary drive up the wild and twisty road as I entered the narrow canyon, turning away from the endless blue ocean at Santa Monica. I wound higher and higher on the steep road, leaving the noisy smog of L.A. far below. Only forty-five minutes from there, but a million miles apart. Rugged rocky cliffs loomed on either side, a ribbon of creek meandered far below, and clumps of pale orange monkey flower and dusty green sage clung to the cliffs. Sunlight glinted on the boulders, changing their colors from red to brown to gold. Slender pine and expansive oak surrounded the homes that clustered in the hills.

The tangy scent of sage and honeyed perfume of wisteria greeted me as I pulled into his driveway. I sauntered up his steep path, passing a grove of trees—orange, lemon, grapefruit, apricot—unkempt, but laden with fruit. At the top of the rickety wooden stairs perched a slightly ramshackle house with a red tarpaper roof and two outbuildings. A profusion of the most beautiful wisteria I had ever seen flowed over the roof and porch with long fluttering clusters of lavender blossoms.

Steven rushed out to greet me, clasped me in a long embrace, and then with a dramatic bow and sweep of his arm, ushered me inside. He was literally dancing with joy that I was finally there, so he could show me his home and canyon. Wide redwood planks paneled the walls of the long living room, and a bank of windows at one end flooded the whole room with sunshine.

"I put them up myself," he said proudly, sliding his hand down one length of the redwood, without actually touching its rough splintery surface. "Old wood from a mushroom farm."

"I tried that in the ceiling of my bedroom, but my arms practically fell off," I said.

"I loved every minute." He pointed to a tall conical Swedish fireplace. "And I put this in. It was my only heat for years."

I stroked its smooth black surface. "Does it draw well?"

"No, but I can make a good fire anyway. We'll have one tonight."

I stepped out to the narrow porch, my hands on the shaky metal railing. The dark mountain curved majestically against the pure blue sky, like a sleeping giant, with layers of hills disappearing into the distance. Between the mountain and us, the canyon plunged downward.

Steven joined me at the rail, his hands next to mine, our shoulders touching.

"I love that mountain," I said. "It reminds me of Mount Konocti at Clearlake where I spent summers as a child."

"When my friend helped me move in, he said I would spend my first year watching the mountain move." He braced his arms, leaning way out. "He was right. It's my salvation. I thank it every day." He grasped my hand. "I want to show you the park. We had fires last summer. That makes the wildflowers profuse."

We meandered the paths, knee-deep in fields of orange poppy and red paintbrush. High green grasses waved on either side, with the mountain we'd seen from his window leading our way. We knelt to admire a flower, trying to identify it, with its fragile color of ivory and five delicate petals with lacy edges.

"Its leaves are long and slender, like a lily," Steven said.

"Look, the petals curve up like half-open fingers," I said. "I wonder what it's called."

"I shall call it 'princess's hand,'" he announced, cupping his own hands to mimic the flower.

"Perfect," I said, laughing at his whimsy. So unlike my parents' scientific attitude. With my father an ornithologist and my mother an amateur botanist, I grew up learning the importance of the correct nomenclature of birds and flowers.

"Here's a *Brodiaea*," I said. "My mother's favorite flower, always a first sign of spring at the lake." I tapped the rounded purple head, with its tiny clusters. "She only taught me the scientific names. I don't know its common one."

He danced ahead on the trail. Fluttering his fingers like rain-drops, he called out, "Here's more flowers, reds, yellows, blues!" He moved with the grace and strength of a leaping deer. "And here's lupine!" He stopped to inhale the heady perfume of the lavender-plumed blossoms and stroked the tender new buds beginning to open.

A long sharp cry cut through the sky above us. Steven pointed to a large bird circling high. "Red-tailed Hawk. My favorite bird—their wildness and that plaintive cry." His eyes followed its circular path until it disappeared far into the blue.

We arrived at a grove of wide-spreading oaks at the top of the hill and sat down in the dappled shade of an old gnarly one, with its secret hollows and crevices, admiring the hazy ocean in the distance.

After a short while, Steven stood up, bowed toward the still-distant mountain peak, put his palms together, closed his eyes, and began to chant. "*Phutam salanang kachami . . . salanang kachami . . .*" The same long repeated phrase over and over, with an even tone and steady rhythm; at the end of each phrase, his voice swirled down and then up, accenting the final "*kachami.*" His sonorous voice was mellow and modulated, yet it resonated firm and strong from his diaphragm. I couldn't make out the words or the meaning, didn't know it was the ancient Pali language. But I could feel its spiritual peace flooding through me, like a Gregorian chant. He rotated slowly around, chanting to each of the four directions, and then ended with his voice trailing out to a final whisper.

That evening Steven built a fire, settled me on cushions on the rug, and poured me a Bohemia, a dark Mexican beer I'd never heard of. I was used to Coors. A Bach cello sonata swept through the room, one of my favorites. While he disappeared into the kitchen, I studied his living room. Like my own, it had dark wood paneling, a cozy informal cabin feeling, with the walls lined with books and shelves of classical phonograph records. The same well-lived-in feeling of casual comfort, with eclectic furniture, not worn, but secondhand. But while I had an antique family piano and a framed embellished wedding certificate of my great-grandparents, he had a stunning collection of Asian art. A silk wall hanging of an orange and green Buddha encircled by saints and elephants; a framed calligraphy of an imperfect black circle drawn in uneven brush strokes; a two-headed wooden dragon with carved gray and pink feathers; a rugged brown mask with black eyebrows and high cheekbones that looked uncannily like Steven himself.

Soon he reappeared from the kitchen wearing a striped apron and carrying a silver tray with a large pottery bowl piled high with bright green guacamole, a bowl of tortilla chips, and more beer. He set it down with a flourish and toasted me with his glass.

I scooped up a huge bite. The lush smooth avocado slipped down my throat, with exactly the right combination of spicy fresh salsa, lime, and fresh chopped cilantro. "Better than the best Mexican restaurant," I said. His face glowed.

We munched and drank until late, the guacamole and beer, and later the plate of gourmet cheeses and crackers, filling us up. I was impressed that, unlike any man I'd ever known, he did not need a real dinner.

Steven's queen-size futon was already rolled out at the other end of the living room, luxurious with its thick quilt of large blue swirling flowers. Before long we tumbled into it. At the height of passion, I flung my hand against the rough mushroom-wood wall. A thick splinter jabbed into my finger. A shout of pain blended with a cry of pleasure. I didn't realize how deeply I was pierced until the next morning when it began to throb.

I was hooked. I was in love with this glorious green canyon, the April wildflowers that surrounded us in carpeted profusion, the majestic mountain, the wildness and beauty and space. I was in love with this man.

Every weekend for the next six weeks, we explored our new passion with each other. We alternated who made the two-hour trip, he to San Diego or I to L.A. At the age of forty-two, I was free and on my own. My son was away at college, my daughter in France for a year between high school and college.

One weekend in early June, I picked Steven up at the train station in Del Mar and guided him along the beach toward the Poseidon, an outdoor restaurant at the edge of the water. The towering silky waves curled, bursting into foamy bubbles on the sand, ebbing and flowing toward us and away. Tall stately Marbled Godwits poked their long red beaks tipped with black ink into deep holes in the sand searching for food. We ordered our favorite snack of hot potato skins stuffed with melted cheese and sour cream.

"I'm going back to Oz," Steven announced. His name for Australia. "In July."

I stared at him, as the ocean breakers crashed over and over onto the wet sand. "For how long?" I asked.

"Four months. I need to finish my book. It's the only place I can do it."

Tears filled my eyes. I couldn't believe he would leave when we were so fresh and new and hopeful. "What about us?"

"I want you to come with me."

I felt spun in two directions. First, he was deserting me, then inviting me along. I didn't even notice that he'd left me out of the decision. "Do you really mean it?"

"Yes." He squeezed both my hands in his and beamed those intense eyes on mine. "Please come."

"How can I? My job—I can't leave it."

"Ask for a leave of absence."

"I don't know. I'll have to think about it." I struggled with my conflicting emotions. "And besides, I've just committed to my mother, to go to Kenya with her for two weeks in August. I can't, I won't, back out."

"Make your trip with her. Then join me for my last six weeks. I shall show you my Oz. Then to New Zealand and Tahiti on our way home. It will be our honeymoon." Was this a proposal or merely his romantic way with words?

He pulled both my hands up to his lips, gave each finger a kiss. "How 'bout it?"

I watched the water churn, a tumbling mix of frothy white and darkest green. He was irresistible. But what a risk. How could I go off to the other side of the world with him for six weeks, after knowing him only three months? Even if my boss said yes, I couldn't afford to be without a salary for that long. And I couldn't not be here for my daughter when she returned from France.

I glanced at Steven, chewing his potato skin with relish, slurping up the sour cream, wiping it off his moustache with the cloth napkin. I turned to gaze at the waves and the godwits.

With sudden clarity, I knew. Right then on that beach, with the wild strength of the surf behind me, I vowed to myself that not only would I go to Oz with him, but I would commit to this man forever, no matter what. Even then I knew it wouldn't be easy. He was impulsive and moody. I knew we'd probably have the usual problems over money, sex, stepchildren. I warned myself there might be other unknown challenges and obstacles. But he met some vast unspoken need and unexplored side of me. I had never wanted something so much in my whole life. I jumped in with both feet on the ground, both eyes wide open.

BICYCLE RIDE

The bamboo branches
caught in passing winds must dance
like helpless humans.

— EDITH SHIFFERT

On a steep hillside
being bamboo for awhile
I absorb sunshine.

— EDITH SHIFFERT

That Friday in Kyoto, after the police took Steven away, I sat all afternoon by the phone. I was dying to take a walk, to get some fresh air to clear my head, but I didn't dare miss a call. At some point, Keiko, Tom's wife, stopped by with a loaf of warm whole-wheat bread and a hug for me. Finally, Tom called. He had tracked Steven down at the local police station. But no other news—he couldn't find out when Steven would be released or what would happen next. At six thirty, Steven dragged home. Withdrawn and depressed, he fell into bed, refusing to talk.

Now, two days later, on a sunny Sunday morning, we drink our tea. "We need to get away," I tell Steven. "Let's go explore today." I swirl the pale green liquid in my cup. Whenever we need to talk something out, we spend time together on a courtship sort of date. Back home in California, walking among wildflowers restored our balance. In Kyoto, participating in the whirl of a festival or meditating at a Buddhist temple does the same. We rediscover why we love each other. Only then can we open up and discuss our issues. But I know our talk today will not come easily.

Steven sets his teacup on the rug by the bed. "Maybe. I think I might like that." He traces the curve of the blue flower on our quilt, then flings it back. "Yeah, let's go. I may end up in prison tomorrow."

Yesterday the lawyer told him he must report to the Customs Police in Osaka every day for Interrogation, in lieu of being put in prison, but he should always bring a toothbrush and a change of underwear, in case the authorities change their minds.

He hesitates on the edge of the futon, his face gray, as if his own words, tossed off lightly, have sunk in. "But where?"

I pull my knees up to my chest, burrowing one last moment in the warmth of the quilt. "Entsū-ji. The book I've been studying says this temple has a meditation garden with a view of the mountain. It's way off in the northwestern hills."

"Okay."

I pull on my corduroy trousers, thinking how reluctant Steven has been during this stay in Japan to take days off. When we lived abroad before, he was always eager for excursions. On our first trip to Japan, we wandered for a month with packs on our backs in the remote countryside along the coast of the Japan Sea. Without knowing any Japanese, we convinced suspicious *minshuku* owners that, in their family "bed and breakfasts," we knew how to sleep on the floor, refrain from using soap in the communal bathtub, and eat raw fish for breakfast.

Before we left home, we promised each other a trip to Hokkaido, the largest of the islands, but that hasn't happened. Lately, Steven rarely has taken even an afternoon off. Although he's free to set his own hours, he's insisted on going to his office every day, even sometimes on Saturday. He says he has to keep up with his hardworking Japanese colleagues, but I resent it. I've come to Japan to explore with him, not to do it all on my own. Now I wonder if the long work hours have been merely an excuse to smoke pot all day.

Leading the way, I cycle out of our Shūgakuin neighborhood. The cold wind blows strong in my face. On my bike I feel safe and deliciously free, in my own private space. Free of the nightmare into which Steven plunged me two days ago.

And even free of him for a few minutes as I speed ahead. When cycling, I am liberated from my struggles with the Japanese language, with bus schedules, with watching anxiously for the right stop. And free from Japanese customs and politeness, as much as I want to learn them.

I felt that same freedom when I first rode off on my new bike, seven months ago in July. I had just bought it all by myself, over Steven's strong objections.

The day after one quarrel, Steven bicycled off to the university on his used bike, a simple one with a narrow seat, thin tires, and no gears. I set out for the neighborhood bicycle shop. Silently practicing my Japanese phrases to use with the shopkeeper, I hurried along the busy street, the sidewalk fish vendor calling out to me, and women of all ages rushing past me doing their morning shopping.

I hesitated outside the shop, searching the rows of bicycles. There were no price tags. I peered in, my heart whirling as fast as the bicycle chains that the man was spinning in order to examine them.

"*Irasshaimase!*" Two men greeted me, smiling and looking up from their work. The shop was one narrow room with dozens of bikes hanging from the ceiling and parts and half-assembled models strewn all over the floor. As the two men tinkered with several bikes at once, the gears ground and the smell of grease filled the air. Steven and I had come here once before, quarreled over the prices, and left without buying one. This time, they did not seem to recognize me. Perhaps we *gaijin* all looked alike.

"*Sumimasen.*" I cleared my throat and swallowed hard. "Do you have any old bicycles?" I said in Japanese, not knowing the word for *used*.

The young man wiped his greasy hands on a cloth, letting the gears cycle round and round on the upside-down bike. "*Hai.*" He gestured for me to follow him out front. He pointed, and said in Japanese, "This one, six thousand yen. That one, eight thousand."

They were different bikes, different prices, from the ones we'd seen before. I couldn't tell if they were better or worse. I pointed to the blue one with the basket. "*Sore o onegaishimasu.* That one, please." He smiled and rolled out the bike and adjusted it for my long legs. He motioned for me to try it. His friendly silence and gestures comforted me.

"*Ii desu ne, dōmo.* It's good. Thank you." I smiled as I climbed back off, handed him the yen, and bowed. "*Dōmo arigatō gozaimasu.* Thank you very much," I added to be sure I was being polite enough. I patted the leather seat, ran my fingers along the curve of the shiny metal handlebars, and climbed on. I rode off down the street, away from home and toward the river.

I had done it. As I flew along the bicycle path next to the Kamo River, I felt as light and free as the white egrets that roosted in the big green trees on the opposite bank. The cool breeze brushed my cheeks, and my legs pedaled faster and faster. I was as exhilarated as I had been in Thailand in '86, when I first rode my bike all alone to the open market near our village. I had bought my first oranges and mangoes, using Thai, without Steven to translate for me or protect me. In Kyoto it didn't matter where I was going. It was only me, the bicycle, the river, and the wind.

Seven months later, cycling toward the temple, speeding ahead of Steven, I can leave all my troubles behind and rejoice in the rim of mountains behind and ahead, the dancing grace of the winter trees, the antique wooden homes, the bold curlicues of the *kanji* shop signs. Now I can be in charge and show Steven the Kyoto I've been discovering without him. This time we're together; it's the two of us against the world of Japan.

Steven's boss Takeda, the lawyer, and the U.S. consulate have all scared me. I have a premonition that in the unknown number of weeks ahead, all I have come to love about Japan will end.

I fear I will be fighting the flip side of Japanese culture that tourists, short-term residents, and even most expatriates never see: police, Customs officials, consulate, lawyer, judge, university president; the restrictive laws and customs; and the frightened reactions of our Japanese friends and colleagues.

My legs stretch out long and straight, my back unkinking as I bend forward in the seat. Since Friday when the police came, I've been waiting to talk to Steven. I've been too bewildered, too shocked to confront him. And mostly grateful he was finally safely back home on Friday night after his long detainment at the police station. There's been no time between the police, lawyer, my students, and Takeda's late-night visits to plan strategy. When there is time, Steven collapses with fatigue, refusing to talk, beaten down and deflated. Or we both fall exhausted into bed, hugging each other in silent desperation.

Takeda says to not tell anyone, not our local Japanese or American friends, not even our family back home. If this story leaks out, Steven will be in worse trouble. Takeda says that's how Japanese society and Japanese law work. There is no one I can turn to for support except for my tiny circle of secret-keepers: our friend Tom and his wife, and Takeda. I am alone and stranded.

I push the pedals sharp and fast. Steven and I agree we must not talk at the house, fearing the police bugged the phone and the apartment on Friday. We suspect that was what the huge bodyguard was doing for so long in our bathroom. On Saturday, we held a hurried, whispered conference on the porch, when Steven reported on his meeting with the lawyer, but even there we felt no safety, no privacy.

We pass through empty narrow streets lined with traditional shops, all shuttered on this Sunday morning, low buildings each touching the next, with dark wood fronts and tiled roofs. When I stop to consult my map, Steven waits by my side, staring vacantly at the closed doors with unseeing eyes.

The treetops of the western hills ahead pierce the pale blue sky like tiny swords. All bundled up, I pedal faster, trying to get warm. We turn into a narrow street that circles up the mountain. As the hill steepens, my fingers tighten on the handlebars, my heart thumping, my shoulders tensing.

I need to know exactly what Steven has done. It feels like a matter of life or death: prison or freedom, isolation or escape, separation or marriage. But I'm afraid to ask Steven the questions, to hear his answers. Afraid he'll resist with his usual silence or litany of slippery excuses: I'm too tired, depressed, coming down with a cold, not in the mood. Or, not now, this is a bad time. I'm not going to let him slither out this time.

I glance back at Steven, who is puffing hard as he pushes on his pedals. I pump each of mine with persistence, one at a time, slower and deeper. I know he needs help getting himself out of this mess; he won't and can't do it alone. I must figure out how our love and marriage can survive.

When we first committed to each other nine years ago, I knew he would not be an easy man. I vowed to myself I would always fight to preserve the marriage. I would not have another divorce. We had already solved and survived many problems: stepchildren, troubled children, stifling jobs, relocation to a new town, the rough isolation of field work in the Thai village. If we couldn't solve a problem, I promised myself I would seek professional help. But as I cycle up the hill, I forget that promise, too caught in the drama of the moment, too isolated, and sworn to secrecy. I keep cycling, Steven dropping further and further behind.

Twelve years ago, I learned a lesson from a former boyfriend about asking hard questions. When he celebrated his birthday with a platonic friend instead of with me, I knew something was wrong, but I kept silent. Two months later I finally asked. My intuition was right; yes, he had slept with her. After that, I vowed to always follow my gut feeling and immediately ask the troublesome question. With Steven, I've learned to do it most of the time. Whenever I falter, I remember that earlier lesson. Now I have no choice.

The mountain grows steeper, the houses thinning out. They are older and more traditional, larger with two stories, more wood, more porches. Jumping off my bike, I wait for Steven to catch up, and we begin walking side by side. A small neighborhood Shinto shrine nestles against the sharp slope of the wooded mountain.

"Let's stop here. We need a rest," I say.

The shrine building perches like a tiny square box on a huge deck. It is made of light brown wood, spare and plain, with none of the usual Shinto decorations, like strips of white paper zigzagging down from the doorway, or thick braided rope tied around an old tree, or colorful plastic pinwheels planted into the garden. The tall and wide main door is closed; the grounds around the building are bare dirt, swept clean. Maybe it is deserted, or not used often. Yet it looks well cared for, well worn and loved, if empty. Together we walk up the long broad steps.

Sitting on the wooden platform, we huddle in the one spot of sun, gazing at the muted greens and browns of the wooden houses and trees below. Steven pulls his pipe out of his pocket and begins to scrape the bowl with that shiny little spoon.

Forcing my rapid shallow breathing to slow down, I face him, sitting cross-legged, my knees almost touching his. "Tell me what happened, Steven."

He doesn't answer and looks down at the wooden boards, pipe in hand, legs dangling over the edge.

"Why did the police come?"

Steven opens his leather pouch, pinches out some tobacco, its fragrance of damp loam and pine bursting into the air. He stuffs it into the bowl with his thumb. "Better you not know," he finally says. With his head down, eyes half closed, he murmurs, "The lawyer says the Customs Police won't question you, but how can we be sure? I don't want you involved. This is my problem."

I rest my fingertips on his knee. "No, this is my problem, too. You've gotten us into it. Together, we've got to get you out." I run my hand over the smooth floorboards that are beginning to warm in the shifting sun, then look up again at his closed face. "You need my help, Steven. You can't do it alone. I've got to know everything, that's the only way I can help you—and help us."

He begins to talk in a low voice. "I had some dope. I kept it in my desk at the apartment. And at the office. I smoked it there, in my pipe. It wasn't much. They wouldn't care about it in the States."

My shoulder muscles relax a bit. "How did you get it?"

"I carried it on the plane."

I clench my fists tightly together. "What about Customs?"

"It was in my shirt pocket—in my tobacco pouch."

"Weren't you nervous?"

Steven sighs. "I didn't think about it. I didn't think it'd be a problem."

I feel like a police interrogator, badgering him with direct questions I know he hates. Still, I refuse to allow his usual meandering conversational style. "You must've felt something. You knew it was illegal."

"Maybe a twinge. I was pretty sure I'd get away with it. I just breathed in, breathed out, and walked through. It was . . ." He glances up at me briefly. "Kind of exciting."

I twist my head to look at the city far below. We've traveled so much together. This can't be the only time. I never thought to ask. I dig my fingers into the flesh of my palms, inside my mittens. "How did the police know you had it?"

Steven puts his pipe between his lips, pulls out a match, and tries to light it. The wind sweeps up toward us, so I reach forward to cup my hands around his to shelter the flame. He blows a few puffs in and out, the aroma of burning pine whirling between us. "They intercepted a package mailed to me, a brown manila envelope sent to the office. I don't know how they knew what was in it."

I stare at him, my teeth rattling so much I can barely talk. No matter the layers of wool, the patch of sun, I'll never be warm again. Where is this heading? As we get deeper into his story, I fear each new question, each new answer. Fear my marriage is in jeopardy. Fear he can't save himself. He will disappear into passivity, depression, or worse. And for the first time, I am afraid of Japan. I don't want to go on with the conversation.

"A manila envelope?" The shaking spreads over my whole body, uncontrollable. "I was at your office that time, you picked up your mail . . ."

He lets his pipe go out and takes it out of his mouth, giving me a blank look.

"Don't you remember? You said, 'Oh, it's from Denise,' and put it aside. I thought nothing of it, meaning to ask you later that evening what her news was. But I didn't want to pry."

I've never liked Denise, never understood their friendship. She's one of his former girlfriends, a stockbroker in her thirties. I reluctantly let him invite her to our wedding four years ago. In our marriage, we strongly believe each of us should have separate friends. We both left behind constricting, traditional first marriages. In this one, we've tried something new: separate friends, separate finances, separate names, even separate cottages on the same property, and no wedding rings. We strive to blend the independence of our single lives with the excitement of our courtship, with the intimacy of togetherness. Perhaps we have erred too far toward independence.

Getting up off the deck, I pace back and forth to get warm, and to put some distance between us. The shrine building and the trees around me are a blur. "Did that one have marijuana in it, too? Why did she send it?" I pause. I know I'm badgering him again. I can't help it. "Did you ask her to? Were there others she sent? Is that what the police found?"

He bends his head, refusing to meet my eyes. "Yes. I only brought a little on the plane. When I ran out, I called her from a pay phone . . . asked her to send me some. The last one the police intercepted. I don't know how."

I glare down at the barren earth around the shrine. If I get angry now, he will clam up. "But—"

Steven pulls his wool hat low over his eyebrows. "I arranged it before we left."

"What?"

"I was afraid I'd run out. Without it, I can't write, can't think straight, can't be creative. You've never understood that. She was going to find a connection, a dealer over here. But she couldn't, so she started sending me the manila envelopes whenever I called."

Walking to the edge of the deck, I contemplate my bicycle, its handlebars glinting in the sun. Maybe I won't stand by him after all. Part of me wants to jump on that bike and ride off, far away from all this. What is his strange connection with Denise? I've never understood the attraction, though I know that marijuana is part of it.

At a pizza restaurant in Santa Monica six years ago, Denise, Steven, and I were eating dinner, along with Henry, Steven's younger son, still in his twenties. Toward the end of the meal, I excused myself to go to the restroom. While I wove my way back through the other tables, I saw the three of them talking intently. As I approached, they abruptly stopped talking, glancing at each other. Feeling uncomfortable, I sat down. What was wrong? I looked at each of them, but no one met my eye. Steven busied himself with the bill, Denise burrowed in her purse, and Henry fiddled with his backpack. After an awkward silence, Steven made a joke, turning the conversation to some frivolous topic. I twisted a long strand of hair with my finger and turned inward, sensing he was hiding some secret. I knew he used superficial chitchat in order to avoid things. Feeling hurt and puzzled, I shoved it aside to ask him later.

Soon we left the restaurant. While I walked with Steven, Henry rushed after Denise to her car down the block. We hadn't even said goodbye to her. When we reached our car, I grasped Steven's arm. "What's happening?"

He straightened his arm, shrugging my hand off. "Nothing. She has something to show Henry. That's all." He grabbed my elbow. "Let's get in."

Steven and I sat there in silence, staring straight ahead. It didn't make any sense. Twisting around to look behind at Henry and Denise, I could see them absorbed in conversation. Then she sped off. He sauntered back to us and climbed into the backseat.

While Steven drove home along the pounding surf of the Pacific, I worried about Henry. He had recently returned from an extended trip to India, where apparently he'd been experimenting with drugs. What were he and Denise up to? Was Steven involved?

The next morning, at home in Topanga, I gathered my courage. We sat knee to knee, facing each other on the rug by the potbelly stove in our bedroom. "Steven, what was going on at the restaurant yesterday—and at Denise's car? I felt left out." I looked steadily into his eyes.

He looked down. "Just buying some dope from her."

"In front of Henry?"

"Yeah."

"And why did Henry go to her car?"

"I asked him to. To get it from her. So you wouldn't know."

"What?" My voice rose as I pushed away from him. "Do you think that keeps you clean, letting your son do your dirty work? What do you think you're teaching him? Look at the manic state he's in."

I walked to the French doors of our bedroom, glaring at the pink and white impatiens in our garden, unable to show my anger directly, or even to acknowledge it to myself. I felt incredulous, but also sad. I had tolerated Steven's smoking, but for him to reinforce his kid's drug use was going too far. I pushed open the garden door for some fresh air. Perhaps he wanted to be caught.

Back then in California, we already had a problem with secrecy and marijuana, both of us refusing to acknowledge it. Neither one of us was being honest.

"I'm sorry," he said, his voice harsh. "It was pretty stupid. I shouldn't have involved you or Henry." He sank into the chair across the room, his legs stretched out in front of him.

I sighed, sitting on the arm of his chair.

He reached up to fold me in his arms. I melted into his embrace.

That was my pattern: gear up the nerve to confront him, back off once I received an apology or quick reassurance, accept, and move on, without noticing he didn't support or even acknowledge my feelings.

Now in Kyoto on the deck of the shrine, the cold wind blows up toward us, scattering the dead leaves that someone has swept into piles. Steven still sits where I left him, his dead pipe cradled in his hand, as he stares at his fingers. I walk along the crack of one of the long boards with slow small steps. I'm trying to break a pattern I'm not even fully aware of. I'm not letting him slide out with easy answers. But I still want to believe him, and am still slow to anger. Instead I feel sorry for his dilemma.

And I want to placate him so he'll keep talking. I'm beginning to sputter with frustration but managing to keep it inside. I don't yet know that at some point it will finally explode all over us.

I sit down a few feet away, my knees dangling over the edge, scrutinizing the green treetops below. "Didn't you know it was illegal, that you were taking a big risk?"

"I didn't think about it. It was such a small amount each time. I wasn't sure of the law, but how would they know?" He picks up his pipe again, stirs up the old tobacco with the metal spoon, once again trying to light it. The wind is too strong. "I thought we'd get away with it. Or I didn't care. I needed it too much."

"Why didn't you keep our agreement? You were going to tell me when you smoked." I'd always wanted to know if I was dealing with a straight man or a stoned one.

"I knew you really didn't want me to, and I thought you'd be mad. I thought I could smoke and you'd never know." He raps his pipe upside down on the edge of the deck to empty it. "I tried to do without it. It had nothing to do with you."

"But don't you see? It has everything to do with me. And with us. You put us both in danger, the minute you packed it to bring along, the minute you picked up the phone to call her."

As I turn to look straight at him, my eyes fill with tears of frustration for the first time since the ordeal began. I'm usually quick to cry at any slight problem or harsh word. Or quick to use tears instead of anger.

When I was a child, my mother taught me to always suppress both anger and tears. Frequently she showed me the only Biblical sentence she had retained from her strict Methodist childhood, after turning her back on all organized religion: "He that is slow to anger is better than the mighty," underlined in her old childhood leather-bound Bible on the shelf. And she punished me for crying, by sitting me down alone in front of my dresser mirror to stare at my ugly, red, swollen face until I stopped. She succeeded with the anger, but not with the tears. But I never learned how to deal with my anger. It always left me shaken and depleted, never accomplishing anything.

Usually any argument with Steven ends with my crying; he softens and I "win," or at least he finally listens to my feelings. But since Friday, I've been too much in shock to cry. I brush away the tears. Like the anger, they will have to wait for later.

"You've been selfish, Steven, very selfish."

Looking up at the blue and white of the wild racing clouds, I move away from him, into a new spot of sun. I've given him power for too long, and he has misused it. Now it's my turn to be in charge.

"I need to know more. I need to know everything." With teeth clenched, eyes narrowed, I pound my fist on the deck. "When did all this happen? When did you smoke it? When did you try to stop?" I'm pushing again; I can't help it.

Steven shakes out his stiff legs as he walks the deck. "I smoked in my office and on my bike. Those have been my happiest times here in Kyoto, riding my bike to work and getting stoned." He rubs his arms to warm up. "I don't remember when I started calling Denise—soon after we arrived, I guess."

His words cut through me. What about all our adventures together? Biking through the chill of the morning along the Kamo River to Japanese class, hiking the mountains with Takeda and whisking green tea over the campfire, slurping cold noodles while floating on the river barge, riding the tram up Mount Kurama and strolling down the paths from shrine to shrine. Those are my happiest times here. With him. Or are my happiest times without him? Studying the arts of *shakuhachi* flute, ikebana flowers, and *shodō* calligraphy; teaching English to young Japanese women; photographing the festivals that swirl with music and color, like the one for elaborate hair styles, or the one for the wild boar. Perhaps my life here is more separate than I realize. More separate than I want. Which has come first, his withdrawal or mine?

"What about trying to stop? When was that?"

He sighs. "I don't remember. I think when I first ran out and she couldn't find a dealer over here for me. I cut way down so I wouldn't have to call her as often. That's why I've been so irritable." He digs again into his pouch, pinches out new brown strands of tobacco, and refills his pipe. "I knew I should stop, but it drove me crazy. It was too hard, too depressing. And I couldn't tell you."

I step over to him and hold him tight, with tears of relief to finally know why he's been so down, and feeling sad that he couldn't tell me, and tender that he can tell me now. Perhaps now we can be honest with each other. I always thought I could tell him anything (the only man I ever could), and that therefore he could tell me anything. But how wrong I've been.

I pull my face back from his cheek. "That's the hardest part, Steven, that you were keeping secrets after all these years we've been together. I needed to know you were depressed, or why you never wanted to go out. I should've noticed. I should've asked." I take his two hands in mine. "But I'm still confused. You said you tried to stop, you were in withdrawal, but you kept calling her to send you more."

The wind dies down, and the morning chill begins to fade as the sun patches lengthen on the boards of the deck. After squeezing my hands, Steven lets go, picks up his pipe again, and makes another attempt to light it. I reach forward to cup my hands around his. He tilts his head back and to the side, so that tiny white puffs float up to the sky. "I was confused, too. I would try to go without, then I'd get irritated with you, my colleagues, the university, Japan. I got scared, called her up, and she soothed me, promised more. I was on a yo-yo. I didn't know how to get out of the loop."

Taking off my mittens, I study my fingers, the lines of my palms. I wonder how it feels to try to stop smoking and not be able to.

In the early seventies when I first heard of marijuana, I was thirty, a single mother with two small children. I quickly learned that marijuana brought out an ugly part of me that I didn't want any man to see: whiney, depressive, and clingy. Fortunately, I'd moved far beyond that before I met Steven. I believed pot-smoking was okay for others, a personal choice for recreation, or even for meditation or creativity. I didn't know the difference between recreation and addiction.

All of a sudden, the last several months make sense. Steven has been irritable, irrational, and explosive, all an extreme of his usual fluctuating moods.

When we first arrived in Kyoto, he quarreled with me repeatedly over my wanting to buy a bicycle. He insisted the one at the shop was too expensive. He had bought his the day after he arrived in Kyoto, from an ad on the bulletin board, proud that it cost so little. He offered to let me use his and said he'd take the bus. But I knew he didn't mean it; he wouldn't really take the bus. And I knew we couldn't share one bike.

I was tired of hunting, and there was nowhere else to look. The following week, over breakfast, I made one last try. "Steven. I really need a bicycle." I took a mouthful of homemade granola, savoring the flavor of honey and almonds. "On the bus, I never know when to get off, don't know how to ask."

He looked up from his cereal, his spoon poised in the air, his voice firm. "Keep looking. People're always moving out."

I laid my spoon down in the bowl. "I looked again yesterday. I made the rounds of all the bulletin boards, at the university, at the Community House." I searched his stony face for clues. "I've read all the ads in Kyoto magazine—the Osaka ads are too far away. I can't wait any longer."

Steven clunked his spoon down on the table and glared at me under his bushy black eyebrows. His voice had turned tight, filled with monotones. "I want to wait till we can get as good a deal as I got."

My granola began to taste like straw. "That's never going to happen. Why not just buy that used one at the shop? We can afford it."

"I don't want to pay that much." He resumed eating, his head down, focusing on his cereal.

My face flushed as I heard my voice rising high and thin. "But, St—"

He picked up the English language *Japan Times* and started to read with his back to me. "I don't want to talk about it." His cereal lay soggy and unfinished on the table.

I stood up and grabbed my daypack. "I'm going for a walk." My head ached with a piercing throb as I headed up into the hills toward Shisendō Temple, one of my favorites. The fresh air cleared my head, but my mind churned as I walked faster and faster.

Why was I waiting for his approval? Yes, it was his money— I'd given up my teaching job to come to Kyoto. But I wasn't used to being financially dependent on Steven—this was the first time—and I was chafing under it. I was used to my own job, my own money, my own decisions.

I strode through the winding residential streets wondering why I let myself get caught up in his price comparisons. It didn't matter whether it was rice or bicycles; Steven was always searching for the best price. Probably it was from his childhood days of poverty in the Bronx. Yet whenever he bought rice, he talked a lot about going to all four local stores to find the best deal—but ended up buying it at the most convenient place.

And what about our teapot? On our recent trip to downtown Kyoto, while wandering among the row of pottery shops, he'd immediately spotted a delicate burnished-gray teapot. It was small and shallow, with an opaque finish. The handle, instead of curving over the top, came out from one side at an angle ninety degrees from the spout, perfectly balanced. Without hesitation, he bought it for our growing Japanese pottery collection. There was no talk of price, no comparison shopping up and down the street for the perfect pot at the perfect price. It was expensive. He loved it. And so did I.

How was that different from a bicycle? Perhaps a thing of beauty or a collection made the difference. A bicycle was practical, a necessity.

I reached the Buddhist temple and entered the empty garden. Sitting on my favorite bench by the koi pond, I watched the huge orange-and-white fish meander in the murky water. I scribbled in my journal, my anger making my writing almost illegible:

Why do I hesitate? He's wrong. I need a bike and he knows it. We can afford it. I'm not going to listen to him. I'm going to just go buy one. Why don't I say that to him. No. I'm just going to do it.

The koi swam slowly back and forth, the sun glinting on their golden scales. I inhaled the fragrance of the moist green water, the velvety green of the moss, and the peace of the weekday summer garden. And then I sauntered back down the hill toward home. I strode up the two flights of stairs to our apartment. "I will buy a bicycle tomorrow," I muttered to myself.

Seven months later, sitting next to Steven on the cold deck of this empty shrine, I now see that I gave only muted sympathy when he frantically complained that he couldn't make overseas phone calls (oh, so that's why; he couldn't call Denise), that the Japanese printer was incompatible with his computer, that his colleagues weren't helping him. He was such a complainer that I didn't take the complaints seriously. I've wanted to say, "Look, Steven, something's wrong, with you. This isn't about the Japanese, the phone, the computer. There's some underlying problem you're not seeing." But I've kept silent.

I'm used to letting him work out his own moods. He has taught me that they will soon pass, something he's learned during his twenty years of Zen Buddhist practice. But why haven't I seen that this black mood was lasting too long? I haven't sensed that he might need help breaking out of his misery.

I yank my scarf tighter around my chin. Perhaps I've been too absorbed in my own Japan, in my own journey of exploration, my art and my new friendships. I've wanted him to take care of himself. He's refused to join me in my quest, so I've ventured out on my own. But that is my lifelong style, to take all the responsibility, rather than make demands of the other person. I wish I'd followed my intuition and confronted him. Or at least gently drawn him out of his shell.

Pulling my mittens back on, I leave him there folded into himself, puffing that pipe, looking out at nothing. I walk around the perimeter of the deck, studying each board, each swirl of grain, moving one foot, one muscle, one leg at a time, in a slow meditation. Coming full circle, I sit down next to him again, looking out at the rooftops. "I don't know what to do, Steven. Didn't you know all this would affect me?"

"I thought I could keep it separate from us. I wanted my secret. I thought I could smoke and you wouldn't know. You didn't need to know how I got it. I was protecting you."

My teeth chatter again, even though the sun now touches the entire platform of the shrine. Every question, every answer, leads to more questions, more doubts. My mind searches back through the previous months. "At Christmastime, why did Customs call us about that package of salami and woolen socks that your son Robert sent us? Remember, they said you couldn't import salami, but did we want the socks?"

"That wasn't connected."

"I think it was. They must've already been suspicious. I don't believe you can't import salami. Was there marijuana in that package too?"

"No, he wouldn't do that."

I take a long drink of water from my bottle. I question our whole time in Japan. How many layers of secrets are there? There must be other questions that I don't know to ask. Yes, he's opened up to me at last, but I fear the unknown, past and future. I believe his answers. Or do I? Can I ever trust this man again? I don't think we're at the bottom of this, but for now I've taken in as much as I can handle.

I offer him some water. "I need to stop now. I'm exhausted. We've got to find a way out of this. Together. I'll do everything I can." Waiting for him to drink, I ponder my options. What else can I do but help him? I can't run back to the States, abandoning him to police and prison. I'm his wife and partner, and I love him intensely. If our positions were reversed, I know he'd help me. I have to pull him into action; if he cannot, I have to take action alone. I don't yet know how I'll rescue him or how I can survive without someone to support me. But somehow I will find the strength.

This is my usual style in this marriage. I think I have to solve everything, not insisting that he take responsibility. I never ask, what are you going to do about this, how are you going to get us out? I know what the answer will be: "We'll know more on Monday . . . I don't know the full charges—or the Japanese procedures. I have to take one day at a time." In the weeks ahead this will continue to be his survival strategy. I pretend to endorse it, but it frustrates me; I prefer to plan ahead and map out a strategy.

My usual style is also to soothe and reassure. I don't ask Steven for an apology. Even for minor offenses, he's slow to give one. I've accepted that, rarely asking for them directly. Today at the shrine I'm too focused on digging out the truth. An apology can come later. As always, I think the truth alone will solve all problems and that an apology won't help. I'm wrong. Later I'll learn that asking for an apology, insisting he take responsibility, and expressing my anger actually work quite effectively.

I hug him tight. "We'll get through this, I know we will. As long as we keep talking. No more secrets."

Steven hugs me back, long and close and soft, whispering, "No more secrets." I don't know if what I'm saying is true, but I'm determined to make it happen.

Hand in hand, we descend the steep wooden stairs to where our bicycles lie on the clean smooth earth. It's felt good to try a new confrontational style. With most of the men in my life, I've feared confrontation, including with my grown son, and my father when I was a child. Yet here at the shrine I'm still only digging for facts, not for the larger problems between us.

We climb back on our bikes and pedal up the arduous hill for the rest of our journey to the temple. The road is too vertical, so we hop off and push our bikes side by side, admiring with silent gestures each tiny garden, with the rows of bonsai plants, towering bamboo, and raked paths. The sky has cleared, the day warming up a bit, and the green leaves of each tree are sharply etched against the blue. As we ascend, the muscles of my legs and arms strain against the angle of the mountain. Glancing over at Steven, I see him fall behind, his face closed up again, eyes cast down, focusing on each slow footstep.

Like the bamboo bending and swaying in the strong late-morning wind, I want to find the strength I will need to endure the days or weeks ahead. My eyes follow the line of one frond all the way down until it touches the ground. I study each individual boat-shaped leaf and breathe more steadily, in and out. Will Steven be strong enough to hold up his end? I can't do it all alone, and I'll resent it if he deserts me emotionally. In a crisis, I know he can be either intensely passive or intensely active, show-ing amazing resilience and persistence. I hope he'll call on those hidden reserves this time.

Has the talk at the shrine changed Steven as much as it has me? A fragile paper door has slid open for me, revealing a glim-mer of fresh air. I can't tell what he's feeling, but I sense his sor-row and his gratitude that I'll stand by him both physically and emotionally. And I sense his silent apology. I don't think I'm fooling myself once again.

Gripping the handlebars more tightly, I forge ahead up the never-ending hill. Finally, Entsū-ji, a Buddhist temple three hundred and fifty years old. As the land levels out, I jump on my bike and call back to Steven, "C'mon. Here it is." The dark wooden temple shines with ancient luster atop the mountain, its tall doors swung wide open in welcome. We walk together along the path of the outer garden, each stepping-stone encircled in velvet green moss. As we pass through the doors, an unseen tem-ple bell tolls twelve times, full and sweet.

The scent of incense and candle wax drifts toward us, and the familiar peace of the temple envelops us, reminding both of us of our years of meditation together. The tension in Steven's shoulders relaxes as he breathes in the power of the temple. I link his elbow in mine as we stroll through the temple rooms and out to the central garden of rock, moss, and sand, enclosed on all sides by temple walls. Mount Hiei soars high above the garden in the distance, as if linking heaven and earth—the "borrowed scenery" I've read about, using natural landscape to enhance the creative composition of the garden. Turning at the same moment to gaze into each other's eyes, we smile, clasping hands. Then slowly letting go, we drift apart, each to find our own spe-cial place to sit and contemplate the sea of moss, the islands of rock, the raked lines of sand, the jewel of the mountain, and the rhythms between them.

THREE BLOSSOMS
IN A QUIET POND
An Interlude of Flowers

A white peony
wide open in the sunlight
no sound comes from it

— EDITH SHIFFERT

In the golden heart
of each white water lily
is there a Buddha?

— EDITH SHIFFERT

Every week I escaped into the world of flowers. My first lesson with my ikebana teacher happened only a few weeks before the police came, when my neighbor Lisa took me along to her class. She had studied ikebana for years and was fluent in Japanese.

That night we bundled up in our winter clothes. The fierce cold bit at my cheeks and whipped around my scarf and wool hat. Lisa led me out the back of our apartment building, through the parking lot, down the tiny side street with the rice shop and the tatami maker's shop, then over the small bridge of the Takano River.

I had been searching for an ikebana mentor to study with, one like Kuroda sensei, my flute teacher, where I would find the same intensity and continuity. The series of ikebana classes I had taken at the Community House in the fall intrigued me with the simplicity and peaceful beauty of the arrangements, but the class's noisy lack of focus left me dissatisfied.

Right after the bridge, Lisa made a sharp left through a narrow slot in a tall, wide hedge. "Here's where we go. You need to remember this hedge." A series of footpaths connected several small old cottages, like a family compound. The third house on the right was Sensei's. The glassed-in porch was lit up, bright and welcoming. Lisa showed me where to put my coat and sweaters, and where to line up my shoes in a neat row with the others. I followed close behind her, copying her actions. We each picked up a bundle of flowers from a pile in the corner, then entered the house through a low door, bending down so that we were already in a bow as we emerged into the warm, cozy tatami room.

Several Japanese women, in their twenties and thirties, knelt on either side of the low table, their dark heads bent, their fingers already immersed in their flowers. The women glanced up at me with shy smiles and nods and murmured the good evening greeting, "*Konbanwa*." The room was heady with the rich smell of moist blossoms, kerosene heat, tatami mats, and young women's scrubbed, unperfumed bodies. The elderly Sensei, with her beautiful, wrinkled face, bowed to me in dignified silence.

Lisa settled me next to her at the table. I ached to get to know these delicate young Japanese women, to be engrossed in their language and their gentle whispering. I was dismayed that I couldn't understand a word they were saying and by how long it would be before I could.

I knelt on my cushion, staring at the low flat vase in front of me on the table, the wide expanse of water in the empty vessel like an open sea, an open book, a blank piece of writing paper.

This class was already different from the ones at the Community House, where the students were *gaijin*, and the teacher a different middle-aged Japanese housewife each time. At those sessions, the teacher demonstrated how to make an arrangement, explaining the rules, then took all of the stalks out of the *kenzan* and laid them on the table. Next, one student at a time tried to make the same arrangement from memory, with no model to look at. The teacher critiqued it, then dismantled it, so the next student could take her turn. Often I was the last student in line. The stems had grown soggy and limp, the bottoms frayed. I snipped each one a bit shorter to firm it up and attempted my arrangement. I tried to shut out the *gaijin* women's giggles and chatter, gravitating toward the calm stillness of the Japanese teacher and entering my own garden, my own pool of peaceful water.

Here at Sensei's house, the students were silently absorbed in their work. I knew they came every week, committed to studying the art in depth, the wise Sensei always there, kindly guiding them.

We each worked on our own. I laid out my fresh bundle of flowers next to my *suiban*, the low flat vase. Then unpacked and separated each flower, laying each blossom's neck over the table edge toward me, so it hung down and was not bent or crushed. I watched Lisa at each step to see what to do.

Sensei had chosen the three kinds of flowers, the shape of the *suiban*, and the style of arrangement. Lisa had told me that Sensei had studied ikebana since childhood, following the Ōhara tradition, one of the main ikebana lineages, founded at the end of the nineteenth century. Today she had created a model flower arrangement that stood in the center of the table. We were supposed to study it from all angles and attempt to copy it. She gave no rules or explanations. We had to figure that out by ourselves. Thank goodness I had scribbled the basic rules in my notebook at the Community House classes: the varying heights of the three main stems; the proper angle of each stem relative to each other, to the vase, and to me; and whether they should slant at forty-five or sixty or thirty degrees.

I peered at Sensei's model, then peeked sidewise at Lisa's ikebana. She whispered to me, "This is the Heavenly or Upright style, one of the basics." I lifted up my first stem, a stately quince branch laden with pink blossoms and buds, and I began. This would be the main stem, I remembered from the Community House, sometimes called the "subject" or "host" in English. I trimmed away the unnecessary side branches and blossoms, in order to accent the chosen blooms and curves. I measured the stalk against the *suiban*, cutting it exactly the right length of one-and-a-half times the length plus the width of the vase. I placed it in the spiked *kenzan*, or frog, toward the back of the vase, at a straight vertical angle.

I tried for Sensei's structure, her angles, her heights, her spaces. But I knew I didn't have to match hers perfectly. Hers was a guideline. Each of ours would be different, and that would be okay.

As a child, my experience with art had been quite the opposite. I had waited in the car with my mother while my older sister sketched the fallen-down barn with her new pencils and sketch pad. Mother told me I didn't know how to draw. She never thought to give me my own crayons and scratch paper and let me try anyway. My mother couldn't draw either, and she had grown up with a sister who could. In her mind, you either had talent or you didn't.

Again, I studied Sensei's model, then watched the student across from me to know what to do next. Tentatively, I took the "secondary" stem, another quince branch, cut it to half the size of the subject, and placed it in front of the subject at about a fifteen-degree angle slanted toward my left shoulder. Then I chose the "object" stem, a fluffy white plume of stock blossoms, cut it to one third the size of the subject, and placed it facing toward me at a low angle of maybe eighty degrees. I gradually added the third kind of flower, two short branches of shiny green camellia leaves with plump buds. Working within the comforting structure of the *suiban*, the *kenzan*, and the imaginary triangle of flowers, I found myself soaring with a new freedom. The simple rules and the flow of my heart seemed to balance each other.

When I finished my arrangement, Lisa nudged me. I could motion to Sensei that I was done and ready, or I could simply sit until she came. I looked around at the other women. As each one finished, she sat back on her heels, hands in lap, and waited for Sensei. But it was not waiting. It was more like Kuroda sensei, my *shakuhachi* teacher, when he stood by the open window before his flute performance, immersed in peaceful meditation.

Sensei shuffled around the table on her knees, making the rounds from student to student, critiquing each one. I discovered I could learn from these other critiques as much as from my own. Sensei approached me, smiled, and kneeled on my cushion as I moved to the side. I didn't understand her Japanese words of praise, but I could tell from the warmth of her tone and face. She thoughtfully adjusted an angle, a placement, a height, a spacing. She studied and studied it. Another tiny adjustment. I watched each one, attempting to memorize what she did. How could such a small change turn my clump of flowers into a floating elegance? Sensei honored what I had done. It was barely a lesson. It was doing ikebana together with her as a guide.

"Now take it all out and try again," Lisa whispered.

Oh, no, I thought. I didn't want to take it down. I'd created this thing of beauty, even if imperfect. Sensei had made it perfect. How would I ever recreate it?

This was not my second-grade teacher tearing up my crayon drawing in front of the class, saying it was wrong, that it didn't look like the perfect house and perfect daisy she had drawn. I wasn't allowed to tear it up myself or to start over. It was simply wrong. But her destroying my drawing forty years ago was not the same as me now in Kyoto tenderly taking all the stalks out of the *kenzan* and trying again.

Mono no aware. The fleeting beauty of the moment, impermanence: all things change and fade. Beginner's mind, no attachment. Perseverance. Each time, your fingers grow stronger, your heart more flexible, your eye more sure. These were the lessons being taught, by doing, undoing, copying the model, not by talking or lecturing.

Now I could understand why my son's college ceramics teacher, at the end of each day of making pots, made the students gather up the clay, lump it together, and throw it back into the can for the next day, to begin again.

I pulled out all the stalks and made the same style of ikebana, new and different while striving for the same. And again I sat in silence until she approached me. She praised, she adjusted. I took mental notes. I sensed that no written notes were allowed here, just as Kuroda sensei had forbidden them. Learning the arts in Japan was an ancient oral tradition, a hierarchy of passing on knowledge from teacher to student, teacher to student.

I attempted it again. As many times as I wanted, Sensei was always there to study and adjust. The silent repetitions with her compassionate guidance took away the power, the fear, the anxiety for perfection. Like *zazen*, like "Writing Practice," it was not good, not bad. I merely did it, like breathing over and over again.

When the class was over, I mimicked the other students' actions, wrapping up my flowers, now cut and used, in the newspaper. From our kneeling position on our cushions, Lisa and I bowed deeply toward Sensei, our palms resting flat on the table and our heads almost touching it. Sensei bowed back, only half as deep, to show her superior position as teacher. Lisa showed me how to pay discretely, slipping the cash for the month into a special envelope at one end of the table. She explained class was once a week from two o'clock to eight o'clock. You went as often and as long as you wanted each month, always paying the same amount once a month, no matter how many times you had come.

I bowed again as I backed out of the room, cradling my flowers, my secrets, these simple stems of beauty. They were hidden away, ready to be unfolded once again at home.

BROKEN VALENTINE

How invisibly
it changes color
in this world,
the flower
of the human heart.

— ONO NO KOMACHI (tr. Jane Hirshfield & Mariko Aratani)

Takeda, Steven's boss, stretches out in the easy chair in the kitchen while Steven and I squirm on the straight-backed chairs at the table. It is the evening after the eighth day of the Investigation. Steven pours sake into the ceramic *tokkuri* pitcher, heats it in the microwave, and lays out *senbei*, the golden rice crackers coated with pungent seaweed that always make me sneeze. As the evening wears on and Steven pours more and more sake into the thimble-sized *choko*, Steven and Takeda gradually sink to the linoleum floor. They sit cross-legged and alternate serious talk with bursts of laughter.

I cannot laugh. Watching from the kitchen table in the corner, I hold back tears as I take tiny sips of sake, unable to let go of the tension hovering above us. Yet I am happy to see it loosen for a few minutes into tentative friendship, with both men smiling, their shoulders relaxed.

Around eleven thirty, Takeda sits up straight, tosses back another cup of sake, and sets the cup down. "You must resign from the university. The board is pressuring me. We cannot wait until the Investigation ends." He sighs, not looking at Steven. This is a long speech for this taciturn man, his face creased with pain and shadow. "I am so very sorry. I have held out as long as I could."

77

I stare into my empty sake cup. Every night this week, they have debated resignation. Some nights Takeda wants it, other nights he doesn't. Some nights Steven does, others he doesn't. I push my cup away to the far side of the table. I can't drink any more. I don't want him to resign. Yet it seems the honorable thing to do. Steven has betrayed both Takeda and the university. But at a university in the States, this wouldn't mean resignation. It might mean banishment to another department, a leave of absence, or a public apology. And in the States, Steven's crime would not be taken so seriously; the U.S. consulate has told me that here in Japan, marijuana is treated more like heroin.

Steven nervously scratches the linoleum with one finger. He sticks his feet straight out, his spine curled and crooked, like a broken toy soldier. I can't tell what he's thinking. His whole identity and his livelihood as a professor are at stake.

Steven rouses himself and fills Takeda's cup. "I'll resign tomorrow."

"Thank you," Takeda says. "Here's what you have to say."

They move to the kitchen table while I grab paper and pencil from Steven's desk. As they bend their heads together, Takeda dictates, and Steven writes. It has to be the proper format with formal phrases, so Steven doesn't worsen the situation.

I carry their sake cups to the table and refill the *tokkuri*. Reaching into the cupboard, I pull out more *senbei* but hold them far from my nose, the fumes rising from their shiny surface like fresh shellac on a hot day. A million questions buzz through my mind, but I don't want to interfere with their process.

Resignation. My mind races then stalls as that word hits me. No salary as long as we're forced to stay in Japan. What if we run out of money? We can't live on my meager income from my rental property in California, or from my few private ESL students here. *Gaijin* are not allowed to work without proper visas. Steven was brought over specifically for this job; legally, I'm not allowed to work at all because I'm on a "dependent" visa. Without a job you aren't allowed to live here, but we are not allowed to leave.

I slide open the glass door, step out on the porch. The black night air cools my cheeks. On the street below an occasional car swishes by and the sidewalk is empty. The clouds hang bulky and silent, and I breathe in my momentary solitude. One cloud shifts, revealing a faint star.

To my surprise, I find myself whispering my mother's three-line prayer:

Give me the serenity to accept the things I cannot change,
the courage to change the things I can,
and the wisdom to know the difference.

I wonder where or when my mother first discovered it. Probably years ago in *Reader's Digest*. I used to find her version in her scrawled handwriting everywhere around her house, especially after my father died when I was twenty-four and she was fifty-nine. One would flutter out when she opened her poetry book to read me her favorite verse. Or when she handed me her wallet to pay for one of our monthly lunches, it would be slipped in back of the twenty-dollar bills. When she sent me to fetch her big old dictionary so she could look up a new word, it would be taped to the inside cover; or when I sifted through her clothes closet to find her peach-colored robe, it would be pinned to the back wall. Every time it annoyed and embarrassed me. How could those simple lines help? But they were not hollow words for her; she embodied those lines in every moment of her life. I didn't know, nor did she, that the prayer was composed by Reinhold Niebuhr, a Protestant theologian, around 1941, and was adapted during World War II by Alcoholics Anonymous.

Now I whisper the words in earnest, adopting her same ferocity. If she could do it, so can I.

Takeda and Steven resume their cross-legged positions on the floor. I grab my *choko* and join them, filling all three cups.

"What does this mean for us?" I ask, trying to keep my voice calm and neutral, though inside I'm quaking.

Takeda glances at the floor, then out the dark window. "Steven's salary will stop at the end of this month." He pauses. "You will have to leave this apartment."

"When?" I ask.

"February 15," Takeda replies.

Today is February 8. Only three more weeks of salary, only seven more days in this apartment. We can't possibly leave that soon. My eyes linger on the low ikebana of camellia and narcissus on the coffee table, on the curving branch atop the fridge that I decorated with purple and orange silk charms from the temples for our Christmas tree, and on the pot of miso soup on the stove ready to heat up for tomorrow's breakfast. Housing in Kyoto is impossible to find and prohibitively expensive.

I look over at Steven. He looks back with heavy lids, his usually pliable face closed up. He reaches out to rest his hand on my thigh. I am as numb as if I'd sat all day in the dentist's chair.

"Where will we go?" I ask.

Takeda gazes into his cup as if it were a bottomless pit. "I'll work something out. I'll arrange everything with the apartment manager downstairs."

As our sponsor, Takeda is still taking care of us, in spite of the pain and loss of face Steven has caused him. Will he tell that apartment manager, with her pinched face and severe gray suit, why we are leaving? When we first arrived, she refused to let us exchange our Western twin beds for a futon, and later she locked up the piano in the Community Room so that I couldn't practice.

Takeda unwinds his long legs, nimbly pushes himself up to kneeling, then standing. We rise too, slowly unkinking our stiff knees. It is past midnight. The men say goodnight Western-style, shaking hands, then pulling close in a comradely hug. Takeda learned about masculine hugs when he lived in Spain. I give him a traditional low bow to show respect. And then, even though it's not common except at Buddhist temples, Steven and I each press our two hands together in front of our faces, in a *gasshō*, to show our gratitude.

Takeda understands. He turns to the door, his face long and shadowed, his shoulders heavy. "I'll come by tomorrow."

In silence, standing side by side at the sink, we wash the sake and *senbei* dishes. I am stunned and can find nothing to say. "Let's sit," I finally suggest.

Steven arranges our two round black cushions next to each other facing the wall and rings our meditation bell. The golden tone echoes through the room. After sitting *zazen* for our usual twenty minutes, we lie down on our futon, curled up like two caterpillars, facing each other.

"I'll call Martha," says Steven. "She'll wire us money if we run out. And we'll count our cash in my desk drawer." He cups his fingers around mine. "I'll teach you the *kanji* instructions at the ATM."

I pull him toward me, refusing to meet his eye. "I'm so worried. Where will we live?"

"Let's see what Takeda finds."

We slip under the quilt and cling to each other, first he holding me, then I him, all night long.

The next evening Takeda stops by to announce that we will stay at his house, in his extra bedroom.

We visited his suburban Western-style ranch house last summer after he took us on a picnic and hike in the mountains, in order to welcome us to Japan and help us escape the muggy Kyoto heat. I remember little about our new home, only the spacious living room with its piano and the dining room corner with its sliding-glass doors where we ate dinner. Takeda's wife and teenage children only visit during school vacations. She tried Japan for several years but could never adjust, so she returned to her native Spain. Perhaps this is why that bittersweet look creases his face, always a hint of melancholy drifting across, as if he were a Kabuki actor who can never quite shake his demons.

The minute Takeda leaves, Steven and I whirl around the kitchen in a dance. We have a place to live!

"I'm so relieved," I say. "But aren't we imposing on him? He's such a solitary man."

"We have to do whatever he says. Let's divide up the chores. What do we need to do these last seven days?"

The next morning Steven pulls out the list of moving companies that Takeda gave him. At last he can leap into action.

"I'll call some of those and get the best price," I say.

"No, I'll do it." He picks up the phone and signs up the first company on the list. They will wrap and pack all of our things and ship them home. All we have to do is sort them into categories.

But the movers call back the next day. They can't ship our belongings home now. They have to store them in Japan. Steven argues, but they won't budge. When we're ready to fly home, they'll ship them. Not before. And we will have no access to them. I fume as I pace back and forth in the five feet between fridge and sink. I am not going to pay for storage. It doesn't make sense. Probably it has to do with Steven's Investigation. It feels like the whole country is conspiring against us. Maybe the police called the movers or vice versa. Maybe they need to search our things again. But I want control of our possessions.

All that week, piles of books, clothes, papers, and files clutter the floors, the table, Steven's desk, my cabinet, and every corner. Boxes are scattered everywhere: half-open, half-full, or still empty. Our two huge suitcases gape open, waiting. I struggle under the weight of one box after another, stacking them at the side of the room. After seven and a half months in two small rooms, I can't believe we have so many things. But it's the uncertainties and the decisions that overwhelm me. What to send to storage, what to throw or give away, what to take with us to Takeda's?

While Steven sorts the papers in his desk drawers, I sift through the books and files in my cabinet. Should I take enough for one week, one month, one year? I choose *The Tale of Genji*, and *Zen Mind, Beginner's Mind* by Shunryu Suzuki, and a haiku book by Edith Shiffert, my seventy-year-old mentor whom I met at my women's group. If I need more, I can go to Kyoto's English-language bookstore. I pack one teaching file to use with my four remaining students; the rest I am forced to let go. Into the box for Takeda's, I add my journal and the supplies for my art lessons: *shakuhachi*, ikebana, *shodō*, and Japanese cooking. Also, my language notebook for my lesson with our tutor Toru. I must squeeze in these lessons during the days ahead; I will need them as my refuge.

Next, I clatter open my closet door and stare at the tall piles of clothes. Will I need spring clothes? Summer? I choose two sweaters, then put one back; choose six shirts, then exchange one for another and return two. Finally, I use a trick of Steven's: pretend or make believe when something is difficult. I pretend I am taking a short trip, snatch two changes of clothes, then add some silk long underwear, in case Takeda's is chilly like most houses here. Probably he owns a washer, and hopefully we'll be out of Kyoto before spring. If not . . . I force my mind toward the kitchen.

I bang cupboard doors open and shut and rattle dishes as I pile them loosely into a box. I don't know if Takeda cooks. I've never seen his kitchen. In Japan they're usually the size of a boat galley. Steven joins me, and we work side by side to sort, choose, and pack. Not trusting the movers, we wrap in newspaper our collection of traditional artifacts: the ceramic sake cups and *tok-kuri* pitcher, the red enamel rice bowls and square *bentō* boxes. I linger over the two pieces of *Hagi yaki*, teacups with a pale mauve lacy glaze from Hagi, the pottery village we visited in the mountains. We won't need them at Takeda's. Or our pots and pans and everyday dishes. Those we can give to our neighbors. But, no, they will ask why, and I'll have to lie.

While I cushion the teapot in multiple layers, I ponder who to tell about our move and how to say it. In Japan, only our small circle knows our secret: Takeda, Tom and his wife, and the lawyer, Fukuda. A week ago, I confided in Clover, my new and only friend here. She's an American artist from the women's group I finally joined only two weeks before the police came. We met for tea, and I blurted out my secret, bursting to tell someone, anyone. And during a recent tearful lesson, I told our tutor, Toru, as he sat across from me with his grizzly, frizzy ponytail. At each lesson since the police knocked, he had asked me where Steven was and why he kept canceling his appointments. By the third time, I broke down and told him our news, which quickly pulled him in as an ally and confidant.

In the States, only our five children and Steven's sister Martha know what has happened. We call them with Takeda's address and phone number but do not use the word *eviction*. I'm too ashamed to tell my mother; I know how much she loves Steven, and I don't want her to hate him for this. Instead, I write saying we've found a nice big house to live in, with a friend. For Kuroda sensei, my flute teacher, I write down my new phone number but offer no reason. For the others in Japan—like Lisa, the woman who escorted me to her Sensei's ikebana class; Suzuki, our former language teacher turned tentative friend; Yoshiko, the woman from the summer hike in the mountains with Takeda; and all of Steven's colleagues—we simply disappear.

At that same tearful Japanese lesson with Toru, I asked him what I should say to my eight students who I must stop teaching.

"I can't teach them at Takeda's house," I said. I could no longer teach them at our apartment, or in the Library upstairs or the Community Room downstairs. Once we'd moved, I wouldn't dare show my face there again.

"You must say your mother is sick and you must return to America," Toru said.

"I can't say that. It's a bad omen."

"It's the only excuse they'll accept."

"Why can't I say the truth, that I'm moving and there's no place to teach?" I held my pencil poised over my notebook. "How do I say that?"

"Okay, but later you'll need the other excuse."

After Toru left, I picked up the phone, my hands shaking. I didn't want to do this. I dialed the first number and said the one Japanese phrase I had jotted down. The student said, "Okay, bye-bye," in English. I said, "I am sorry, bye." My Japanese on the phone was almost nonexistent. No chance for conversation, only awkward pauses. I wanted to ask for their addresses so I could keep in touch, but I wouldn't be able to understand their answers. One by one I worked through my list of students, crossing each one out as I hung up the phone.

I keep my four favorites, who happen to live in the neighborhood. Yuki was my very first student. Last July, Steven found her for me. He was smoking his pipe, waiting for me under the huge sprawling tree in front of the apartment house. Yuki and her mother tentatively approached him, asking if he knew of an English teacher. He said, yes, my wife. When I joined him a few minutes later, he introduced us and launched my ESL teaching career. She soon became my most loyal student, an eager twenty-year-old with a passion for both English and her golden Labrador.

Now, I ask her if I can teach in her home instead of at my apartment. It's unusual for a Japanese person to allow this; homes are private, places to withdraw and relax away from the rigid rules of society. They are not for strangers or *gaijin* teachers. But she agrees, even enthusiastically.

Makiko and her two little girls are new students whom I already teach at their home. They lived in New Jersey and know Western ways. I'm always greeted with excitement and served Western-style tea and homemade cookies.

As I ride the elevator one day up to our apartment, during that last endless week of packing, the words of a large poster jump out at me, in both English and *kanji*.

A Valentine's Day Party!!
For all apartment house residents and their Japanese friends.
In the Community Room at one o'clock.
Looking for volunteer musicians.
Sponsored by the University Japanese Women's Society.

February 14! Our last day here. My heart flies up to the top floor and out the roof to the sky. For them, a Valentine's party; for us, a silent, secret farewell. I will play my *shakuhachi*! A perfect way to say goodbye. The moment I open the door to the apartment, I rush to the phone to call the woman in charge.

At my next flute lesson I ask Kuroda sensei for guidance. He merely nods, giving me neither a no nor a yes. No hints, no advice, but agreeing "Kyorei" would be the piece to play. He implies I'm still too much of a beginner. Undeterred, I ride home on the train, determined to practice hard every day.

At last Valentine's Day arrives. I gather up my *shakuhachi* and folder of music and walk with Steven downstairs to the large Community Room. High-pitched conversation bubbles through the air; clusters of women and children sit at the activity tables, already busy creating Valentines and origami. The room is crowded with both *gaijin* and Japanese, most of whom I've never seen before.

Steven and I separate, each mingling with the crowd in our own way. I've never seen such a big gathering at our building. Where do these people come from? Usually they hide away in their apartments, and only a handful show up for the periodic sponsored events. I have attended every one, eager for the opportunity to be part of the university community: observing a lacquerware craftsman at work, learning the intricate way to dress in the many layers of a kimono, or practicing the chanting of Noh drama.

But I haven't reached out to any of the *gaijin* women from these events. I've missed a rich opportunity here, a six-story building full of potential friends from a variety of cultures, all with one thing in common—adjustment to the Japanese culture. Instead I've tried to befriend the Japanese, but without success, since most of them are hesitant to form friendships with us foreigners. This is a transient *gaijin* population, with new residents coming and going every week, their fellowships or temporary jobs finished. I haven't yet learned the value of a short-term friend, or even of a one-time friend, and that I can have exhilarating interaction, no matter how brief our time together. At first I was shy, and then, like many of the other *gaijin* couples, I clung to Steven and our tight coupledom, uniting against this puzzling foreign world.

Now it no longer matters. We're leaving, with no chance of making friends out in those suburbs at Takeda's. And I've nothing left to give a friend; I'm too depleted and preoccupied. I can't offer what my best friend back home claims I give her: a calm, comforting serenity, with optimism and insightful feedback. Today I have only Steven and my *shakuhachi*.

I search the Community Room for the Japanese woman in charge and ask her where I'll be playing. She shows me to a circular area in one corner of the room where she's arranged a cushion on the rug with a chair next to it. I can choose which way to sit. She says I'll be the only one playing. I panic, stage fright flooding in. I expected supportive fellow musicians. I think of my junior high school cafeteria, where I was required by my teacher to perform in competitions, standing up alone, the linoleum floor slick, the shrill silver flute echoing off the bare walls, the blurry faces of the other students staring back at me. I arrange my *shakuhachi* on the chair, fumbling with the folder of music as it almost slips to the floor and scatters.

"What time will I play?" I ask.

"I don't know," she replies. "It depends how the party goes."

I drift from one activity table to the next. At the Valentine table I sit with a group of Japanese women and children. Our scissors snap, colored papers fly, paste sticks to our fingers as we rustle in the piles of lace and sprinkle glitter all over the table. The children giggle and the women cover their mouths whenever they laugh, while they watch me to see how an American does it. At the origami table, I let the children teach me with their experienced, nimble fingers. They laugh at my misshapen, lopsided boat, and I join in.

At the *shodō* calligraphy table, I spread out a smooth, absorbent piece of creamy rice paper. I close my eyes for a moment, then dip my brush into the thick black ink, rolling the long bristles into a pointed globe, coated with ink. I peek at the Japanese woman next to me to see how to hold my brush, where to start on the complex *kanji* character in front of me. She nods and smiles. I know the basics from my weekly class, but each time I'm a beginner. I peer at the orange-inked *kanji* model set up in front of us, trying to copy its suggestive rough curves and ups and downs. The model *kanji* means winter rain, the leader always choosing something appropriate to the season or occasion. As we work, the black of the calligraphy jumps off the white paper, and the camaraderie wraps around me as we bend our heads to the paper, our brushes poised. No laughter, but a silent meditative concentration, touched with occasional sighs of frustration or delight. One of the Society women circulates, helping each of us with a horizontal stroke, a circle, or a trailing end point. She holds my hand loosely in hers, guiding it. Then a silent laugh of encouragement, and "*Jōzu desu ne.* Good, you're doing great." Which of course I am not. She selects a fresh sheet of paper. "Here, try again, and again."

I look around and catch Steven's eye. He is circulating the room, practicing his Japanese with the Japanese women, talking with animation to *gaijin* of both sexes. He gestures in expansive circles, raising his bushy black eyebrows for emphasis. With almost his old bounce and a hint of his usual mischievous gleam, he watches the handwork at the tables or moves to the food table to munch on sticky sweets, salty rice crackers, and tea. His troubles are well hidden as he plays the part of charming foreigner.

As I dip my brush again, the odor of the ink, sweet and pungent like a smoke-filled bat cave, makes my stomach lurch. My brush wavers. When will the leader call me to begin playing? Will I be able to make a sound on my flute? What will my life be like at Takeda's? I re-dip my brush, close my eyes to envision the *kanji* shape, and reenter the world of *shodō*.

Steven and I meet up at the game table, where a large poster in the shape of a big round cartoon face, blank without features, is pinned on the wall. We try to puzzle out the rules. It's a version of Pin the Tail on the Donkey but with exaggerated face parts to pin on instead of a donkey's tail. One middle-aged Japanese woman with short permed hair and playful eyes sits down next to us and transforms it into a language game, teaching us the words for cheek, eyebrow, mustache, and chin. Steven and I each take a turn. With my eyes closed tight, hands held out stiff in front, I stumble toward the blank face, surrounded by squeals of glee.

In the midst of the laughter, someone grasps my upper arm from behind. I jump in surprise. It is the woman in charge. Time for the concert. I turn away, seeking Steven's face. He squeezes my hand and whispers, "Good luck. I'll be there with you." I follow the woman to the opposite corner of the room, my legs almost dissolving into the rug. On a low table, an ikebana beckons me, a Japanese plum branch with small pink blossoms, chosen to be appropriate for the winter season.

I kneel on the cushion in traditional *seiza* style, my legs tucked under me, and smooth my wool plaid skirt around my knees in a semicircle. With shaking hands, I spread the sheet music out flat on the rug. "Kyorei," the ancient meditative song Kuroda sensei played as if in a trance, at my first lesson. At his insistence, I have memorized it, the only piece I ever have in all my years of flute playing. But today I can't take the chance that I might forget even one note.

Since I warmed up in the apartment earlier, I should be ready. But I'm not. Still too much of a beginner after only four months of lessons. If I become too nervous, I will lose my breath and be unable to play. I'm sorry I signed up for this. But I was so eager to give with music what I couldn't give with words.

Again I am in that junior high cafeteria, halfway through a flute piece, when my face flushed and sweat trickled down to my chin so the mouthpiece slipped away from my lips. There I was, unable to make a sound, unable to finish the piece. After that, I refused to take lessons from any teacher who insisted that I perform.

Maybe now I'm beyond that. But the *shakuhachi* is even more dependent on the breath than the silver flute; it requires a relaxed breath and a relaxed diaphragm to produce any sound at all. Discreetly, I dry my sweating hands on the cloth handkerchief I've hidden under my skirt.

A half circle of Japanese faces looks up at me eagerly. They are mostly women, kneeling in *seiza* like me. A few tall *gaijin* are scattered in back. How dare I presume to play the *shakuhachi*, their instrument, for these women? I haven't studied the required seven years needed for any traditional art here. If only I had excused myself from the party for ten minutes to go upstairs, warm up again, and meditate. Too late now.

I take three solid breaths and try to smile, then catch Steven's eye. He's sitting in the back row. I'll play for him.

"Today, I will play 'Kyorei,' 'Empty Bell,'" I say. I recount the legend that Kuroda sensei told me, of the disciple hearing the beautiful bell and making a flute out of a piece of bamboo to match the sound. I mention my years playing silver flute, my lessons with Kuroda sensei, and that I've only studied *shakuhachi* for four months.

They all nod, their faces serious, but kind. Women in Japan never play *shakuhachi*; they play *koto*. Only a *gaijin* would dare try. They know it usually takes months to blow the first sound.

I raise the flute to my lips and blow the first note, my trembling fingers steadied by the familiar silky roundness of the sturdy bamboo. Breathy, but it does come out. Thank goodness *shakuhachi* notes are supposed to be rough, like breathing in and out through a length of bamboo. I play the next note. Then the whole first phrase. The sound is low and soft, but I am making music.

My mind wanders. I dread the move to Takeda's house. Will it work out or not? I panic and look at Steven. My lips and throat tense. My diaphragm coils like tangled roots. When I blow again, no sound comes out. I try again. Still no sound. I pause, lower the flute, offer a pale smile. "When I get nervous, it's difficult."

Eyes closed, two full breaths. I try again. A small sound. Too weak, but the breathy pattern of long low notes floats into the room. Then it fades. The harder I strain to make a sound, the tighter my throat and belly, the weaker the note. Until no sound at all, just air whispering through the bamboo. Sensei was right. I am not ready.

I lay my flute across my lap and bow deeply. "I am sorry. I cannot finish the song."

They clap lightly, with both wise understanding and expectations of success still in their eyes and smiles.

"I'll finish with a folk song." I haven't planned this. I don't especially like Japanese folk songs; they aren't slow and meditative. But Sensei insists I learn them because they're good for my technique and show me a different side of Japanese culture. Fortunately I've brought along my folder of music.

I pull out "Kisobushi," a folk song from the town of Kiso. It's one of the most popular folk songs, easy to play, fast and spirited, high and melodic. Every toddler learns it at home. I don't announce the title, merely launch into the first line.

I glance up at the Japanese faces beaming at me. By the second line, they all join in, with thin, reedy, high-pitched voices, singing out the words, women and children alike, eyes shining, heads bobbing with the rhythm. The room floods with song.

Kiso no naa nakanori san
Kiso no ontake san wa nan-jara-hoi
natsu demo samui
yoi-yoi-yoi.

The boatman of Kiso
ferries the wood from Kiso's Ontake mountain.
How is it?
Even in summer it is cold.
Yoi-yoi-yoi.

I'm playing loud and strong, the spotlight off me. I offer them this gift of song, this hidden goodbye. Bittersweet joy pours into my throat and out my flute. I repeat the last chorus, lingering on the final tone in the air before laying my flute across my lap. I lean forward with a bow, my head almost touching the floor.

They clap and clap, smiling and buzzing with talk, then crowd up around me. "*Jōzu desu ne.* You are so talented. You play beautifully. *Dōmo arigatō gozaimasu.* Thank you for knowing our songs." It all tumbles out in a mixture of Japanese and English.

I'm warmed and comforted by their pleasure. Steven sits down next to me, pats my thigh, and leans forward to murmur in my ear, "You did fine. They loved it." He helps me up from my *seiza* position, my legs and knees stiff and numb, and hooks his elbow in mine.

The next morning the movers arrive. They are four men in black. The two slight and small men wrap each item with slow precision. They finger my blouses and dresses, tilt my ESL books, and rifle my stacks of field notes. With my hands in my lap, I sit watching them, my thoughts rushing back to that day the police knocked. The two heavy and strong men carry the boxes downstairs, load them into their truck, and are gone.

The minute they leave, Steven and I tackle the apartment with mops and buckets. The sharp cleansing powder stings my eyes and sends Steven to the porch sneezing and coughing. I attack the dirt with a vengeance as if it can absorb my submerged anger and despair. We scrub and scour the inside and outside of every surface—closet, cupboard, drawer, stove, and fridge. Working peacefully side by side, we never question who will clean what or who will clean more, as we did at home. Here, we have a common goal. We know the high Japanese standards of cleanliness and the sourness of the downstairs manager. We don't want to be fined or called back to do more.

As the day wears on, we drip with sweat, in spite of the cold wind that blows in when we open the porch door for air. We don't talk much, but we work as if scrubbing could destroy the evidence, erase the fear and the lies, give us our lives back. With a silent mindful concentration, we lean into the task, like the meditative work practice of a Zen *samu*.

The watery winter sun streams through the open door and mingles with the strong scent of soap, drying my sweat and giving me little prisms of hope. Maybe things will be better at Takeda's. This apartment has smothered us: the scene of Steven's crime, the place of our "house arrest," the black knock on the door.

Finally, we stand back and admire our work: the empty space echoes around us, the floors and cupboards shine, the carpet stretches cool and clean. It's like new, as if we've never lived here.

Late afternoon, Toru, our ponytailed tutor, arrives and helps Steven and me load up his miniature Toyota, until it overflows like a bulging clown car. They trudge up and down the elevator until everything—our suitcases and endless boxes and bags—is piled at the curb, while I heave boxes, cram bags in corners, and fit things in like a jigsaw puzzle.

Steven climbs in the passenger side. Before they drive off to Takeda's house, Toru pokes his head out the window. "Guard your stuff or else people will steal it. They'll think it's public property."

I sit on the curb to wait and survey our bulky mound of possessions. We're taking too much to Takeda's. But these things are all I have left in this twisted, upside-down world. And I want the homey familiarity of my own peanut butter, oatmeal, my favorite haiku book. If only I'd also saved out those two teacups from Hagi, with their fragile beauty. I poke the bags of rice, beans, and whole-wheat flour and rattle the bottles of oil, sake, *shōyu*, and *mirin*. I can't face throwing out these staples. Surely Steven will resume cooking at Takeda's. For him, creating a *nabe* stew or poaching a *saba*, mackerel, in wine sauce is a serious art form. And I will cook too. There won't be much else we can do while we await the next step of this mysterious plodding Investigation.

I stand up and pace the curving sidewalk, staring down at the cracks of the concrete. They've been gone too long. The round trip should take about thirty minutes. What if someone sees me? I can say we're moving to a friend's house. That's all they need to know, but even that prospect shames me. After checking my watch, I glance up at the dark mountains in the distance, the trees fading to nothing in the approaching dusk. I pull my sweater tighter around me. I haven't brought my coat downstairs for this February day, feeling too overheated from all the cleaning.

Finally Toru and Steven reappear, grinning and joking as if they were schoolboys on a field trip. They have to make three or four trips, and each time they grow more jovial and bonded, managing to turn this into a game. I envy their camaraderie yet am happy Steven can rise above his worries. Loaded up again, off they whirr.

I huddle on the last hard suitcase until Steven and Toru pull up for the final load. I urge Toru to take some of our food, at least the oranges, the spinach and cabbage.

He shakes his head. "Thanks, I don't cook. I live in one small three-mat room. I only eat out."

He struggles to make ends meet on his tutoring income. He probably eats at tiny neighborhood hole-in-the-wall places, where a large bowl of noodle soup costs almost nothing.

"Let us treat you to dinner tonight," I say.

He nods in agreement, flashing a smile as they drive away. The curb is now deserted.

I climb the three flights to our empty apartment, one hesitant step at a time. Sitting on the floor by the glass door, my legs straight out in front of me, I stare at the growing dark. There's nothing left to do. No one to say goodbye to. I want to tell Lisa, my ikebana partner, that we're leaving. Or walk down the hall to another neighbor, the Japanese woman who escorted me to her tea ceremony classes downstairs. But I don't have the courage. Instead I hide in the apartment in limbo. Even if I had friends here, I wouldn't be able to tell them my secret.

Steven touches my arm. He has walked in the door, his step light, his face clear. He pulls me up. "Let's say farewell to our home here."

He leads me to the other room and begins chanting a Buddhist chant he learned in his Thai village. "*Phutam salanang kachami . . . kachami . . .*" His sonorous voice floats through the emptiness, his face serene, almost trancelike as in meditation. His head bowed, eyes closed in concentration, hands in *gasshō*, the Japanese prayer position, each foot lifted one at a time, slow and steady. His ritual and posture warm me as I follow a few steps behind, also with *gasshō*, and bow. This sounds like his ritual that enchanted me on one of our first dates, during our wildflower walk on the Topanga mountaintop.

He circles each room, pauses on the porch, and stops at the front door. We face the kitchen one last time, give a final *gasshō*, then walk arm in arm to the elevator.

Downstairs the sour manager woman rustles her stack of papers at the counter. I hesitate at the door. Convinced she knows our secret, I was hoping for one of her faceless assistants.

Steven doesn't seem to care, or maybe he wraps himself in his armor again. He steps forward and smiles, radiating charm, as if an accomplished actor. "Good afternoon. Here's our key. Anything we need to sign?"

She glares at him. "That's been taken care of," she says through thin, unmoving lips.

I shove our box of leftover pans and dishes onto the counter, refusing to meet her eye. I mumble into the box, "We don't need these—perhaps a new person will." Covering my face with my hand, I walk out.

Through a blur of tears, I peer out the car's window at our soaring apartment house with its sprawling tree, at the hot French loaves in the bakery window, the fishmonger weighing silvery fish, the glistening apples and eggplants rising in pyramids at the corner stand, and the closed doors of the Berg Café, my favorite place for tea.

WALKING WITH THE TREES
An Interlude of Nature

Bent but not breaking
the trees of the bamboo grove
a strange wind blowing.

— EDITH SHIFFERT

Walking with the trees
flowing water, and mountains;
mind empties and fills.

— EDITH SHIFFERT

We had our first adventure with Takeda seven months ago, on a hot, muggy July day, soon after we arrived in Kyoto.

The day before, Steven had arrived home on his bike, his wet shirt clinging to his back and sweat pouring down his cheeks in spite of the brown bandana he had tied around his forehead, Japanese style. I was sprawled on the carpet in front of the small rotating fan, with all the windows flung wide open, having just emerged from a cold bath in our deep Japanese tub.

"Takeda's taking us to the mountains tomorrow, for a hike and a picnic," Steven announced with a grin, as if presenting me with a gift.

Mountains! Hiking! My two favorite things. And a rare chance to escape the oppressive humidity and congested city. I could already imagine the fragrance of the pines and the tingle of the cool mountain air against my skin.

The next morning Takeda parked his car in front of our apartment building and jumped out, tall and confident, his face fresh, open, smiling. This was a new Takeda. He was not animated like this a few weeks ago, when I saw him briefly at the welcoming party. Then he was wearing his Japanese professor face, impassive and taciturn. I studied him as he climbed into the driver's seat. He was handsome, with a craggy mountain-man look, an angular, dark-skinned face, and a short thatch of black hair, with no hint of gray. His body was lean, strong, and muscular.

As we settled into the backseat, Takeda introduced the woman sitting next to him as Yoshiko, with no further explanation. She twisted around to us with a warm smile, a low warble of a laugh, and flashing dark eyes. "I am so very happy to meet you," she said in perfect English. She was slender and wiry, maybe in her forties. Loose black curls, pulled back simply behind her ears with two combs, fell almost to her shoulders. Her hairstyle was more Western, not the usual tight perm of Japanese women over forty, nor the sleek straight hair of younger women. She seemed instantly at ease with us, unlike the shy reserve of many Japanese women. I was curious who she was and how she was connected to Takeda.

I leaned back, looking out the window as we wended our way out of the bustle of city traffic, leaving the narrow streets and crowded buildings behind. Takeda and Yoshiko chatted in the front seat, mostly in Japanese, but some English for our sake. Comfortable spaces flowed between their talk, the silence of a communal journey. Takeda's head of black straight hair leaned close toward her dark curls. Laughter and excitement punctuated the mood up front, while a camaraderie and lightness seemed to ripple between them.

Yoshiko turned often to chat with us. She missed *gaijin*, and the opportunity to speak English. In Africa where she had spent two years doing research with her husband, she had worked with many English-speaking colleagues. I remembered meeting her husband at the welcoming party, attended only by male professors and me, the token wife. I wondered where he was today.

We wound up into the mountains outside of Kyoto, the road steep and curving, soon entering a pine forest. I opened my window to drink in the fragrant air. I felt the same tingle of happy excitement I used to feel as a child, heading off in June to spend the whole summer camping with my family, in the mountains and forests of Montana, Idaho, Washington, and northern Mexico, where my father did ornithological research. As the car climbed higher, I scanned the peaks in the distance, all covered in dense forest.

Takeda was Steven's boss. The boss-employee relationship is a complex one anywhere, but especially in Japan, where relative position and mutual obligation within the hierarchy are crucial. Even more important, Takeda was Steven's sponsor. To work in Japan and to be at a university in Kyoto, one had to have an official sponsor and host. Takeda was responsible for Steven's well-being and all of his actions, both personal and academic, in a paternalistic sort of way. In the Japanese system, Steven owed Takeda allegiance, and Takeda owed Steven protection (and me, too, as his wife on an official "dependent" visa). Takeda had arranged for Steven's office, bank account, and our apartment at the university building for international faculty. Steven had turned to him with every problem: when the office computer and printer repeatedly broke, or when the telephone failed to receive or make overseas calls, or when the apartment manager refused to remove the Western beds so we could buy a futon instead.

The two men had also quickly become friends, even though friendship was never completely equal with one's boss. They were both in their late fifties, respected professors with successful careers, devoted to their research, and nearing retirement. They cared about their children profoundly yet rarely were able to see them. More important, they seemed to share a poetic soul, a quirky sense of humor, and a history of melancholy and pain that they had risen above. Takeda and Steven had found an instant rapport and bond.

Maybe today would be my chance to get to know a new side of Takeda. He turned off the steep mountain road, slowing down as he entered a village. He and Yoshiko searched for a certain house; clearly they'd been here before. They conferred with each other, made a couple of wrong turns, and then Takeda cried out, "There it is!"

We three waited in the car, watching Takeda walk to the front door of the modest cottage nestled at the feet of a towering grove of bamboo. He knocked repeatedly and circled the cottage, calling out someone's name in a low voice. Returning to the car, he conferred again with Yoshiko in rapid Japanese.

"*Dōzo*. I think it's okay. *Ii desu ne*," she said to him, in a mixture of the two languages. While he returned to the house, she translated. "He says the old woman isn't home. He hates to do it without her permission. But she's always let us before."

He circled the stand of bamboo as if searching for something, then pulled out of his pocket a leather sheaf, and from that, a long sharp knife. Working hard and deliberately, he sawed back and forth at one bright green stalk of bamboo. Finally he cut one piece, about eighteen inches long. Later, I would connect it to the bass *shakuhachi* that Kuroda sensei would demonstrate, with its full-bodied tone. The length and smooth round shape were similar, but Takeda's was a shiny yellow-green instead of a burnished gold.

"What's he doing?" I whispered to Yoshiko.

"You'll see." She smiled.

Takeda returned to the car triumphant, his grin directed at each of us, while he raised the bamboo piece high above his head, as if he had just won an Olympic race. Again, I would later be reminded of Kuroda sensei, the way his handsome face switched rapidly from serious and formal to passionate delight when focused on his art; for Takeda the mountains, for Kuroda the music. Except Takeda's face was rugged with that hidden pain, while Kuroda's was serene and smooth.

Takeda stowed the bamboo in the trunk, jumped in the car, and drove on. I nudged Steven with my elbow, whispering behind my hand, "What's it for?" He shrugged and smiled, unconcerned. My style was to ask questions to draw the person out, finding that most people liked to talk about themselves. Steven, as usual, was content to let the mystery unfold. He didn't like to ask questions, preferring to wait for the answers to come out during conversation. Perhaps it was his anthropologist side that held back, the "participant-observer."

The car climbed higher, the forest thicker and darker green. All pines and cedars now, no more mixed forest of deciduous trees, no more bamboo. Far below us in the narrow valley, a stream rushed wide and milky blue; occasional small houses clung to the hillsides, and rare road signs pointed to distant, unseen villages.

I wondered how long a drive it would be, and where he was taking us. I knew we were in good hands. But most Americans would supply some of this information to make the foreigner feel at ease, or to show off their country, explaining the sights, scenery, altitude, and route.

I sat back, embracing the rush of cold wind on my face and body, the seat no longer sticky with heat. Squeezing Steven's hand, I pointed out a thin ribbon of a waterfall that began high above our heads; it laced down a vertical cliff, weaving through rocks and fallen logs, with white foamy bubbles and clear silver curls, finally disappearing far below. Steven squeezed back, gesturing toward a hawk circling above the cliff top.

After what felt like half the day, but was probably only two hours, Takeda pulled off the road. "Here we are," he said. I crawled out of the car, stretched, and surveyed the layers of mountain ridges above and below us. I was famished. I wanted to ask where we would picnic, how long the hike would take.

From the trunk, Takeda and Yoshiko pulled out an odd assortment of bags and boxes, overflowing with food, pans, knives, bowls, a grill, and two folding chairs. They loaded us up in a haphazard manner, like vagabonds, with bags hanging off each shoulder, boxes teetering in our arms. No backpacks, no picnic baskets. Only Takeda had a knapsack, an old-fashioned brown canvas one, small and loose with no frame.

When we were all loaded up, Takeda tucked the bamboo piece under his arm.

"What's it for?" I asked.

"It's a secret." He smiled and started up the trail.

We struggled behind him up the path. Was this how the Japanese picnicked and hiked, or merely Takeda's style?

The path was narrow and steep, with scratchy bushes close on either side. I paused to inhale the invigorating air, to study the variegated shades of green silhouetted against the sturdy blue of the mountain sky. I was reminded of backpacking in the High Sierra, leading my boyfriend and my two young children, ages nine and eleven, over snowy eleven-thousand-foot passes. Now, shifting my heavy bags to distribute the weight, I bounded on ahead.

Takeda led, followed by Yoshiko, me, and Steven bringing up the rear. He was puffing and lagging behind, sweat dripping under his headband down onto his cheeks. But he bravely returned my smile and pointed with a free finger to the peak soaring above us, covered with pines, soft and furry like a friendly black bear. We all walked in easy silence, our attention on the weight of our gear, the rocky trail, and the beauty of the mountains. In spite of the cool air, I too grew hot with the exertion, sweat dripping down my back. The awkward bags pulled at my shoulders, sometimes slipping and sliding to the ground. How much farther could it be? Was Takeda wandering, or did he have a site in mind? This was a strange picnic. But I was determined to push on.

After about half an hour on the trail, we descended down into a small narrow canyon.

> The voice of a stream
> far, far below this high path
> dimly we hear it.
>
> — EDITH SHIFFERT

Chilled air rushed up from the bubbling stream below. "This is it!" Takeda shouted as he plunged downward toward the water, dumped his gear on the ground, and propped the bamboo piece upright against a big boulder that marked our site.

I followed him to the bank and sank to my knees, submerging my wrists in an icy pool and splashing my face and the back of my neck. The air felt like a frigid gust from an icebox. The stream cascaded down the canyon, with the ferns and the moss on the rocks creating green lace and velvet along the edges. Over the lullaby of the water, a hidden bird warbled.

Again I was back in the High Sierra at a forest campsite, cooking pancakes over an open fire, meandering lush meadows strewn with alpine wildflowers, sleeping outside under a black sky studded with a million brilliant stars. I wanted to stay in this icy canyon in the Kyoto mountains forever.

Takeda and Yoshiko worked as a team, unpacking and directing us where to set up the folding chairs and picnic blankets, where to stack the pans and bowls. It felt as if we were setting up camp for a week. Takeda built a fire ring out of rocks and asked me to gather firewood.

Scanning the rounded bowl of the pine-needled forest floor, I was reminded of my childhood, when my father would send me out with instructions to collect wood the minute we arrived in camp. It became my favorite job, alone at the edge of the warm circle my parents created, alone with the forest, the trees, the birds, on a crucial task that I, as the baby of the family, could do, and do well.

I returned to Takeda with my load of wood and watched him build the fire, handing him kindling and snapping pieces in two with my knee to make the appropriate sizes. He puffed on the fire to get it going, then sat back on his heels.

"I like to come to the mountains in the winter," Takeda said. "My favorite time. Only my snowshoes and small knapsack. One December I spent a week here, camping in this very spot."

"It must've been very cold," I said.

"Not for me. The white beauty, the white silence, the sculptured softness."

> Into my silence
> taking the grove of bamboo
> and falling snowflakes.
>
> — EDITH SHIFFERT

We watched the flames leap and grow. When the fire was roaring and crackling, Takeda wedged the metal grill among the rocks to level it.

Steven had helped Yoshiko set up the cooking area on slabs of flat rock, the way my mother used to do in our campsites. Purple eggplant, white onions, and yellow summer squash adorned the gray stone, the shiny purple catching pockets of sunshine that filtered down through the trees.

Suddenly shouts echoed down the trail. Yoshiko looked up with a laugh and a welcoming call. It was her husband and their two children, ages seven and nine, also bundled with packages, bags, and boxes. She ran up the trail to greet them, relieving them of some of their load. After quick introductions, the children dashed to the stream to play, giggling and calling to each other. Her husband pulled out a bottle of whiskey, settling himself in a chair by the fire. He offered the whiskey around. Only Steven accepted a small token glass, sitting down in the chair next to him.

Takeda retreated to a quiet part of the stream, up from the splashing children. He sat on the ground cross-legged for a long time, whittling with his pocket knife, shaping his piece of bamboo, in fierce concentration.

I walked over to watch him work, squatting down silently at a respectful distance. Here was another face of Takeda's. Like a Kabuki mask, it seemed poetic and sensitive, yet tragic with fleeting shadows or sudden withdrawals, and with that mysterious melancholy hidden behind it.

Again I was reminded of my father, with his intense focus and companionable silence. Maybe this was why I seemed to feel comfortable with the Japanese, since silence and open spaces were so natural for them.

"Steven tells me you both do *zazen* each morning," he said, without looking up.

I nodded.

After putting down his work in his lap for a moment, he swept both arms in a circle toward the mountain. "The mountains are my meditation," he said, his face suddenly aglow like a sunrise.

"They used to be mine, too. I miss them," I replied. After watching him work a bit more, I murmured, "Thank you," and walked toward Yoshiko to see if I could help.

"Come, look what my husband brought. Help me cut it up," she said, patting the rock next to her. She held up a huge slab of raw, bloody beefsteak.

I closed my eyes, swallowing down the nausea.

"What's the matter? Are you okay?" said Yoshiko.

"Yes. But I'm not used to red meat." I reached for the knife and the beefsteak. "I've been a vegetarian for over twenty years— I only eat fish, and occasionally chicken."

She snatched it back. "I admire vegetarians. Here, you do the eggplant."

"Please, let me cut the meat." I was determined to do my share and experience this picnic in full.

We worked together, sitting close on the flat stone. I struggled with my hunk of meat, the spongy red flesh fighting against my fingers, the blood dripping down my wrists to my elbows. I tried to meditate as I carved the chunks into strips, noticing each slow movement of the knife and finger, and each breath, in and out.

When the meat was finished, we chopped the vegetables into thin slices for the grill, our knives resonating through the forest as they chimed onto the hard rock surface. She told me more about Africa, how she missed the camaraderie with her husband working side by side on his research, the intellectual clarity, the equality she felt as a fellow researcher, and her fascination with learning the new culture.

"That's exactly how I felt in Thailand," I said. "I miss that total immersion in daily village life. And working together— attending every ritual and festival. He talks to the villagers, and I videotape. Or surveying the women weavers—he asks the questions, I take notes and photos. And then each evening comparing our field notes."

"Now," said Yoshiko, "I'm just a housewife, caring for my husband and children all day long. I love them, but . . ." She paused. "Here I must be a proper Japanese wife." She reached for another piece of squash. "But in Africa, I was a foreigner—I could do or be whatever I wanted."

"That's what I want here in Japan—to try out new ways of living my life."

Takeda, now radiant, approached us, holding up the stalk of bamboo. "Where's the sake?" he asked Yoshiko. She flung her hand toward her husband.

The four of us watched Takeda as if he were performing a sacred ritual. First, he held the bamboo horizontally over the fire, low enough to warm it, high enough not to burn it. When he decided it was exactly the right temperature, he tipped it to a forty-five-degree angle and, drop by drop, poured sake down its throat until it was almost full. Apparently he had cut it so a node at the bottom held the sake in. He returned to the fire, keeping the stalk at the same forty-five-degree angle. Holding it over the fire at exactly the right height, he then tipped the angle down just enough so it wouldn't spill out the top. He cradled the bamboo, rocking it back and forth over the flame, his face intent and serious but with an occasional playful half-grin.

Finally, he gathered us around the fire ring. After taking the first sip, he passed the warm bamboo around the circle. It felt like a tea ceremony ritual, or the passing of a peace pipe. Or perhaps of a toke of grass. I never found out if this was Takeda's private ritual or a common Japanese custom. The warmed sake slipped down my throat, delicate, with a hint of sweetness, a hint of rice, a smooth silvery liquid that warmed me to my toes. At that time of day, about one o'clock, on an empty stomach, it flushed right back up to my head, making me woozy. We passed the bamboo holder round and round until it was empty. Takeda propped it up against the big boulder next to our campfire.

Yoshiko and Takeda grilled the strips of steak and slices of vegetables over the fire. She had steamed white rice in a pot on the corner of the grill. My companions all ate standing up around the campfire, using pottery bowls and chopsticks. I picked out veggies from the grill, piled them on my rice, and sat on a rock at the edge of their circle. I wanted to be part of the group, but even more I wanted to immerse myself in the pines and ferns.

After lunch, Yoshiko and I squatted at the stream, washing the dishes and chatting. She rested her soapy hand on my forearm. "Let's go to Katsura Imperial Villa together. It has formal gardens and reflecting pools—all from the seventeenth century. Maybe next month?"

I covered her hand with mine. "I'd love that."

"I'll call you, and we'll make a date."

We packed up all the food and equipment, and then she wandered downstream with her children. Steven and Yoshiko's husband settled by the fire again, Steven drinking sake, the husband whiskey, the two engrossed in conversation about their university research.

Takeda had disappeared upstream. After an hour, I figured he must have gone on a hike. I was sure he wanted solitude, but I wished I could've gone with him. I longed to cross the stream to investigate the path on the other side. Instead, I sat on the mossy bank, relishing my own solitude. I followed the path of the water with my eyes as it threaded its way from rock to rock, curve to curve, always in motion, always exploring each nook and cranny as it meandered down the valley.

I didn't know these woods, and hesitated to hike on my own. Even though Japan was unusually safe, I'd seen signs posted in similar places warning women to be careful. Maybe strange men lurked there. Or maybe poisonous snakes or wild boars. From my years hiking in the Sierras, I could recognize the diamond-back pattern of the rattlesnake, and I knew what to do if I encountered a black bear. But here I didn't know what was poisonous, what was dangerous.

When hiking with Steven at home in the States, I would often leave him under a tree to doze or read while I wandered confidently up the trail on my own. After nine years together, I seemed to have lost the strong, adventurous independence that I prided myself on before I met him; we had become coupled and interdependent. Something kept me at his side. Perhaps an extra closeness grew when we were living together in a foreign country, daily trying to figure out the new culture.

At last Takeda emerged out of the dense bushes upstream, his eyes clear, his cheeks reddened with color, a serenity on his face. Again, he reminded me of my father, glowing with a boyish joy when returning to us at our campsite, after his day alone on the trail studying the birds he loved.

Takeda strode to the campfire ring and stoked the fire back to life. Rummaging in his knapsack, he pulled out a bundle of Japanese silk and unwrapped a small ceramic teapot and one large tea bowl, both of them the sturdy raku style, with rough asymmetry and a brown-gray glaze. Also, a bamboo whisk, and a thimble-sized silver tin of *matcha*, the brilliant green powder used for formal tea ceremony. He handed Yoshiko a small dented metal pan. She filled it with water and nestled it at the edges of the coals to boil. Sitting down on the soft pine needles near the fire, Takeda motioned for us to circle around him on the ground. With his usual concentration, he whisked the tea in the bowl until it was high and frothy. He solemnly rotated the design of the bowl outward and handed it to me for the first sip. After my one sip, I rotated the bowl again and passed it on. Around the circle, each one took a sip, Takeda drinking last and finishing the bowl.

> Rekindling our fire
> the greens of pine, moss, and fern
> one bowl of shared tea.
>
> — Patricia Dove Miller

After that, we loaded each other up and staggered up the trail back out of the canyon, with our burdens a bit lighter this time. The cicadas rang out their evening chorus. We hiked back up into the daylight at the top edge of the valley, the sun low but not yet set. Steven and I climbed into Takeda's car, Yoshiko with her children into her husband's.

As Takeda loaded our picnic supplies into the trunk, I noticed the leather sheaf that held that long sharp knife. "Takeda, what about your bamboo sake holder?" I asked. "We forgot it."

He gave a quiet chuckle. "No, I leave it on purpose. I offer it to the stream before I go. It belongs there."

As we drove off, he glanced at me in the mirror, raising an eyebrow. "We'll cut a new one in the fall. I'll take you to my favorite mountain in the north, we'll see the *momiji*—the leaves turning color—and the wild pheasant."

Golden gingko leaves
pheasant's feathers flash crimson
we sip green tea.

— PATRICIA DOVE MILLER

PART II

Takeda's House: Kyoto

SHUTTERED WINDOWS

Leafless plum tree
barren clothesline flapping
waiting, waiting.

— Patricia Dove Miller

A safe house. A real home, spacious, with two stories, a garage, a front yard, in a quiet residential neighborhood. No more cramped two-room apartment, vast six-story building, and noisy streets. It's a bland suburban ranch-style house from the seventies. Not like our home in California, with its redwood paneling and cascading wisteria. But now any place will do. I welcome its anonymity, its dry winter lawn and empty circular clothesline.

The first day Steven and I unpack together, working closely side by side. In Takeda's galley-sized kitchen, we stuff my jar of peanut butter into a corner of his cupboard and squeeze our one eggplant and cabbage onto a shelf in his fridge. The kitchen is dimly lit, with no counter space. So cluttered and crammed with his food that we can barely move around in it.

"Where'll I put all this food?" I hold up bags of rice and beans.

"C'mon. I'll show you." Steven grabs the bag of *shōyu*, oil, and sake bottles and leads me up the narrow steep stairs to the spare bedroom. It's piled high with Takeda's boxes, suitcases, and old clothes. And all our stuff from the apartment. We'll never be able to unpack it or fit it all into this house. Sitting on the floor, I paw halfheartedly through our belongings. I try to make order of the chaos, separating our things from Takeda's, stacking them into categories of food, clothes, books. If only I could know how long we'll be here.

Finally giving up on the task, I wander across the hall to peer into Takeda's upstairs bedroom. The unmade bed is strewn with pajamas and open books, the table littered with coffee cups, the floor covered with piles of dirty clothes and empty plastic bags. I turn away from the clutter and back toward Steven, who is waiting at the top of the stairs. "But where's our room?" I hear the hint of desperation in my voice, but I can't help it.

With a flourish, he tucks my elbow in his and escorts me down the stairs, as if we are marching to an altar. Our own wedding four years ago, when we strolled through a path of wildflowers and streaming Thai banners, on a bluff overlooking the shimmering Pacific, feels eons away right now. I realize he's trying to cheer me up, so I put on a smile and pretend enthusiasm.

"Here's the entry hall," he says, sweeping his arm toward the spacious area, as large as a small porch. A polished wooden table dominates the space, and a row of shoes is lined up in a designated place on the floor by the front door. Walking down another narrow hall, we enter the big living room, which is neat and uncluttered. A pair of ceremonial raku tea bowls rests on an ikat cloth atop the piano, and a print of a Botticelli painting hangs above. I slide into the soft couch, remembering the room from the one time we came here last summer. He had pointed out the piano in the far corner where he practiced each evening for his weekly lesson. In the other corner stands the rectangular dining room table where we ate dinner that evening, and looking out the open window, I had breathed in the fragrance of lush grass and leafy fruit trees in the front yard.

Today that window is shuttered tight.

I jump up and stride toward it. "Let's let in some light." I reach for the cord to raise the inside blinds.

"No!" says Steven, his palm sharply raised. "Takeda says we have to keep them down. All the time."

"What! Why?"

"The neighbors. They mustn't know we're here."

Takeda has told him they might make idle gossip or tell the newspapers. If the news breaks, it will hurt Steven's case because the authorities will be harsher with him, to set an example to other foreigners.

"Who's he fooling? The neighbors will see us going in and out." I cover my face with my hands. I can't live in a house without windows, without light or air. I'll suffocate.

"And we have to keep our bikes hidden behind the garage." Steven curves his arm around my shoulders, trying to comfort me. "C'mon, Pat. It's his house, and we have to obey his rules. We're lucky to be here."

This will be Steven's repeated mantra over our days here, one of acceptance and resignation, in contrast to my rebellion. And my anger. Always aimed at windows, Takeda, or the police. Never at Steven.

I glare at him and stomp down the hall, noticing for the first time the silent black phone in a nook on the wall. I thought this would be our home, not our prison.

"But where's our room?" I repeat.

"That last one on the left." Steven trudges along behind.

I shove open the door. A small square room, with narrow twin beds. Photos and children's drawings cover every inch of the walls. The shelves are piled high with books, trophies, and knickknacks. The closet, too, is stuffed, with clothes of all sizes and toys on the floor. I yank open the dresser drawers—more clothes crammed in. Takeda's teenage kids live in Spain. But this is still their room, intact like a shrine.

Sinking onto one of the beds, I pull a pillow to my face. "Where will we put anything? How can we possibly live in here?" I say. I should be brave, but I can't right now.

Steven slips into the room and sits down next to me. "We have no choice, I'm afraid." Another one of his mantras. He holds me while I give in to weeping.

Pulling away, I survey the Venetian blinds at the windows. "I suppose we can't open these either?"

"That's right."

I stretch out on the bed and lift the blinds a few inches to peek out. A lone plum tree not yet in bloom, and the dilapidated clothesline, sagging on the dead winter lawn. Down the street, not a person in sight, no life visible behind the neighbors' doors. With a sigh, I pull myself up and try to sound cheerful. "Let's bring our two smallest suitcases down and see what we can do." Steven follows me up and down the stairs, like an obedient puppy.

I push aside the rock collection, toy cars, flags, ribbons, and dried flowers, and stack the school papers and stuffed animals in a corner. I leave one suitcase on the floor to live out of and heap the rest of my clothes on the shelves. Next to my bed I lay out my alarm clock, flashlight, bifocals, and *The Tale of Genji*. I prop up three photos: my eighty-seven-year-old mother, my son, my daughter. A seashell I brought from the beach in California, and my one-inch-high Buddha statue.

I bought that statue thirty-two years ago, when I was pregnant with my son, carried it to the hospital when he was born, and have carried it ever since when I've traveled. It wasn't until this year in Kyoto that I learned he wasn't a Buddha at all, but a Chinese god of good fortune and joy, his fat belly a sign of luck and plenty.

After unpacking as much as possible, I carry a small bundle of my dirty clothes to the large tile bathroom. Next to a traditional deep Japanese tub stands a fancy Western washer, so unlike the one on our apartment porch, where one of us had to watch each cycle and move it manually to the next step. By guessing at the *kanji* characters on the knobs, I manage to work it. I hang the wet clothes on the clothesline in the front yard. An odd place for a line, where all the neighbors can see. They will wonder what woman is living here. But Takeda didn't say not to use the clothesline. And I won't get caught. I'll bring them in before he returns tonight. I realize I'm rebelling—it's childish—but it gives me a perverse pleasure. After hanging all my clothes, I leave the yard and glance back at my underwear, flapping in the cold wind, revolving round and round on that circular line.

Takeda gave Steven only one house key and acted surprised when Steven asked for a second one. But I must have my own key so I can maintain my independent life. I don't want to be tied to this house—or this husband.

That afternoon Steven and I wander the neighborhood, following Takeda's vague directions, looking for a place to copy the key. Along one bleak and treeless street stretches a handful of stores that have sprung up one by one like afterthoughts amidst the suburban development. We search, ask questions, make wrong turns. The shopkeepers look through us, as if we're invisible, unlike in our old bustling Shūgakuin neighborhood, where we were welcomed with friendly curiosity. I'm feeling so paranoid I worry that they, too, know our secret.

Finally we find the crowded hardware store. With elaborate sign language we convince the hostile clerk to copy the key. We check out the one forlorn grocery store, more like an expanded 7-Eleven, with wilted produce and no fresh fish. As we walk home through the bland suburb with nothing for dinner, my fingers curve around the smooth edges of the key in my pocket.

The days at Takeda's drag along, each one blurring into the next. An uneasy lull, not knowing what will come tomorrow. Waiting. For the Investigation to end, for the hiding at Takeda's to end, for us to be allowed to fly home. Behind these darkened blinds, my world shrinks by half. Steven's shrivels to almost nothing. Most days I escape the house to search for a haven of music or nature, or to keep my commitment to my four remaining students. Other days I withdraw into the house, afraid to go out, avoiding any interaction. I take long naps in my narrow bed, read the next chapter of *Genji*, practice the next piece for my *shakuhachi* lesson.

There is a lot of silence in the house. Mostly I welcome it. All three of us seem to perch here, living around the edges.

Takeda is rarely home. We never find out where or how he spends his time. I know he works long hard hours at the university. I imagine he eats at soba or tempura restaurants near his office. He probably takes long solitary hikes in the mountains, no matter the weather.

Takeda is welcoming, but he remains aloof. He and I slip past each other unobtrusively with a nod and a half-smile, almost invisible, putting up our protective masks to hide our emotions. I tiptoe around the house, avoiding him because I'm too ashamed. In spite of my resistance to Takeda's rules, I'm grateful he's opened his home to us. But I'm too aware that none of us know how long we'll be stuck with each other. And too aware of Steven's betrayal. Why has Takeda taken us in, when he's been so wronged? Apparently it is the Japanese way—or maybe it's just Takeda's way. As Steven's "sponsor" in Japan— and his friend—he still feels responsible for him on a personal level—for his actions, for his well-being. And feels obligated to take care of him and protect him. Even if it means breaking the sanctity of his home.

I also avoid Steven, who sits in the easy chair in that darkened living room behind those shuttered blinds, doing nothing all day long. I don't want to be dragged down by him. His gloom drifts through the house like a cold dense fog.

On my calendar each morning, I cross off another student who was scheduled and then cancelled; perversely, I pencil in the amount I would have earned in yen, as if I must tally all that Steven's wrongdoing has cost me.

I can't teach my students at Takeda's. I fear even asking him. What would the neighbors say if strings of young women began coming to his house? I loved the glimpses into Japanese culture that these diverse women provided. To study the GRE with the woman who wanted to attend graduate school in Australia; edit the Indonesian graduate student's masters thesis on mangrove swamps; help the young socialite converse with her friends in English as I accompanied them on outings to the department store; simulate grocery shopping with the young secretary; or debate with the nursery school teacher the similarities and differences between my traditional Ōhara style of ikebana, which emphasizes freedom within structure, and her modern Ikenobo style, which favors wild, unconventional forms and materials. Without my students, I feel lost, isolated, unanchored, like a long stem of kelp severed by unseen hands, left to float the sea and eventually break into tiny fragments.

One day at Takeda's, I open my taped-up box of treasures and pull out the blue silk case with my *shakuhachi* snug inside. Silvery cranes soar toward a shimmering moon on the case's fabric. As I load it into my daypack, along with a sheaf of sheet music and my lavender notebook, Steven wanders in from his daily post in that easy chair in the dark living room to ask where I'm going.

"To my lesson. I've got to leave early. It's a longer route, and I don't know the way."

"Please don't go. Stay home with me." His brown eyes plead.

"I can't live without my music, Steven. You know that," I say, with a warning edge of steel in my voice. I won't let him take my music away from me.

He hangs his head and turns away. "I shouldn't have asked."

"I'm sorry. I can't give it up, and I can't take you with me."

He shuffles away down the hall but soon returns, his footsteps a bit lighter.

"I'll walk you to our new *densha* station. Takeda showed me the way when I went to the Customs Police yesterday."

"C'mon. I can't be late."

As we leave the house, Steven opens the door quietly, and we peer up and down the block to see if it's empty, hoping no neighbors are peeking out. We sneak out the door, hurry down the street, and round the corner.

At the station, Steven clings to me, pulling our hips tight against each other, both of his arms clamped around my back. His voice is muffled as he burrows into my shoulder. "Pat, I feel desperate. I don't know what they're going to do to me."

I pull away and glance around, embarrassed that someone will see us. Back in 1993, the Japanese didn't hug or kiss in public, rarely even held hands. Fortunately, the platform is empty at eleven in the morning. "You'll be okay," I whisper, only half believing it. I don't know how to pull him up. And part of me, the angry exhausted part, doesn't want to. I want to escape his miserable gloom. I am drowning, barely able to keep my head above water.

I pat his arm. "Walk home the long way. Get some exercise. Take a hot bath. I'll see you about four." I throw out my list of suggestions, recognizing he is too down to take any, except maybe the bath. As I board the tram, I call over my shoulder, "Take yourself out to lunch, that *kaki furai* oyster place we found." The doors close behind me.

In Kuroda sensei's upstairs studio, I bask in the golden warmth of the tatami, munch the juicy tangerine slices he shares with me, and sip green tea out of a delicate *chawan*. He recounts the folklore legend for my new piece, "Itsuki no Komoriuta," "Itsuki Lullabye," about a servant girl on the southern island of Kyushu. Then as usual we work on it together: he models the piece, and I try to mimic his style and tone.

Toward the end of the hour, he surprises me by cutting the lesson short. "I show you something. We stop now."

While I clean my flute and slide it back into its blue silk case, he brings out the book he is making for his children, beaming with pride. "We go in April. I want they learn about Thailand. See map I draw?"

I linger, pouring over his detailed maps of Northern Thailand with admiration. He has created a beautiful hand-bound book, decorating its pages with the elaborate curlicues of Thai script. The maps are annotated with Thai legends, historical facts, and comparisons between Thai and Japanese Buddhism, and between the Thai king and Japanese emperor. He has illustrated them with drawings of Thai animals, plants, and weather patterns of cloud and monsoon. Immediately, I'm reminded of Steven's and my days living in Northern Thailand, when he introduced me to his village and taught me about similar aspects of the culture. A time when we were happy and close.

"Please ask husband, what more to put in book."

"I know he'd love to help." Anything about Thailand always cheers Steven up.

I walk home from the station, refreshed after my time away from Steven and the dark house. He flings open the door with a smile, and with open arms he embraces me. I'm not sure I'm ready for such closeness. Still I'm relieved he's feeling better. He holds me for a full minute. Then he grasps my hand and leads me into the living room.

"Look, I've made us a fresh pot of *gyokuro*." This is a high-grade special tea made from the first picking of the tips of new spring leaves. When brewed, they are the color of bright moss after a rain, with the fragrance of newly mown grass in the sunlight. He's trying to revive our old morning habit, shifting it to afternoon. For a while, we sip in silence, but not with the easy camaraderie of our former ritual. He fiddles with the dregs in his cup, rocking them from side to side. I can feel his tea-making spirits plummet.

"Let me tell you about my lesson."

Over the years, Steven has taught me the value of storytelling, and he always loves mine. "We worked on a new piece, about a young poor girl that's sent away from home to be nurse-maid for a rich family. She can only go home twice a year. She sings over and over about wanting to return home."

Too late I realize this topic is not going to cheer him up. I notice his gaze go vacant. I've lost him.

"And he's going to Thailand!" I tell Steven all about the intricate handmade book. "He wants me to ask you lots of questions." I run to my room for my notebook, returning breathless. "Where should he go, what should he see?"

Steven lifts his eyebrows at me, stretches his legs way out, his elbows behind his head, lost in dreamy thought. "First, they should see the Emerald Palace."

We list a few of our favorite adventures from our time in Thailand: choosing Hill Tribe textiles at the lively market in Chiang Mai; outside of Chiang Mai, climbing up Doi Suthep, the hilltop temple; floating down the Mekong River from Mae Sai to Chiang Rai. Steven pauses, his face animated, no longer stony. "Wait. Let's invite him and his wife to dinner. I'll tell them everything and cook a green curry." He loves nothing better than to cook his Thai specialties and regale his guests about the culture of the villagers he studied. He lived among them so long that they became almost family to him. But he hasn't cooked a thing since the police knocked.

I jump up to hug him. "I'd love to repay him for all he's given me." I cross the room to sneak a look out the slats of the closed blinds. "But how? Where? We can't have guests here."

Steven closes his eyes and slumps back in his chair, folding his body away from me, like a stepped-on sea anemone.

I meant to cheer him up and instead I've slapped him in the face. Mentally exhausted, I flee to my narrow bed in our shuttered room. I sleep curled up into a tight ball, waking up hours later, groggy and unrested.

The next day I decide I need a nearby haven, and I search for the local shrine. I miss Saginomori shrine in our old neighborhood, with its wooden bridge over the stream, the multicolored pebbles shining beneath the water, the sweet-smelling soaring pines where the egrets roost. Ever since the police first knocked on our door, I walked to that shrine every evening, once Steven was home from the day's investigation. The fresh air and exercise cleared my head after a day waiting by the phone for news. At the shrine, I followed the Shinto ritual in front of the outdoor altar: clapping my hands, ringing the bell-rope, and bowing in prayer to thank the spirits for one more day of Steven safely home, one more day not in prison.

I was raised with no formal religion, my father a devout scientist-atheist. But these Shinto shrines draw me in, with their worship of every part of nature—tree, rock, sky, and stream. I like their simplicity, beauty, and silence. I don't really believe in the Shinto spirits or understand the religion. But Saginomori soothed me anyway and answered my search for solitude and nature, as when I backpacked at eleven thousand feet and worshiped the glory of a Sierra mountain peak.

Now I search Takeda's neighborhood. I've learned that every neighborhood has a shrine. I wind along the walking paths that thread between the suburban houses, and, finding a stream, I meander beside it, until I emerge at a busy street lined with used-car lots. After crossing the street and rounding the first noisy corner, I discover Hachiman Shrine hidden away in a grove of trees. On an island in the middle of a small quiet pond, a bronze statue of a dove nestles. A low bubbly fountain gurgles, echoing the music of the live doves in the courtyard beyond. This bronze dove is as large as a human. Most shrines are dedicated to a specific animal or spirit that symbolizes certain myths or supernatural powers. This one must be for the dove. Years later I learn that the dove at this shrine does not equal peace as it does for us Americans, but rather war.

I enter the shrine courtyard and sit down on a wooden bench next to a round bronze bell that is taller than I am. Flocks of doves swirl around me, their feathers a pattern of honey brown, eggshell white, and sunset pinkish gray. Their long, pointed wings beat rapidly as they swoop from courtyard to rooftop and back down to the bell. Their voices croon "*poh-poh*," their heads bobbing up and down as they waddle at my feet.

I cast my eyes down toward the courtyard stones and meditate, breathing in and out, with the cooing of the doves like the echo of a meditation bell. I began my daily meditation practice four years ago, after visiting Steven's *Rōshi* in Okinawa. Now during this crisis, I've increased my meditation to three times a day, and it helps sustain me.

At sunset, the ringing of the bell next to me startles me out of my reverie. Rung by unseen hands, it sings out a golden sweetness.

> As the sound fades
> the scent of the flowers comes up
> the evening bell.
>
> — BASHO (tr. Robert Hass)

I jump up to run to the shrine kiosk before it closes and spy a white ceramic whistle shaped like a dove. How perfect for my mom, who has always identified with this peaceful, gentle, musical bird, long before it became a peace symbol. Since it was her birth name, she grew up surrounded with images of doves. Later she was both amused and proud that she, with the last name of *Dove*, married an ornithologist and quickly grew to love birds as much as he did.

I point to the dove whistle. "*Futatsu onegaishimasu.*" I hold up two fingers, one for Mom, one for me.

> Small doves
> leave the nest
> each day a mother returns
> her voice ever more mournful
> more distant.
>
> — KATH ABELA WILSON

I also buy one wooden *ema*, a small rectangular plaque with a painted picture of two doves facing each other, to add to my folk art collection. The elderly woman behind the counter rattles off Japanese, pointing to the outdoor altar behind me, at the head of the courtyard. Hundreds of these wooden *ema* hang there, covered with candle wax drippings and bird droppings, smudged with smoke, and faded by rain. I understand she wants me to hang my new *ema* there. That's the custom, to pray for good fortune, happy marriage, successful exam, or new baby, and then hang the plaque at the altar so the wish will come true. As I clink my yen piece on the worn wooden counter, I blow into the whistle and, smiling at the woman, make soft *hoo-hoo*s. Before leaving the shrine grounds, I sneak past the altar, my *ema* concealed in my pocket. I don't look back, convinced I can feel her eyes on me. Later I will wish I'd bought two *ema*, one to keep and one to hang on the altar, wishing for Steven to stay safe and for me to find courage.

As I reenter the world and retrace my steps toward home, I notice with a new calm perspective the gentle modulations in the hum of traffic, the glint of each shiny used car, the curved design of each roof tile on the suburban houses. I pause by each bend of the stream, then sit down on a mossy bank to search for a stone. Perhaps a flat thin one to skip on the quiet pool farther along, or a burnt orange one to shine in a low ikebana vase, or a smooth round one to curl into my palm in my pocket. Here is yet another haven for me to retreat to.

Before my life with Steven, I escaped from my troubles by wandering the windswept beaches of the Pacific or by backpacking in the High Sierra. Living in Topanga with Steven, I escaped to my own cottage on our property, or into the views of the mountain from our porch. But back then I was too focused on the intensity of our new love affair and did not nourish my desire for nature and solitude. Here in Kyoto, I gradually learn that I need these moments of quiet repose, not only as escape from my troubles, but also to maintain my daily equilibrium.

Today's "afternoon" nap is a bit late, but it's pure pleasure. I climb into my bed, the only place that is truly my own, snuggle under my blanket, and immerse myself in the next chapter of *Genji*. Before I doze off, I sneak open the shutter for a last bit of light and for a view of the plum tree, its arms raised to the sky.

⁂

I don't know exactly what Steven does these days at Takeda's. Mostly, he stays home alone, waiting for the Investigation to be over, sitting in that easy chair in the dark living room, behind those closed-up doors and windows. He has no office, no colleagues, no computer. He could work at home on his current research project, but he has lost all his usual energy and drive. He has no lessons, no havens, no bike rides to turn to.

He worries all day about his next trip to the Customs Police, now every few days instead of daily. Once a week he visits his lawyer, Fukuda san. Sometimes he goes alone, sometimes with Tom, who found this lawyer through the connections of his Japanese wife's family. Tom has become like a loyal son, providing encouraging companionship and crucial translation during the legal sessions.

Steven clings to these visits to the lawyer's peaceful, plush office like a lifeline. He is treated with a calm respect and served cup after cup of green tea by the silent "office girl." He trusts Fukuda san's knowledge of Japanese law. But nothing ever seems to happen there. The lawyer cannot speed up the case, or help in any tangible way, or even tell Steven what will come next and when.

On rare occasions Steven cooks a dinner for Takeda and me. He bangs around that cramped kitchen, Takeda joining him to watch, with a *tokkuri* of sake in hand. They bump into each other as they choreograph their movements in the tiny space and laugh together like in the old days. But Steven has lost his touch; the meal comes out lackluster, a bland broiled fish with rice. Not like at home where cooking was a creative art, as he experimented with combining various cuisines: Thai, Chinese, Italian, Egyptian. And not like our second date in his redwood-paneled living room in Topanga, when he made me his luscious guacamole.

I encourage him to resume his weekly pottery lessons at Sato sensei's house. After the police knocked, he stopped going, too busy with the daily Investigation to even consider it.

"But what if I get there and Sensei won't let me in?"

"He's an artist. Maybe he won't be as intimidated as your colleagues are." But I am not convinced myself. There is no way to know.

"I can't take the chance," he says.

Sometimes Steven and Takeda sit up late drinking sake, after I've gone to bed to read. Or if Takeda doesn't return until past midnight, Steven sits up drinking alone, sunk into that same soft chair in the living room, maybe listlessly reading outdated issues of the English-language newspaper, or merely staring at the floor.

One morning over our breakfast of cold cereal, I ask him what he and Takeda talked about the night before.

"We sat in silence mostly, listened to a Mozart concerto."

"What kind of silence?" I ask.

"Mostly comfortable." He puts down his spoon and looks up. "How can he be so kind to me?"

"Maybe we help his loneliness."

"He was my best friend, and now it's all twisted. I try to talk to him but I've nothing to say. I can't tell him how ashamed I feel. He starts to discuss our research or our colleagues, like we used to. Then he sees the pain in my eyes, and I see it in his. And he stops."

"And then?"

"We talk about the rainstorm or when spring will arrive or the prime minister's latest doings in the evening paper. Then he puts on the Mozart." They used to banter over the differences between Italian opera and Japanese Kabuki, in those weeks before the police arrived.

"I told him how grateful I am," Steven adds.

"Me, too," I say.

Other than Takeda, his boss turned reluctant host, Steven's only contacts are Toru, our ponytailed tutor turned friend, and Hiroki, his Buddhist colleague from a distant university. Both of them are outsiders, too, in their own way. Both have spent time in the West. Also, they know and accept our secret.

Toru is a maverick in Japanese society, with his long hair, freelance teaching, hand-me-down clothes, and no steady salary or wife. The opposite of the short-haired, clean-cut, black-suited "salary man" who takes the subway to work each day, returns home late and tipsy, and struggles with the office hierarchy and obligations. A sad, but often true, stereotype. Toru slips easily and unobtrusively through the cracks in the rigid conformity and restrictions of Japanese culture. He works for an American boss so is free from the usual hierarchy. And he lived for many years with the Quakers in Philadelphia. He does not fear reprisals for his friendship with Steven.

Somehow Toru manages to entice Steven out of the house. He zooms by in his car at spontaneous random moments, snatches him out of his chair, and drives him off to a café or bar far away from Takeda's, and outside the university district as well. He understands that Steven will be embarrassed if he runs into those colleagues.

The only colleague Steven is able to confide in is Hiroki. The ones from the university avoid him, never calling or stopping by. We never find out why, although we speculate. Perhaps Takeda never told them where we are. Perhaps he told them not to contact Steven. I imagine Takeda erects a wall of silence and vaguely evasive excuses. Perhaps they know a hint of the secret and close ranks to protect Steven's privacy, to not leak to the press, and to protect themselves. They might fear contamination from his crime, merely by dint of association. They might fear police questions, or ostracism by friends, family, or other professors; they might even fear arrest.

On the other hand, Hiroki works at a separate university, several hours away in Kanazawa; once a month he attends the research meetings of Takeda's group in Kyoto. Ever since their first meeting, Hiroki and Steven became close friends. Hiroki has a devout daily Buddhist practice and frequently attends weeklong or monthlong *sesshin* retreats in Japan and abroad. His practice is similar to the one Steven had in the States before he met me.

Steven discovered Zen Buddhism twenty years ago, in the seventies, during the personal crises of his divorce and the death of his best friend. He plunged into it with intense focus: meditated daily, became a serious member of a Zen center in Los Angeles, attended periodic weeklong *sesshin*, and studied for years with a Japanese *Rōshi*. Once we lived together, he cut back to a steady home practice of daily morning meditation. He offered to teach me, but I resisted for years, insisting that walking in the mountains was my meditation.

Now in Kyoto, his practice nourishes him. After the police knocked, Steven let his practice lapse, but soon, at my urging, we began to sit morning and evening together.

His friend Hiroki never deserts him during our time at Takeda's. He calls him frequently and usually is able to lift Steven's mood temporarily. First they discuss Hiroki's own research, but they quickly turn to their troubles, both Steven's and Hiroki's. He is in a committed relationship with a married woman. It will be ten years before they are finally able to marry. Hiroki understands what it is like to live a bit outside the norms of society.

These days, I never go to my ikebana class. But my bundle of flowers still waits for me in a bucket of water on Sensei's glassed-in front porch, whether I pick it up or not. I have continued to pay my monthly fee. I miss the feel of silky blossoms and cool water, the soft murmur of my fellow students, the silent communal spirit, the gentle hands of Sensei.

But something holds me back. It all seems too hard—to ride the bus, speak Japanese, to smile and be polite, to follow the ikebana rules. At the time, I blame it on Steven's moods that deflate me, on Takeda's secrecy that stifles me, and on the sudden urgent meetings with the lawyer that seem pointless, but Steven insists I attend. I don't understand that it's me: frozen and depressed, unable to reach out to anyone. I've no energy to take care of myself, much less to be creative with flowers or anything else. I'm not aware that I can't seem to separate myself from the crisis or from Steven. And that I need the ikebana to rejuvenate me.

Finally, one day after teaching Yuki, my loyal and enthusiastic twenty-two-year-old student, at her home in my old neighborhood, I stop by Sensei's house on a whim. The lesson with Yuki has invigorated me, with its challenge of finding the right way to help her, our playful role-playing as she struggles to learn the English phrases she needs to shop for clothes, and her ancient, traditional wood-paneled home, with its spacious peacefulness.

At Sensei's, I pick up my weekly bundle of flowers from the porch and ride the bus home to Takeda's, the flowers bulky and wet in my lap, my nose buried in the scent of yellow forsythia and purple iris. I have the house to myself for the first time since we moved in. Takeda and Steven are off together somewhere. I don't know where or why. Perhaps meeting for a beer at the end of the day, somewhere far from the university. Maybe Takeda will fill Steven in on his recent meeting with the university president, about the continuing reverberations from Steven's crime.

Now I can play with my flowers at leisure. After searching all over his house for a vase, quite certain he must have one, I find a low, wide oval bowl, with crackly gray and white glaze. Similar to the size and shape of a traditional vase, it will be perfect for the ikebana. In the solitude of the empty house, I create my arrangement at the dining room table, using the basic "Slanting" style from the Ōhara school. I work with one bloom at a time, pausing to remember Sensei's rules and the way she would adjust my flowers. I check that each of the three main stems are at the proper complementary angle and face the proper direction, that the height of each one is slightly different, and that none touches or overlaps another. I step back to admire it and make a final adjustment to the angle of the iris. I've never done one on my own before, but I can do it! I can create a garden pool of beauty without Sensei's guidance. And I forgot how comforting it is to sink into the meditation of the flowers.

I wander each room for the perfect place to display my ikebana. I need a plain background so the architecture of the arrangement will be distinct, and an open space around it so the viewer's mind can soar with the blossoms. I choose the table by the front door and, with a joyful contentment, wait all afternoon for the two men to arrive home.

When Takeda enters the hall, he stands in front of my ikebana for a long time studying it, and then pulls up a chair facing it, so his face is the same level as the flowers. He absorbs each detail, the way I've seen him study the design on the inside of a raku tea bowl after drinking the liquid. Steven kneels next to him, doing the same. At last, they both stand, gaze down one more time at the arrangement, then turn and smile at me. Steven squeezes my shoulder and plants a kiss at the base of my earlobe, whispering a husky, "Thank you." Takeda bows low toward me for several moments and then silently drifts up the stairs to his room.

That is the only ikebana I do at Takeda's. Suddenly there is no time for flowers.

GOLDEN LETTERS

And what is mind
and how is it recognized?
It is clearly drawn
in *sumi* ink, the sound
of breezes drifting through pine.

— IKKYŪ SOJUN (tr. Sam Hamill)

The next evening, Steven is twirling me round and round the
entry hall as if it were a ballroom, almost knocking the fresh
ikebana askew. He has just returned from the lawyer with news.
It is the twenty-fifth day since the police knocked; we've lived six
long days at Takeda's, which have felt more like six weeks.

"What's happened?" I ask.

He pauses and with a somber face announces that there are
still no decisions about his case. But then he flashes a broad grin
of contained excitement. "The Investigation is over! I don't have
to go to the Customs Police station anymore."

We dance again, and I twirl with abandon and relief that
there will be no more waiting by the telephone, no more terror
that he won't come home each evening. It is over. But no, it is
not.

"Wait, stop," I say, breathless and dizzy. I rest my hands on
his shoulders. "But what now?" Fear creeps into the edge of my
voice. Fear of more waiting, more not knowing.

Steven fills me in on the details. The Customs Police will now
prepare their final report to send to the prosecutor. They will com-
pile the hours of questions and answers that Steven has endured
during the last three weeks. Then they'll decide what action to
recommend to the prosecutor. Once again we must wait. We both

fear the police report. We don't know if there are other options besides prison. The lawyer has been no help with that.

Gradually over the last few days Steven has been telling me about the Investigation. It's been coming out in dribbles and spurts. Mostly he hasn't wanted to talk about the tedious and endless procedure he has endured at the Customs Police station each day. Eight hours a day for seventeen days. That to him felt more like seventeen weeks. And to me also, at home waiting by the phone. Never knowing if this would be the day they'd decide to put him in prison, instead of sending him home to me. Several policemen took turns questioning him, always very polite, very kind, offering him continual cups of green tea, plenty of breaks, and a choice of delicious menus for lunch. One man asked a question in Japanese, the translator repeated it in English, Steven answered in English, and the translator translated it back into Japanese for the policeman. Back and forth, back and forth, between the three of them, until the next break. During the break, the secretary typed that series of questions in both languages. After the break, that section was read to Steven in English, and to the police in Japanese, to see if both sides agreed to all of it, and then they all signed it. And on to the next section of questions.

During the long breaks of transcription, Steven meditated or wrote haiku in his head. And sipped more green tea. His twenty years of meditation practice kept him going, kept him sane. Some days he brought the haiku home to me, stored in his mind, but we never thought to write them down.

Now Steven guides me gently to the dining room table and sits me down. "There's one thing we can do," he says. For the first time in weeks, his face looks hopeful. "My lawyer says I must gather as many Letters of Recommendation as I can, from my university colleagues. To show I'm a serious and respected senior scholar. And mustn't be sent to prison."

I jump up, sputtering. "That's absurd! How can that possibly help?"

"This is Japan. There's nothing else to do," Steven replies, his voice soft and steady, with yet another one of his mantras of survival.

He plunges into the new mission with zeal. At last he has a task and a chance to redeem himself. Phone calls, faxing, and xeroxing consume his days. I drag along behind, not really believing in this project. I don't want to spend hours shuffling papers. Yet I'm thankful he has something to do. Maybe it will help after all.

First, he calls Jim in San Francisco, his closest friend and colleague of thirty years and another Thai specialist. Steven sits on the floor below the phone nook in the hallway, his hands shaking as he dials the number. For once his wit can't help him, but his strong friendships may.

"I got busted!" he says, trying to make a joke of it in his usual way, as if it is no big deal, but his voice cracks and fades away. In a halting voice, he tells Jim exactly what he needs. The Letters of Recommendation must be faxed immediately to Tom, his son's friend, the only person we know who has a fax at home. The Letters can be in English, but they must be handwritten. With a long history of calligraphy, the Japanese value handwritten letters and documents, but not typed ones.

"What!?" shouts Jim into the phone. "I never handwrite. Haven't since grade school."

"It's the only way. Type it first if you want. Then copy it out, or have Joann do it." I can hear the quaver in Steven's voice. He rarely asks for favors. "Please. I need your help."

Jim's voice thunders back over the line, filled with gruff concern. "I'll do it. Tomorrow. We'll get you out of this. Don't worry. We're here for you."

"Wait," Steven says, and then he finishes the instructions. The letter must stress his professional qualifications, his experience, his character. As if he were applying for the most important job of his life.

One by one, Steven dials each university colleague, in California and North Carolina, in New Zealand and England. Every call grows harder and harder. E-mail is still rare, and international phone calls are expensive, cumbersome, and often marred by static. But each friend responds with warmth and haste. They aren't shocked by the crime. By U.S. standards, it seems petty. But, from Steven's story of the Investigation and the threat of prison, they quickly grasp how serious it is here.

When Steven's sister hears about the Letters, she insists on taking charge. She coordinates the Letters from San Diego: makes follow-up phone calls to confirm they are all actually written and when; has them faxed to her; faxes them on to Tom's for us. This lifts a heavy burden from us.

The lawyer tells Steven he should also solicit Letters of Recommendation from his Japanese colleagues. But how can he? They aren't supposed to talk to each other. He does receive a Letter from Takeda, from Hiroki, and from a more senior colleague, a former mentor, in Tokyo. These Letters arrive written in beautiful, curving black calligraphy that will need no translation.

The Letters in English pour in. Each day Steven calls Tom to see if any have arrived, and how many. Steven takes the bus to Tom's house, picks them up, and walks to the corner stationary store to xerox. He no longer is allowed to use the machine at the university.

Every time, he pleads with me to come along. Some days I give in, some days I don't. One morning he seems especially desperate. He's still in bed, and I'm rushing around the room, pulling on sweater and corduroys.

"Please come today. I can't do it by myself anymore," he says.

"I have a full scheduled day. I don't want to cancel anything."

"These Letters are too confusing. You're better at it, more organized."

"I hate it, too, you know."

"Please," he repeats. "It's going to help us get out of here."

"I'm not so sure about that."

"C'mon. What's your schedule?"

I open my calendar, already messy with cancellations and cross-outs. "Tea with Sally at ten. Remember her? From my women's group, the young woman with the baby. And a meeting at KIS at eleven thirty. And two students in the afternoon."

"See Sally another day or change the meeting at the school. Come for part of the time."

I study my calendar, my back to him, fiddling with my pen. I don't want to. It's his job. I'm sure he can do it by himself. Why can't I just say no? I've already cancelled Sally twice, both times at the last minute, when Steven insisted I attend meetings with the lawyer. And the Kyoto International School. I've networked for months to arrange these rare and precious appointments and am just beginning to succeed. I want to study their teaching methods to use when I return to my school in California, where I teach Japanese culture to second graders.

Steven sits up, rests his head on my back, and wraps his arms around my belly. "I'm so lonely."

I pick up my address book, open it to Sally's number, close it again. I shut my eyes, chewing on my finger for a moment. Then I walk to the hall and dial her number.

"Sally, I'm so sorry. I've got to cancel again. I really want to see you. That trouble I mentioned with my husband—it's come up again . . . "

"Don't worry, really. I've been there. Let's just reschedule."

She seems fine with it. I am not. After we first met, I procrastinated calling her for weeks, lost and then found her phone number, and finally dredged up the courage to call. Later, when we finally have tea for the first time, she will be leaving soon for the States. I'll have missed the chance for one of those brief yet valuable friendships typical in Japan. And I'll blame it on Steven.

Next, I find the number for KIS, and stand there with my hand on the phone. This one is harder, the fourth time I've cancelled since this all started. The first time I walked into KIS, I felt immediately at home. It's a small private school, like the one in Santa Monica where I taught, with the same philosophy and atmosphere that I admired: brimming with creativity, innovative methods, and liberal ideas, and staffed with energetic, smart teachers dedicated to their vocation. Before the police came, I often fantasized about staying on in Kyoto and teaching there, having already forgotten the challenge of maintaining discipline in the classroom. At KIS, I've already observed the Japanese-language and calligraphy classes, scribbling pages of detailed notes, and shooting rolls of film. Today will be the tea ceremony class. I can't miss that.

Still, I dial the number and explain to the principal that I have an appointment with my husband and can't come this week.

"That's fine," she says, exactly as Sally did. "Come next month. We'd love to see you."

I hang up and stomp down the hall. A month seems forever. I fear it will never happen. It has been delicate to arrange this collaboration between my Japanese-American friend at the Urasenke Tea School and the teacher at KIS. I have no energy left to try again. I'm sure something else will interfere. And maybe it no longer matters.

Urasenke, one of the major tea ceremony schools, sponsors these outreach programs all over town but usually doesn't allow *gaijin* observers to enter their closed circle. I'm merely an occasional student, not a serious committed one signed up for the usual seven-year stint needed to study any traditional art in Japan.

Several years ago, after I finished my first private tea lesson with my Urasenke friend, he asked me, "What about the tea ceremony do you like the best: the beauty, the tradition, the rules, the artistry of the utensils, or what?"

"The meditation of it," I replied, without pausing to consider. This is what draws me to every one of these traditional arts. Today's tea event at KIS would have brought together my fascination with this meditative art form and my interest in teaching Japanese culture to American schoolchildren.

I grab my daypack from the bedroom and storm out of the house. "See you at the Xerox store at ten." I fume as I race toward the *densha* station, then veer off to take the long way instead, walking across the vast stubbly field toward the bus stop.

I am fed up. Too many cancellations. I miss my art classes: learning a new braised tofu dish from my cooking teacher, the pediatrician who loves to cook; sitting silently at the low wooden table next to my *shodō* teacher, mimicking his hand gestures as he flourishes black circles and fading lines on white paper; learning realistic Japanese idioms from Toru, to use out on the streets when I need to buy shoes, instead of stilted book grammar. I miss the bustle, color, and music of the daily neighborhood festivals: the Turnip Festival, where soup is made in huge cauldrons and then served to the audience at long communal tables; the Hairdo Festival, where young women parade in their finest silk kimonos, displaying their intricate multilayered upswept hair arrangements, which are studded with gold combs and baubles; the Warrior Festival at a temple in the forest, where men in fur aprons shoot bows and arrows in a stylized ritual.

I still seem to drop everything for Steven, whether for a small event or large crisis. I haven't yet learned that I don't always have to put my husband's needs and career first, like my mother did. I can have an artistic passion in my life, separate from Steven, that will both anchor me and keep me moving steadily on course, and that will help with these decisions and contradictions. I'll understand when to choose my husband, when to choose myself, and when to compromise.

At ten o'clock, I meet Steven at the stationary store in our old Shūgakuin neighborhood. Even though Steven has been here often, the grumpy owner does not welcome us with a friendly "*Irasshai*" greeting, bow, and smile, like most shopkeepers do who take pride in their shops and in their regular customers. He doesn't rush to clear off the piles of merchandise stacked on top of the small, old-fashioned Xerox machine in the corner, but waits until Steven asks politely. Then he huffs as he drags out the dusty machine into the crowded aisle so we can reach it. Customers push around us as we stand working for hours in the cramped store. We take turns, bending over, laying in each piece of paper, thumping the cover down, waiting for the slow *chunk-ka-chunk* as the heat spreads up into our palms and each single piece of paper laboriously slides out.

I grow restless and hot in the stuffy store. He can do this by himself. Why did I agree to come? The papers seem endless, with numerous copies required for each person: the Customs Police, the lawyer, the translator, the court. And one for us. And the original for the prosecutor.

My back aches, and the ink fumes choke me. I remember one day twenty years ago when I was a secretary in the psychology department at the university in La Jolla. All day long I'd been xeroxing and typing endless copies of research papers, letters, grant proposals, all in the days before computers, when one word change meant retyping the whole page. I stood at the machine after a Christmas party, the taste of beer in my mouth, thinking I'd squeeze in one last copy job before I went home for the weekend. The room was stuffy and cramped, the machine noisy, drowning out the chatter and clink of the party down the hall. A young graduate student burst in and shoved his one-hundred-page thesis toward me.

"Here. I need this by tomorrow morning."

My face flushed with fury. Maybe the beer gave me courage. I shoved it back at him. "Here. Do it yourself. I quit."

I rushed out, slamming the door in his surprised face, his mouth hanging open, his words sputtering, "But, but," as he still held it out to me.

I was fed up with four years of secretarial tasks, of doing other people's work, especially men's. I didn't care if they fired me. I would do no more. Besides, I worked for the professor, not for this student. I knew I was seen as the quiet, compliant one. Well, no longer.

The next day I was not fired. My boss gave me some data to analyze and cut back on the secretarial tasks. It was the start of my university research career.

I stretch out my aching back and help Steven gather up the messy, disorganized sheets of paper that have spewed out on the floor. We bow our thanks to the unfriendly owner and back out of the shop.

We trudge across the street to the cozy warmth of the Berg, my favorite café when we lived in this neighborhood. Even though it was right around the corner from our apartment, I didn't discover it until the day the police knocked. That day, after they took Steven away, Keiko brought me a loaf of bread from this café, to cheer me up. After that I came here often as a refuge from Steven and the stifling apartment.

Now, the fragrance of hot cinnamon pastry and the symphonic music of Beethoven greet us. After grabbing the metal tongs, small plate, and tray, I circle the open shelves stacked with a wide variety of French and Danish pastries. I savor each one in my mind before finally deciding on a cinnamon roll and a lemon-custard Danish. I choose my usual table in the back with the garden view. We both order *kōcha*, the black English tea always served in such shops, which comes with a pitcher of milk. I drop into my chair, munch sweet pastry, sip hot tea out of the delicate, floral china teacup, and let the music envelop me. For a moment it feels like none of this has happened.

Steven begins to sort, organize, and staple the various copies.

"I can't handle this chaos," I say. My voice rings tight and high in my ears. "You do it. I need to sit and drink my tea."

He looks at me and smiles. "You've done enough."

I sit back and watch without a word. I didn't like the way he did the xeroxing. I wanted to sort the papers at the machine and organize them as they spewed out. He wanted to grab the xeroxed confusion and sort it here. For most tasks, we tend to have different working styles, whether it's how to add a column of numbers, how to cook a soup, or how to deal with the plumber. We've learned to each do it our own way and then compare notes, or to divide the chores from the outset. And to admit to each other that both ways are valid, just different. Today, I'm not feeling so generous. This mess of papers is the mess he has made of our lives.

While I delight in my hot tea and swirl bites of lemon custard in my mouth, he methodically works, until the job is done. His way.

"Wait," I say, as I scoop a stray paper off the floor. "Have you read this one?"

"No."

"It's from Sam." A fellow faculty member at his university at home.

> . . . despite the fame and honor that he has achieved in his career . . . he has managed to remain a most unassuming person, who lives and dresses quite modestly, giving the

wrong impression of not being as important as he is. This is part of his character, which is more concerned with matters of the mind (and soul) than with material objects.

Steven grasps my hand, closes his eyes, a slow smile spreading over his face.

"He goes on and on about you."

What distinguishes him among the people in this department is . . . his . . . consideration for the rights of the individual. He has taught me to respect other people's point of view . . . taught me to be generous, to be understanding, the way he is understanding, to be fair, the way he is fair.

We linger over our tea as I extract one letter after another from the neat pile. "Here's your cousin Teddy."

He has always been a source of great strength for me . . . and a dear friend . . . dedicated his entire life to unselfishly bridge the gap between Asian and American cultures, to being a model father and family man, and a close and caring relative. He has in many ways led an exemplary life.

My voice falters as I read, unable to find the words for the joy and gratitude that I feel.

"I never knew they thought those things," he murmurs, "that they cared so much."

"I didn't realize you asked our children to write Letters, too. Listen, from Alex." My son.

He is a wonderful, kind, brilliant person. He has been a marvelous addition to our family. He is a very scholarly and serious man . . . a very calm spiritual man who practices Zen meditation and karate regularly. We love him very much . . . We miss him and want him home safe.

"Steven, they all love you," I say. He needs this boost to his ego, even if it never helps him get out of trouble. And I need it, too, I guess, a reminder of his good qualities and strong relationships.

Finally, Steven stands up to leave and looks down at me, his face relaxed and clear of pain. "Let's take these to Suzuki sensei tonight." He pauses. "But what if she won't agree to take on the translations?"

I finish my last sip of tea and stand up too, carefully clasping the precious Letters to my chest. "I'm sure she'll be kind to us."

Suzuki san and I first became friends as we wandered among the magentas and golds of the flaming fall leaves at a nearby shrine, while admiring the exquisite porcelain pottery of Steven's teacher. Steven and I had attended her weekly classes at the private language school ever since summer. When I discovered her interest in the traditional arts of Japan, I invited her to the ceramics exhibit. We continued to meet periodically for an art show and lunch, even after I stopped her classes and switched to Toru as a private tutor.

But ever since the police came, I've been afraid to call her, not knowing whether she would be friend or enemy. Language schools have to be careful; they cater to young foreigners and must uphold their strict drug-free reputation.

A few days ago she suddenly called me at Takeda's, her voice warm and friendly. Dismayed at not finding me at our old number, she had searched and searched, finally tracking us down. She heard from someone at her school that we were in trouble, but didn't know why. She wanted to help and immediately invited us to dinner at her apartment. This meant a big new step in our friendship, since Japanese rarely invite foreigners to their homes. But, like Toru and Hiroki, Suzuki and her husband are familiar with the West, having lived in London for many years while her husband studied for his doctorate. Without hesitation I accepted, not asking Steven, merely announcing we were going.

This evening, as I dress up in my one fancy outfit, a maroon silk blouse and matching wide trousers, I feel excited to be going out for a change. But during the tram ride, Steven's worries rumble out. What if Suzuki refuses to translate the Letters, not wanting to be involved, like the other Japanese? Can she do it fast enough? What if she won't accept payment for it? And how to bring it up? He doesn't want to ruin a peaceful evening with a business transaction that might sour the friendship. I try to not let him dampen my mood, but his anxiety is contagious. Will she really welcome us as she did on the phone? And what about her husband? He's a history professor at the same university as Steven and may feel differently.

The Suzukis fling open their apartment door and usher us in with big smiles and Western-style hugs.

"Please, I am Fumiko. This, my husband, Hideo," Suzuki says. Another big and rare step in Japanese friendship, to be invited to use their first names. Maybe everything will be all right after all.

Their home is luxurious: white, airy, and spacious. I didn't expect wealth from a professor and a part-time language teacher. They are in their forties, with no children. As they escort us down the long hall to the living room, I peek into the various rooms that open off of it.

The Suzukis have created their home as a cohesive work of art, decorating it with objects from both Japan and their frequent travels abroad. A semi-abstract Italian collage hangs above an antique English desk. Centered on an antique coffee table are two modern Japanese bamboo sculptures. They transform the traditional basket form into golden abstracts, reminiscent of clouds or butterflies. The Suzukis are clearly serious collectors of exquisite taste. This reminds me of the artistic elegance of the home of my first mother-in-law, the first person to introduce me to the traditional arts of Japan. But more important is the warmth and friendship the Suzukis offer us.

Steven and I settle into the smooth leather couch, sipping our thimble-size *choko* of sake. A Bach sonata plays at low volume from the next room.

Fumiko says with a gentle hesitation in her voice, "Last night, you see newspaper? Or TV?"

Steven's whole body stiffens, as does mine, both our cups stuck in midair.

"What do you mean?" he says.

"You are there, your story."

"His photo, too?" I ask.

"No."

"Thank god," I reply.

Fumiko continues, "Two or three lines in newspaper about university professor and marijuana." She pauses. "And his name."

Steven's face remains impassive, Japanese-style, his eyes riveted on her face. My heart pounds like a woodpecker against a tough tree. Our secret is out. What does this mean? Maybe now we can lift the blinds, fling open the windows. It will be easier not to hide behind our secret. But . . .

"Will this affect your case?" I say to Steven, and then I explain to the Suzukis, "Takeda and the lawyer have said it would. That a lot of publicity will make it worse, the police and the judgment stricter."

Hideo replies in a quiet voice, "That is true here, to save face, to show example, to show precedent. It is different when it remains behind closed doors."

"But the Investigation is over. Who leaked it to the press?" says Steven, his voice tight and thin.

"And why?" I ask.

Fumiko starts to rise from her chair. "Want to see it?"

"No," we both say at once, with a blunt emphasis.

Part of me wants to know the black-and-white reality of it, but the bigger part of me wants to flee from it, to keep it hidden away in Fumiko's back room, too afraid it will tell me more than I can handle.

And ten years later I will discover I was right: it was more than I could have handled back then. My best friend will Google Steven's name for the fun of it, will discover the article and send it to me.

> Customs officials said they will file a complaint with the
> Osaka District Public Prosecutor's Office against Solomon,
> 58, a professor of . . . mailed from Los Angeles inside a
> hollowed-out book . . . found 27.5 grams . . . street value
> of $960 . . .

As I read the fresh printout from the web, my hands will shake, nausea rise, and my heart thunder so hard I cannot breathe. A jumble of new facts and an avalanche of old buried emotions of anger and fear. In Kyoto in '93, I never knew about the book, the number of grams, the street value. Those actual black-and-white numbers and that hollowed-out image will haunt me. I will want to rip the paper in a thousand shreds. Instead, I fold it in a million creases like a failed origami and stuff it in the far back of my desk drawer. Once again, I will think, how devious of Denise, how stupid of Steven. If I had read it back then, I might have flown home to the States without him.

Sitting in Fumiko's living room, I push away my despair at the news leak. I pick up my cup of sake and try to hear what Fumiko is saying. She has rushed on to talk about their last trip to Italy, pointing out their newest Italian painting.

Steven lets the conversation roll on a bit. He squints at me, biting his lip, then leans toward Fumiko, his elbows on his knees. "Perhaps this is a good time. I want to ask you a favor."

Hideo pours Steven another cup of sake.

"*Hai. Dōzo.* Please, yes. What can I do?" Fumiko says.

Steven quickly explains the translations that he needs and then sits on the edge of his chair, his back tense, awaiting her response.

"I want to help." She shuffles through the pages. "Yes. Very easy. When do you need?"

They easily negotiate price. The translations will be ready in three days, and then he'll bring her the next batch.

"*Kampai!*" Hideo lifts his cup, and the four of us toast with another round of sake.

Steven and I lean back into the couch while Fumiko flutters into the kitchen. She returns with a mosaic Italian tray laden with doll-size antique Japanese plates. She offers us *shimeji bataa-yaki, nasu-no-miso,* and *agedashi dōfu*: mushrooms sautéed in butter, eggplant broiled with miso, and tofu warmed in broth. In rapid alternation, Steven and I fill the Suzukis in on the main facts of our story. They only knew rumor, gossip, and now the news article. Soon we meander into discussions about our aging parents, Italian art, British history. We linger in the living room before dinner, drinking sake, munching the hors d'oeuvres, and laughing together. Relief pours through me. At last I feel normal again. They know our secret and love us anyway.

SPLINTERED TELEPHONE

A lone plover skimming the waves
dusk, the Omi Sea
and with each soft cry,
my heart, too, like dwarf bamboo,
stirred, longing for bygone days.

— KAKINOMOTO NO HITOMARO (tr. Sam Hamill)

The silence is broken. Our secret is out. I've been bottled up too long and now am about to explode. I need help from a *gaijin* confidante, but I'm not used to asking.

The next day I call to invite my new friend Beverly for tea, and we agree to meet that afternoon. She directs me to her house, right around the corner from Takeda's. When I knock on her door, I'm puzzled why she doesn't invite me in. I realize the plan was unclear on the phone. Maybe she's adopted the Japanese custom of meeting with friends in public places, rather than at home. I glimpse the corner of a rocking chair, a folded knit shawl, a sunny picture window. I long to curl up there and linger over a welcoming cup of tea. But she hurries me down the path, suggesting a nearby teashop.

We walk through the dry stubbly fields and empty lots between her house and the main road, picking our way through the yellowed weeds and making small talk. I am bursting to tell her my secret, but can I? How will she react?

I first met Beverly in the fall at a party at our apartment house. We didn't connect at first. Like so many Westerners I met, she seemed to cling to her *gaijin* circle, not interested in Japanese culture. I thought I wanted only Japanese friends and tended to avoid the *gaijin*. I didn't realize then that not only was I wrong about Beverly, but that both types of friends were valuable.

Soon after the police came, I rediscovered Beverly at a festival that celebrated the seventeenth-century teahouses surrounding the Urasenke Tea School. I walked the stone path of the garden and entered the dark wooden house. The muted swirls of the natural wood grain beckoned me down the hallway. Beverly stood in front of a display case, looking at the traditional dolls dressed in their colorful, stiff kimonos. We stopped to talk. Now that she wasn't with her *gaijin* friends, I felt an unexpected kinship with her. We were both reading *The Tale of Genji* and were fascinated with the arts of that medieval Heian period—the tea, poetry, flowers, and kimonos. She was here on sabbatical from her university in Iowa where she taught Medieval French history.

To my delight, I discovered she lived only a block from Takeda's. This time I asked for her phone number and promised I would call. As I left the teahouse, I folded the slip of paper into my purse, happy to have a phone number at last.

The teashop Beverly and I enter is the elegant kind that serves only English black tea and French pastries. Beverly chooses a small spindly table in the middle of the room. All the tables are busy with dressed-up Japanese women, wearing silk blouses and woolen skirts in muted colors. They are too close to give us privacy, but I hope they don't understand English.

The room is cozy and the windows steamy from the cold February day outside. I face the kitchen and the continual parade of trays laden with pastries, cakes, and cookies. Beverly faces the window. She orders only tea, gesturing to her plumpness with an air of acceptance. I order *kōcha* and a chocolate-and-whipped-cream pastry. Its rich sweetness comforts me as I sip my hot black tea with milk, out of an English china teacup with a design of interwoven pink flowers. We exchange a few more pleasantries, and then she says, "So, how're you doing?"

"Terrible. I'm in an awful crisis. May I tell you?"

"Yes, of course. Please do."

I blurt it all out, oblivious to the other women around me. Except for my Japanese friends, Fumiko Suzuki and Toru, I've confided my secret to no one but Clover, my American artist friend. But that was soon after the police came, and so much has happened since then. I've not been allowed to tell anyone else, not even my friends back home. It helps that Beverly is a total stranger. I tell her every detail: what Steven did; the police knocking and searching; Steven's daily Interrogation by the Customs Police; the lawyer and our "house arrest"; the resignation, eviction, and move to Takeda's; the closed blinds and need for secrecy; the frantic compiling of Letters of Recommendation; and the news break yesterday. I speak of my exhaustion, despair, and fear.

She listens and listens, with her hands folded under her chin, her round hazel eyes focused on me. She doesn't say much, merely nodding and murmuring for me to continue. When I finish, I sit back, drain the last of my lukewarm tea, and scoop up the last puff of whipped cream from my plate. Beverly pours me hot tea, then cups both her hands over mine. Our eyes meet, and she gives me a slow wide smile.

"I'm so sorry. My relative went through something like this. I'm not free to talk about it, but I understand how terribly hard it is."

"I can't thank you enough for listening. And for understanding." I close my eyes, brush my hair off my forehead and away from my cheeks. Raising my eyes to hers, I say, "I feel as if a huge boulder has rolled off my head and down the mountain."

As we walk back toward our neighborhood, she leads me on an easier path, a longer route that avoids the rough field. Maybe I've found a new friend, I think. But I don't realize that I'm too caught up in my own anguish to ask about her story. I don't understand it then, but this time Beverly gives everything to me, and for the next friend, I will be ready to give my all to her.

The next morning when the phone rings, I hesitate to answer, my hand pausing on the black receiver, struggling to honor Takeda's rules. He's told us not to pick up, that if anyone learns the truth of why we are here, it will hurt Steven's legal case. It's never made sense to me, but I've been trying to follow his request. But now the secret's out and the danger is over. Unfortunately, I will soon learn that for Takeda, it is not over yet.

For the moment I'm glad I've answered. It's Beverly inviting me to her house this evening to watch President Clinton give an important speech on TV. Her group of American friends will be attending. I've no interest in American politics right now. Still, I say yes, grateful to be included. I realize I should push myself out of the house.

All afternoon I brood about the party, growing more and more nervous. Even though Steven's news is out, or maybe because it is, I still feel raw. I want to shrink from all contact, hide behind these blinds and under the covers. What if these other women have heard about Steven? What if they judge him, and me, harshly?

I call Beverly back. "I'm not feeling well. I can't handle crowds right now. I'm sorry."

"That's okay, either way. But there'll be only two or three of us, and you don't have to talk. You could just have some company."

"Thank you very much, but I can't." Instead, I take a prolonged walk, aimlessly wandering a distant neighborhood, and then fall into bed for a nap. When I awake, my eyes ache from depression and fatigue. The walk has exhausted me, and so has the nap. Nothing clears my head. I should've gone to the party.

I wait over a week, way too long, for my next call to Beverly. Wait until I am desperate again, from a new crisis. Even though

I've ached for friends, I haven't had the energy to pursue a real give-and-take friendship, like the ones I have at home. I haven't properly understood the importance of forging a rich network of friends. To be there for them, and they for me.

Beverly answers the phone, very out of breath. I clear my throat and pause. "How 'bout meeting for tea this week?"

She heaves a huge sigh. "I can't possibly. I fly home in three days, I'm in the middle of dust and brooms and mops, I have a goodbye party every night this week," she says, all in one breath.

"I'm right around the corner. Let me help you clean."

"I'm sorry. No, thanks. I've gotta go. Bye."

I fling myself on my narrow bed in the still-shuttered room and weep, giving into self-pity. I'm not invited, of course. No one is giving me goodbye parties. With Beverly, I've missed my chance. I didn't reach out to her when I could have.

On the other hand, I've come to value these fleeting friendships. No beginning, no middle, no end. A "green tea" friend. Whether we share black tea or green tea, the rare beauty of the green becomes my image for these evanescent Kyoto connections. In this transitory world of *gaijin* and expatriates, they come and go, whether for brief or long sojourns. Like a clear delicate cup of green tea, each sip is savored in the moment for its unique color, aroma, and flavor, with a brief glimpse into its hidden complexity. And then it is gone, and I am left with the intricate design in the bottom of the cup to ponder.

The next morning I'm sitting at Takeda's dining room table writing a lengthy letter to my mother about Steven and our troubles. I'm alone in the house, the blinds still drawn to that winter lawn with its empty clothesline. Ever since our troubles began, I've written her only short notes, never calling her. Her letters repeatedly ask, "Why did you move? Where are you living? Will you move again?" Unburdening my secret to Beverly has freed me to finally tell my mother.

In my whole life I've never poured my heart out to her, always resisting her bossiness, her thinking that she knew everything about me. Twenty years ago, the first summer after my divorce, she said, "I never liked Tim anyway." I seethed. All I could hear was that she had disliked my husband for the past twelve years. I wanted her support, not misguided empathy.

The first time I dared open up to her was ten years ago, before our trip to Kenya on a San Diego Zoo safari. She was in her late seventies, I in my early forties. It was our first and only trip together, just the two of us. I wrote to her, "I really want to go with you, but I'm a person who needs a lot of solitude, and I'm worried I won't get it on a group tour." What I meant was, I'm not sure I can room with you because you're too talkative and won't give me space. To my surprise, she read between the lines, reassuring me it would be fine. In fact, it was. Years later she admitted that each afternoon in Kenya when she took her afternoon nap, curling up on her side with her face to the wall, often she didn't sleep and she always rested longer than needed. Her way of giving me what I had asked for.

But my letter to her from Kyoto is a real test. I want to reach out to her in a new way. I don't tell her every detail as I did with Beverly, but I write the truth, a bit softened: Steven's marijuana use, the resignation, the move to Takeda's, the waiting, the not knowing when we can return home. I end by saying, "Please understand and forgive."

I wait anxiously for her answer. Ten days later, by return mail, I receive it. She writes, "I forgive and I understand. I love Steven very much." After rereading it several times, I smooth out the crinkly airmail stationery, fold up her spidery handwriting, and slide it back into the fragile air envelope. Then I tuck it into a safe place in my drawer between my embroidered handkerchiefs.

But her letter also adds, "No one else needs to know." And I obey. She means my brother and sister. And even my Aunt Sylvia. A secret from my siblings doesn't bother me. We've never been close. But I've always been close to my favorite aunt. With her creative free spirit, she was my fantasy mom when I was a child. I often wanted to be part of her family, with her rambunctious house, artistic homemade clothes, and lack of concern for social etiquette.

Later when we're finally back home, I will visit my aunt and yearn to tell her my secret. I know she, too, will understand and forgive. But the voice of my mother in my head stops me: "Mustn't tell. Don't air our dirty linen." A lesson drummed into me since childhood.

And I will spend a weekend at my mother's desert house with my mother and my sister. My sister pours over my photos, insists on hearing me speak Japanese, admires my ikebana of desert flowers, and listens intently to my *shakuhachi*. But then she probes and probes, asking me the same question over and over, "But why did you keep changing houses?" She can sense something is amiss. She can smell a lie. I will hold firm and silent, with Mom's eyes on me. Maybe she is right. She worries about widening the existing rift between us sisters. But I want to tell my sister my secret. If only I could be alone with her. I would be ready to chip away at the layers of concealment that still linger, to release the weight of heavy stone.

On our tenth day at Takeda's, Steven returns home from his weekly visit to the lawyer with a drooping walk. Yet when he looks up, the glimmer in his eyes puzzles me. "Good news or bad?" I ask.

"Both. My case now goes to the prosecutor. There'll be no trial, no chance for Fukuda san to present my case or defend me. The prosecutor will decide what to do with me."

I give him a full-bodied hug, then, sitting back down next to him, I cradle his hand in mine. "Prison?" I whisper. That word is on our minds every day but is rarely spoken.

"It still could happen." He grasps both my hands, and we stare at each other in silence.

I can see the tight fear in his eyes and can feel that same fear gripping my chest like a coiled snake.

"That's how Japanese law works. Tom translated it clearly."

"How many weeks will the prosecutor take?"

"Nobody knows."

I pace around the four corners of the living room rug. My voice rises. "More waiting?"

He bounces up and spins me around. "That's the good news. Right when I was bowing goodbye to the lawyer, he stopped me abruptly and said, 'The prosecutor is away on vacation so can't possibly begin deliberations for a week. If you want some time away, go now. For a few days. But don't tell anybody.'"

I am perplexed that this conservative lawyer would break the rules. From the beginning the police have warned Steven that they must always know where he is and be able to reach him by phone at a moment's notice. This is instead of putting him in jail. He's been warned that if he were younger or held a less-respectable job, he would be in prison already.

I've been yearning to escape Kyoto, have even dreamed of going off by myself. Perhaps to visit my cousin Andy, in Kyushu, the southernmost island of Japan, where he's doing research. Or to attend a silent meditation retreat at a Zen temple. Or to travel to the far north of the country to stay with my former ESL student. Or even to fly home.

But I will never, can never, leave Steven. The pull to stay is too strong for me to go away, even for a weekend. I'm afraid to leave him home alone for a whole day. I don't know whether he is suicidal or not. There may come a time when I'll have to escape for my own sanity, when I can no longer help him. But that time has not yet arrived.

If Steven and I go away for a few days, I suspect he won't be able to really escape his troubles, but I pray he'll find some relief. I know he's planning the trip for my sake.

That night after dinner we tell Takeda our plan. It's a rare evening that he is home with us. He encourages our escape, probably delighted to be rid of us for a bit and reclaim his private space. We ask him where we should go and if he can help us. We must leave tomorrow.

He pulls out a map and points to the Kii Peninsula. I've often fantasized about going there, wanting to stand on the southern tip of Honshu, the main island of Japan, surrounded by the ocean on all three sides. Flipping through his catalog of *ryokan*, the traditional Japanese inns, and the train schedules, Takeda books our hotel and train without even consulting us. The Tsubaki Inn that he chooses sounds too modern and luxurious for me and is located somewhere along the coast, instead of at the tip as I wanted. But I agree to everything, grateful for anything. Takeda writes down detailed instructions: where to buy our tickets, departure and arrival times, train numbers, phone numbers.

Neither of us think to ask Takeda about the prices, although I'm sure the trip will be more than we're used to paying. When I ask Steven, he says, "It doesn't matter. This is a special escape trip. We'll pay whatever it costs. I'll pay for it all."

As I toss a nightgown, change of clothes, and *Genji* into my brown backpack, I worry about our limited funds. Our stash of cash in the drawer from Steven's salary is dwindling. They won't allow either of us to work. And if we ever have to leave Takeda's, housing will be very expensive. There could even be a big fine for Steven's crime.

I search my mind for solutions. Wiring and transferring money internationally is very complex, whether to access our U.S. bank accounts or to receive money from Steven's sister. In case Steven suddenly goes to prison, he showed me how to use his bank card, to withdraw cash from our meager savings account. We stood at the windy ATM machine, the traffic roaring behind us, while he taught me the shapes of each *kanji*, which to push for each function. I memorized each one by tracing the lines and curves into my palm over and over again.

At dawn, Takeda sneaks us out the front door, rushes us into the car hidden behind his house, and drives us to Kyoto station. We could take the local *densha*, then connect to the subway, and on to the *eki* to catch the train, but our packs would be bulky in those small compartments. I think Takeda is trying to protect us. As usual I can't read his silence in the car; it seems calm and accepting, like in the mountains when he was whittling that bamboo sake holder. But now he has that edge of pulled-in self-protectiveness that he often carries around the house.

He drops us off with a brusque, "*Ja mata*, See you later," and a curt nod of his head. I expected he would jump out and help us at the ticket counter. The agent will not speak English, and buying tickets is confusing. One time Steven and I mixed up the words for *to* and *from* and bought a one-way ticket *from* Nara instead of *to* Nara, not discovering it until we tried to board the train. Now, with Takeda, I feel hurt and helpless, wanting to be cared for, even though I tell myself he's done more than enough for us and is probably eager to speed back to the rare solitude of his empty house.

As I watch him drive away, I bite at my nail and tear away a loose piece. What if the police call looking for Steven? What will Takeda say? He must have a plan. But I didn't ask.

When we arrive at Osaka Station, we run through the hordes of commuters and competing loudspeaker announcements, searching for the train to Tsubaki. As we pass a bank of pay phones, Steven insists on calling his sister, Martha.

"No," I say, "we don't have time." The train leaves in fifteen minutes, and we haven't located the right platform yet. I don't know how to find it among the overwhelming confusion of dozens of tracks and trains, all running in different directions, all with signs I can't read.

"I must tell her where we're going," he says, lifting the receiver.

I can't stop him. I stand with my back to the wall, my arms wrapped tight around my chest, my shoulders drawn taut up to my ears, and glance at my watch every thirty seconds. When his news turns to chat and he begins to laugh at his sister's jokes, I glare at him.

I recognize that he needs his sister. But I want him to myself for three days. If only we can pull together a bit on this trip, recapture some of our old playfulness and curiosity. I remember when we wandered a remote peninsula in the North, with no reservations and only our backpacks and a Japanese dictionary, stopping to watch the fishermen pull in their fleet at dawn and sampling their catch of raw fish.

I interrupt him once, twice, three times.

"We'll miss our train. You've got to stop," I shout loud enough so she can hear, and I pull at his arm. Finally he hangs up, his face relaxed and replenished, as it always is after a talk with Martha.

I push him along, and he runs with me toward the tracks. We peer at each *kanji*, trying to match them with the ones on our ticket, and ask each conductor, "Tsubaki? Tsubaki?" They send us scurrying up and down the numerous lines of track. Finally, we come to the biggest engine I've ever seen, its enormous silver snout looming above us. It seems alive with its winking high glass windows and the lines painted under its nose like a closed-mouth grin.

I stare up at the two huge *kanji* written on the side of its face, trying to decipher the cross, hook, and dashes of the first one. Suddenly I recognize the *kanji* for *red*. The second character must mean *tide*! *Red Tide*, the nickname Takeda told us about, for this train that will carry us all the way to the sea. I had been looking for *Tsubaki*. I know *Red Tide* doesn't refer to the English connotation of lethal shellfish. Instead I imagine us lingering along a shallow low tide with the glow of a red-gold sunset reflecting on the shimmering sand.

We find our reserved seats, stow our luggage, and sink into the plush fabric. This is not a *densha*, the little tram, and not a *shinkansen*, the high-speed bullet train, but rather a first-class old-fashioned real train, comfortable and elegant. As it chugs out of the station, the cushiony seats cradle us. We look at each other and laugh like partners in crime, giving each other a surreptitious embrace. We've run away from the police, and no one knows where we are, except Takeda and Martha. I want to stay on the Red Tide forever, just the two of us.

The next morning, the wild sun-drenched blues and whites of the ocean surge against sculptured rocks, directly below the window of our fourth-floor room at the Tsubaki Inn. For a moment, I am transported to the rhythmic surf of the Pacific Ocean in California, where sitting on the beach in Del Mar, munching stuffed potato skins, I first committed myself to Steven. Now, three tatami mats, fragrant as sweet alfalfa newly mown in summer, completely cover the floor of our room. The soft tufted futon almost fills up the space. It's stuffed with dense cotton and is much like ours that we put in storage, with its design that looks like the soaring wings of a heron in the sky. The maid rolled it out for us last night, and she will soon fold it back up and spread out the eight-course breakfast of miso soup, sashimi, seaweed, pickles, and rice on the low table by the window.

The phone rings. Oh no! The police have tracked us down. I panic. A room phone is unusual in Japanese inns. But my son Alex's strong voice booms over the line, as clearly as if he were next door. It seems a miracle he can reach me from his home in Seattle to this remote little coastal town in Japan. He has searched me out, calling Takeda's, reassuring him he is my son, and urging him to give out my Tsubaki number. Takeda resisted, but Alex pushed. For a moment I panic again. Who else will Takeda give our number to?

I lean back against the wall and talk and talk. I speak freely, no bugged phone, no more secrets. So far we've only told our children the bare-bone facts. Now I can pour out all the conflicting emotions and legal details of our ordeal of the last four weeks.

Steven sits on the other side of the room, half-listening. He gazes out to sea, his face and shoulders free of tension.

Alex plies me with questions. When must we return to Kyoto? What's the next step? When will the prosecutor decide?

"We can't seem to figure out how the system works," I say.

"I know. Sounds typical of Japan. You never can figure out what they're feeling or thinking—or what's happening. They hide behind those polite and vague words and expect you to follow blindly along." He too has lived here.

"The waiting must be hard," he adds. He'll talk to a lawyer friend of his who's lived in Japan and see if there's any way he can help. Alex tries to distract me with stories about his work on the Alaskan fishing boat and his new job as a cook in a Japanese restaurant.

"I'll call again next week," he says.

And then he is gone. I too gaze out to sea, at the fine ink-brush line of the horizon. Oh! This is the Pacific! It stretches thousands of miles east to the coast of California and the bays of Puget Sound. When Alex was in high school, he spent a year as an exchange student, in the mountains outside Hiroshima. Missing him, I stood on my California beach, with the ocean foam swirling around my ankles, realizing he stood on his Japanese island. I looked out to sea, comforted by that vast emerald blue water connecting us. Here in Tsubaki, our situations are reversed. Now that I've heard his voice, I feel able to go on. I have a home and a son I will see again.

After breakfast Steven and I travel south for the day to Kushimoto, the village at the tip of the peninsula. The hotel van drives by a long curving stretch of beach on the way to the train station. The water shines crystal clear yet blustery, and fishing boats are propped up with poles to prevent them from falling over on the low-tide beach. If only we could stop and meander here, like we used to do at Topanga Beach, where we made a game of identifying the godwits and the whimbrels.

The train south inches along the edge of the wild, rocky, surf-laden coast. The interlacing greens and blues of tree and ocean, farm and sky, remind me of that first trip together by train along the New Zealand coast, when we'd only known each other for three months. Now, I feel the same freedom and joy of traveling alone with Steven, surrounded by beauty and speeding toward an unknown destination to explore. He is subdued, but his eyes drink in the seascape. Turning to me, he says, "I'm happy you're here."

We pass a placid cove with a huge piece of sculptured drift-wood among the rocks. "Look!" he points. "It's shaped like a human-sized cormorant drying its wings." He looks up and down the empty train car, then hops up to act out the drooping wings and waddle of the bird. A laugh bursts from me, my shoulders shaking. Steven is one of the few people that can make me laugh, but this is the first time he's done it in the last thirty days. He chuckles back low and loose.

I imagine kidnapping him and traveling forever, never returning him to Kyoto. When we travel, Steven is like my father on our summer camping trips, the only time he is truly relaxed and carefree, totally with me. But today is different; it's an escape from police and prison. I haven't yet learned that we can't return to that idealized past—not on this trip—and maybe not ever.

As we walk out of the Kushimoto train station, the endless expanse of the Pacific reaches out on three sides of us. At a seafood restaurant overlooking the sea, Steven orders fresh crab, and I the *saba shioyaki*, salted grilled mackerel.

He deftly picks out the fine pieces of crab flesh, then offers them to me with his chopsticks, as if he were nurturing a baby bird. He grins when I accept them into my palm.

After lunch, we explore the aquarium, stopping at the outdoor tank on each level to admire the local fish. But I don't like them all caged up. I want them to leap over the edge into the ocean and swim away.

At a pier at the end of the aquarium, I see a row of glass-bottom boats. "Let's go," I say, rushing Steven down the ramp. I pay, and we jump aboard exactly in time. No decision, no indecision. None of our usual, "Shall we?" or "Do you want to?"

The boat chugs far out into the harbor. It is a small one with a deep draft in the water. The captain sits on deck on a pedestal seat. We passengers sit far below on benches with glass on all four sides, peering out at murk, gloom, and bits and pieces of floating stuff. When the captain turns off the motor, we drift in sudden silence among the coral. The swell of the waves rises and falls in slow motion, like an enormous breathing meditation. Schools of fish meander around us in the green-black water, hundreds of big and little ones, a rainbow of colors. I become part of their world, like when scuba diving in La Jolla, swimming among the fish. But here I can breathe my own air. Not like the time I gasped for oxygen with a leaky tank that forced me to scramble over the reef toward shore, scared I would drown. Now, gliding along in the glass boat feels like entering a secret garden, or a forbidden cove. We are a floating aquarium. Except we live in the cage and the fish glide free.

The day after we return from Tsubaki, the black phone in the hallway rings and rings and rings, shattering the quiet of the house. Steven and I are lying on our twin beds, reading, after a vigorous morning bike ride to Takaragaike Pond. Takeda's out as usual, and there's no answering machine. Steven refuses to pick up, fearing a colleague looking for Takeda. The phone rarely rings, and I always still struggle whether to answer. But I'm mellow from our trip, and besides, the secret is over. I've only broken Takeda's rule twice, for Fumiko and for Beverly. And now it might be Alex or my friend Clover. Or the lawyer. Or even the police.

Finally, I roll out of bed and saunter to the phone.

"Hi! Is this Pat? This is Denise calling from L.A. How are you?"

I slide to the floor, stunned into silence, the receiver dangling in the air. Denise, Steven's drug dealer. How did she find Takeda's number?

My mind flashes to Steven's promise, during that bike ride to the deserted shrine, when he first confessed to me how he sneaked marijuana through Customs, and how whenever he ran out, Denise mailed him more. He promised he had only called her once, soon after the police came, and that he never would again. He'd called from a phone booth, not daring to use the apartment phone. I was still believing his promises.

"Hello? Hello?" she demands, her voice grating and loud. "Is Steven there?" As if she has no idea what's going on, as if this is a friendly chat.

I pound my palm against the wall. "Get out of our lives. You've ruined us. Don't ever, ever call here again. Don't ever contact him again." I slam the phone down as hard as I can.

Before I can pull myself up off the floor, the phone rings again. "I don't appreciate being talked to like that—" she begins.

"I said, get out of my life!" I slam the phone down again so hard the clang reverberates down the hall. I want the receiver to splinter into a thousand pieces.

I stomp into that cluttered shuttered bedroom where Steven sits on the bed listening. Standing tall above him, I pace the floor, shaking my fist, the tears streaming down my face. He shrinks smaller and smaller to the back of the bed against the wall, his knees pulled up to his chest, peering up at me from under his lowered brow.

I seize his open book and fling it at him, screaming, "You've pushed me too far. I can't take any more."

Steven raises his head and opens his mouth to speak.

"Your stupid lies. And this woman. What's going on? How dare she call here as if nothing has happened."

"She just wants to see if I'm okay—"

"Don't you say a word. It's my turn now. You listen hard." My stomach clenches. I'm going to be sick. "You are the one who's ruined our lives. You and that woman."

He's given up trying to answer me. He merely sits there, listening, his shoulders slumped, his eyes closed, his head drooping.

I grab my hairbrush from the bedside table and throw it at him, right above his head. I don't know if I want to hit him or scare him. The brush strikes the wall, breaking in two. My eyes search the room for something else to throw. I want to hit him, pummel him, hurt him, with all the force of my body.

"Why do I put up with you? I've been patient and loyal, like my mother would've been. Except my father would never have done such a thing." I pause to catch my breath and drop to the floor, like a broken doll. "You've ruined Japan for me."

Steven jerks his head up, but his face remains closed, either blank or numb. Never before have I shown him this kind of anger. He probably didn't think I had it in me. And yet I suspect he's been dreading this for weeks.

Pulling myself up to the bed, I sit opposite him. For the first time, I feel calm and cleansed by my fury. My anger runs clear and strong, a completely new feeling.

I take a solid breath, and another. I know what I have to say, what I have to do, even if it means I will lose him. In a steady, steely voice, I say, "If you ever contact her again in any way, I will leave you. Forever." I don't focus on the marijuana, the lies, the secrets, only on the other woman, and all that she represents. He has gone too far. As fierce as my love for him is, he's crossed a line over which I cannot follow him.

Steven looks as if he's in shock, his face blanched and sagging. He inches over next to me, taking both my hands in his. Holding those liquid brown eyes on mine, he takes two ragged breaths, searching my face. "I promise. I will never," he shakes his head, "never contact Denise again. Please, please, believe me." He strokes my cheek, brushing away the salt. "I don't want you to leave me."

Tears slip down his cheeks as he reaches toward me. I accept his arms, tentative around me, and slip mine around him, also tentative. We sit there a long time in silence, holding onto each other.

Finally, I unlace my arms and his, and then I lean back. "I need some time to myself," I say gently.

At Hachiman Shrine, I sit on the stone bench, watching the doves flutter and swirl up to the bell, to the sky, down to the courtyard, and back up, in a continual circle. They coo over and over in their sweet mournful voices. At the altar, I pull the rope twice to ring the bell, clap my hands, and bend my head to whisper thank you to the spirits for the courage.

At home, Steven has left me a note on my nightstand saying he's gone to visit his pottery teacher, Sato sensei, for the first time since the police came. I smile. At last he's venturing out of his shell. I nestle into the warm blankets for another long nap, this time dreamless and untroubled.

The telephone screams once again, breaking into my post-nap dreaminess. I climb out of bed one limb at a time, stretch, and force myself to walk to the phone, afraid it is Denise again, determined to deal with her with a new calm strength. So caught up in my own marital drama, I don't hesitate to answer it. I pick up the receiver, pausing before I hold it out a few inches from my ear.

"Hello," I say in English, not using the usual *moshi moshi* that the Japanese and Steven always do. I hear a flood of a foreign language, not Japanese. A woman's voice. Maybe French, maybe Spanish. Spanish!

"I am sorry. I do not understand," I say.

The voice switches to accented English. "Is Takeda there?"

"No, I'm sorry, he isn't. I don't know when he'll be back."

A loud silence on the other end. "Thank you." She hangs up before I can respond.

Steven returns home before dinner, his face tranquil and rosy. He tells me how nourished he feels, after digging his hands into clay once again. Sensei and the students, both Japanese and *gaijin*, accepted him with a quiet warmth, much as the Suzukis had. He had been avoiding his pottery class, dreading a door slammed in his face, hostile stares, or a polite steely silence. But yesterday our friend Tom, Sensei's neighbor, called to say that Sensei saw the story on TV and kept asking how Steven was doing, urging him to return.

I mention the puzzling phone call. "What do you think we should do?" I ask.

"Nothing. Whoever it was will call back. It probably wasn't Takeda's wife. She knows we're here and would've said her name." He slips on his coat and ties his shoes. "C'mon. Let's go to dinner. I'll mention it to Takeda later."

We think nothing more of it and go spend the evening at the home of our Dutch friends. I'm still distracted by the phone call with Denise, her grating voice, my slam of the phone still spinning in my mind. And in spite of my new clarity with Steven, I'm still reeling from our confrontation, like a sailboat heeling over in the gale of a storm. I didn't stop to think of writing Takeda a note. But it doesn't matter who the caller was or what the state of their marriage. As grateful and cautious guests, we should've left a note. Or not picked up the phone in the first place.

Steven and I don't return to Takeda's until very late that night, so Steven doesn't have the chance to discuss it with Takeda.

The next morning, our fourteenth day at Takeda's house, Steven and I both stumble into the kitchen to make tea. Takeda is at home for a change. We greet each other with sleepy smiles and bows. Good, I think, maybe the three of us can have tea together, a chance to spend some time with Takeda.

But Takeda frowns, his gaze on the floor. "Steven, I must talk to you. After your breakfast. Alone. In the living room."

Steven and I glance at each other. What could be wrong? I scoop up my teacup and disappear to the bedroom. Sitting up in bed, I sip my tea and stare out the half-open window blind, at the barren plum tree.

About a half hour later, Steven opens the door.

"What's happened?" I ask.

He scowls and slumps against the dresser, his arms folded across his chest. "That was his wife who called yesterday. She's angry. He spent hours on the phone with her last night, trying to calm her down, trying to explain. She won't listen."

"Oh, no," I moan, setting my cup down and sitting cross-legged on the bed.

"He says you shouldn't have picked up the phone. He'd told you not to."

"But I thought it might be Denise again."

"I know," he sighs and sits down on the edge of my bed. "He says we're ruining his marriage. She doesn't believe you're my wife and not his lover, doesn't believe I'm here too. She hates people in her house, even friends." Apparently, even though she no longer lives here and rarely visits, she still thinks of this house as hers.

I scoot over next to him, our knees and hips touching. "Can't you talk to her directly and explain, call her right away or maybe write her?"

"He says absolutely not. It won't help. There's no going back. For him it's the last straw. Believe me, I argued and pleaded. He won't budge."

I open the blinds all the way and study the empty clothesline and deserted street. Did the neighbors tell his wife about us, even before she called? I search my mind for all I've done wrong here with Takeda: hanging my nightgown on that line, leaving the house boldly instead of sneaking out, answering that black phone. But I've tried to show my gratitude: arranging the flowers for him, keeping the house neat and clean, tiptoeing around to give him privacy and the space to practice his piano. And Steven has cooked him dinners and offered companionship, staying up late drinking with him. But all of that pales compared to what I've done by answering the forbidden phone one time too many. We thought his wife knew about us. We didn't know he had added that to his list of secrets. It wasn't only the police and newspapers he feared; it was his wife as well. We were caught in the middle of his marriage, whatever their story was.

I snap shut the blinds. "What's he want us to do?"

"He's kicking us out."

I choke on my last sip of tea, cold, bitter, and too strong. "Maybe I should talk to him. Or to her. Woman-to-woman."

"No. He doesn't care anymore. He's washed his hands of us."

"Did he give us a date?"

"No. But we must leave right away. We can't stay on like this. He won't even talk to me."

He wraps me in his arms, and we clutch each other until our breathing finally slows down, matching one another.

I ride my bike alone to Takaragaike Pond. Sitting under my favorite weeping willow, I scribble furiously in my journal, trying to sort out my muddled anger—at Takeda, at Steven, at myself. Trying to understand my tumbling mix of emotions and to let go of the pain and move on. The ducks paddle aimlessly, and the clouds flicker shadows on the murky surface of the water.

> White goose floats, croaking
> old woman chants by the shore
> ancient, plaintive song.
>
> — Patricia Dove Miller

Too caught up in my own pain, I don't see that in rebelling against Takeda, I've also hurt Steven. I have caused this pain, this problem, this eviction.

At dinnertime, we bike back to our old Shūgakuin neighborhood to one of our favorite *nabe* restaurants, nestled in the green leafy garden next to the aged wooden walls of Manshū-in Temple. At the table, Steven pulls his notebook out of his pocket. We spoon hot rich broth into our empty stomachs and pick out delicacies of shrimp, shiitake mushroom, and tofu, with our chopsticks. And plot our next move.

THE SEARCH
A Long Dark Hallway

So you must persist
in asking where my heart goes
all the long, cold night.
Like following trails left by birds
who vanished with yesterday's sky.

— KOHO KENNICHI (tr. Sam Hamill)

The very next day, Monday, March 1, we begin our daily search for a new place to live. This means endless days of hunting: by phone all morning, trudging the streets all afternoon. We can't find housing ads on any of the bulletin boards, and we can't pin up our own ads because we can't give Takeda's number for call-backs. We stop at every phone booth for yet another dead-end call and hunt for addresses we can never find. We forget to stop for a bowl of soba at a corner noodle shop. We forget to slip into one of the temples, hidden between busy shops, to kneel in front of a formal ikebana. We forget to sit by a koi pond to follow the fishes' meanderings.

The first morning Steven takes his turn at the phone, sitting on the floor in Takeda's hall, the long spiral cord curling up to the nook in the wall. His right palm sweeps upward in broad gestures as he talks to the four friends on his list, asking each one about housing. After his calls, he joins me at the dining room table, walking with a new bounce in his step, invigorated by the conversations. I've been scouring the ads in the daily English-language newspaper and the monthly English magazine. We've chosen a time when Takeda is not home, and I've flung open the window blinds by the table.

Steven reports, "Tom has nothing. He suggests the guest-houses." This is where young *gaijin* stay when they first arrive to look for teaching jobs, friends, adventure, and support from each other.

"I've heard they're noisy, dirty, full of wild partying college kids." I sip my tea, wondering if we could stay in Tom's upstairs office a night or two while we hunt. But he's lived in Japan a long time and is married to a Japanese woman. I know the Japanese rarely invite people to their homes. I wouldn't want to impose. We aren't really his parents after all.

Steven tilts back in his chair, his hands clasped behind his head, his face hopeful. "Toru says it'll be easy to find a place. Tomorrow night he'll introduce us to his boss. He'll find us something for sure. Apparently, his boss knows everyone, both Japanese and *gaijin*, at all levels of Japanese society."

Steven hesitates. "And Lane has offered us a space." He lurches his chair forward with a bang. "A storeroom out back in their garden, empty, with no heat, no bathroom."

I flinch. "That sounds hard." I remember our recent dinner at the home of the Lanes, our Dutch friends. It was the evening after Denise called. They fed us *stamppot*, hot mashed potatoes mixed with melted cheese and minced carrot, and warmed us with laughter and the antics of their two small children. "We could buy a heater, and maybe Tom would loan us a futon."

"Lane said we could use a bathroom in the main house."

"I guess we should look at it," I say, without enthusiasm. "But they have a big two-story house. I wish they'd offer us refuge in there, even for a few days, while we keep looking." I wonder if they're afraid they'll be stigmatized by associating with us or by taking in a "criminal."

"That's a lot to ask," Steven answers.

Before I knew Steven, I often took in troubled friends. One time, my friend Mary wept into the phone. She had recently left her fiancé and had no place to live, no job. She slept on the narrow mattress on the floor of my den for several weeks, until she regained her balance. When my children were teenagers, I sometimes helped out their schoolmates. My son's best friend Chad often sought after-school refuge at our house when he was having conflicts with his parents. Once he pitched a tent in our backyard and lived in it for a month. I'd offered him the use of the den, but he said he wanted fresh air and space.

Several years later, he walked up the path to my house, his grin wide as he proudly held up his new baby daughter. "Thanks for that time," he said. "You helped me get on my feet."

We talked for a while about where his drifting had taken him, how he'd ended up with a GED, a steady job, now a family. As I watched him walk back to his car, I felt proud of him, as if he were my own son, and happy I'd been able to play some small part in helping him.

Now in Kyoto, thinking of the Lanes and then of Tom, I feel our positions are reversed. I, as a parent, am aching to be taken in and cared for by an adult child, or by a friend. I'm so obsessed with finding a place to stay, and with my yearning for a home, that I expect everyone to see our need and our desperation and to offer us a place for a night or two. But we never even ask, and we certainly never admit our desperation.

Steven refills my cup of tea and continues the report of his phone calls. "I called Quinn at his office. He suggests the guide-book for hotels or inns, and, of course, guesthouses." I haven't yet met Mr. Quinn, his new American friend, an English teacher at a local college. "I suggested we have lunch soon, but he said he was too busy this term to get together at all."

"That's odd. I thought he really liked you."

"I don't know. He seemed distant and formal on the phone, and cut the talk short, adding it was better to call him at his home number next time."

Quinn will explain to us later, when we are finally leaving Kyoto, that he was afraid to see Steven or be seen with him, or even talk to him on the phone. His Japanese wife was sick, and he'd been at that college so long. He didn't dare lose his job and feared being unable to find another one. He had heard many stories of *gaijin* being fired for associating with someone involved with drugs or the police.

I take my turn on the floor below the phone nook. Before picking up the heavy receiver, I gaze down the long hall for a moment toward the empty ikebana vase. I riffle through the pages of my address book, looking for the most likely contacts, and then call my small list of friends and acquaintances. First, my American friends; they seem less scary, even the "green tea" friends who I barely know but feel a strong connection with. Many are not home. Few people in Kyoto have answering machines in '93, and besides, I can't leave Takeda's number. He'll be furious if he receives a string of calls from strangers. The ones I do reach offer sympathy but have no ideas. They've found their houses through friends or colleagues. One has a friend with a vacant apartment but no way to contact her; she's on leave in the States for three months.

Finally that evening I talk to Clover, my artist friend, who's here for a year on a grant. The Japan Foundation arranged her housing. "Have you tried the temples?" she asks.

"I've read they only take serious religious students—previous *gaijin* didn't follow the rules and ruined it for others. Besides, they don't take women."

Clover says, "What about the hotels and *ryokan*?"

"The police say we aren't allowed to stay in one—I'm not sure why."

Before she hangs up, she offers to go with me to look for a place. I should say yes. She would be more uplifting than Steven. But I'm too caught in my tight coupledom, thinking we need to solve everything together, not realizing that time with a friend would blow in some fresh air. I'm still not accepting that I need help.

Next, I dial Sally's number again. She's one of my "green tea" friends. We've chatted on the phone frequently but have only managed to meet once for tea. I ask about housing. She's in "going home" mode: headed back at last to the States, frantic with packing, busy with farewell parties, switching gears from the Japanese mode to the American one, and with no more time for new friends and experiences. Her words rush out, all in one breath: her house is not available, she has no ideas, she is sorry, and goodbye.

I am at the end of my list. Suddenly I remember the woman I met at the December pizza party at my Japanese language school. Another "green tea" moment, as we compared hiking trails in the Kyoto hills. She told me she would be leaving in March. I scrounge through my old language book for her phone number. At last I find it jotted on the back of one of my final exams. Now on the phone, she says without hesitation, "Yes, it's available." She describes her traditional wooden house with its many beautiful and spacious rooms and porches.

I lean back, eyes closed, relaxing my shoulder blades against the wall.

"But I better check with the landlord," she adds.

I sit on the floor waiting. Within two minutes, the phone jangles. "I'm so sorry. I wish you'd called last week. She found a tenant yesterday."

I hang up the phone. Biting my upper lip, I stare down the endless windowless hallway. Finally, I drag myself up off the floor and go look for Steven, who perked up after his phone calls but now sits in the living room chair, frozen and passive, while I report on mine.

His mother used to sit the same way, immobile and stiff in her straight-backed chair, always wearing dark glasses and a sour look, with a sharply down-turned mouth. I only knew her when she was eighty, living in her single room in the retirement home. But Steven describes her as sitting that way ever since age thirty-six, when her husband died.

When I first lived with Steven, he suffered frequent depressions, something I'd never seen during our year of courtship. One time his mood was so severe and lengthy that he went to bed as if physically ill. He wouldn't get up, wouldn't tell me what was wrong, and refused my offerings of food, drink, sympathy, or distraction. I panicked, packed him into the station wagon, and drove us south to San Diego for a weekend with his sister. I didn't think of calling a therapist, even though we both had used them in the past. Instead, I depended on Martha, who was a therapist herself. It never occurred to me that his mood might be related to his habitual marijuana use.

Even when I pulled into her wide circular driveway with its huge sprawling elm shading the lawn, Steven merely sat there, not moving, head down.

"C'mon, Steven. We have to go in," I said. I felt like I was talking to a child as I grasped his arm and guided him out of the car. "I can't take any more, Steven. I don't know what to do with you." I thought I had to bear his ups and downs with patience. But my tolerance was depleted. I shoved his floppy tweed hat into his hand. "You don't seem to understand how much your black moods affect others," I snapped.

His head jerked up and he touched my arm. "I do know. I'm sorry. Let's go in," he said, his voice barely audible.

His depression was never that bad again. Until Kyoto, when his moods once again plummeted. I am fearful for him but once again never think of finding a therapist, even though when we first lived together I vowed that if we ever had trouble, I would find professional help. It never occurs to me to call our friend Dr. Lane, a therapist, for a referral. Steven's mood pulls me so far down, I can barely think straight.

But I am determined to keep seeking a home. While Steven sits frozen in his chair, I pick up the circled newspaper ads and plod back down the dark empty hall to my post. I slowly force the receiver to my ear and dial. With the first call there's no answer after dozens of rings. The second brings a volley of rapid Japanese, then a stunned silence at my slow clear English, then an abrupt hang-up. The third is halting meager English, alternating with my minimal Japanese, until we both give up. The fourth person appears to speak passable English.

"What your number please? Husband call you."

"I am sorry. I have no phone. When may I call back?"

"So sorry. Bye-bye."

She seems suspicious. Is it my lack of a phone? Or maybe it's my foreignness, or she's used up her few English phrases, or maybe she doesn't want me to realize she's alone in the house.

The fifth call is a success. The man speaks English, and he has a room for rent at a reasonable price.

"Yes," I say, "my husband and I would like to come see it."

He dictates a long series of complicated directions while I scribble them in my notebook. None of it makes any sense. Japanese homes have no addresses, and once off the main boulevards, most of the streets have no names or else *kanji* characters we can never read. In person, they usually sketch a little map for you. Over the phone, I can't follow anything. With this man, I try one more time, jotting down the bus number, the *chō* or neighborhood, but then get hopelessly lost again.

"Thank you very much," I mumble.

"Come any time. I always home," he says.

"We'll come tomorrow," I say, certain that we won't. The directions feel like a maze; we'd never be able to locate his house. I drop my head to my knees, papers scattering all over the floor. How does anyone ever find housing here? I take a deep breath. One more call, and that's it.

Finally, the sixth call works. I scramble up from the floor and rush down the hall. "Steven, Steven, I found something!"

My triumphant voice rouses him. He lifts his head, a half-smile softening his face. "Tell me about it."

I perch on the wide arm of his chair, my arm around his shoulder. "It's a whole house for rent in the far southwest of town. We'll see it day after tomorrow. Wednesday, ten o'clock."

My eyes rest on Takeda's piano, with the Botticelli print hanging above and the raku tea bowl below. I forget for a moment that our collection of pottery is in storage with no way to retrieve it. Instead I imagine what it'll be like to have a home of our own again, remembering our two *Hagi yaki* teacups, with their lacy mauve glaze.

The next evening, under a cold clear sky jeweled with stars, Steven and I follow Toru to his boss Knutsen's house. We wind through mossy rock-lined streets in the hills above Shirakawa Dōri Street. We've been invited to Knutsen's to discuss housing, lawyers, and Steven's predicament. Ever since we first met Toru, he's been flooding us with tales of Knutsen. He seems to have a lot of vague businesses and ventures; no one knows exactly what they are, not even Toru. I can't remember any of the details, only that he's an American expatriate who leads a so-called "wild and crazy hippie" lifestyle.

"You'll love him," Toru says. "He's helped me with everything. I owe him my job, my house, my life." Like everything else about Knutsen, it remains a mystery how he's saved Toru's life. But Toru is clearly in debt to his superior, and in the Japanese system of hierarchy, this means absolute loyalty.

"I'm sure he'll help you with everything. He's been through drug scares himself. And he always manages to wiggle out."

"What do you mean?" I ask.

"He never tells me much. Just hints at big troubles with the police, close escapes from being thrown in jail. He's lived here for thirty years. He knows the system."

I look at Steven, not quite believing that this Knutsen could be so shrewd, so bigger than life. My husband walks in silence, merely listening. Asking questions is never his style. But tonight he doesn't even engage Toru in conversation to draw him out as he usually would. As in Thailand, when he sidled up to a Hmong farmer, shared a smoke over the fence, chatted about the farm. That's his kind of anthropology, never a direct inquiry; instead he lets the conversation meander.

We turn the corner, and Toru pauses outside Knutsen's house. "By the way, you'll see two women here tonight; the older American one is his first wife, the younger Japanese one is his second wife. They all live together, the three of them, with their assorted children."

I shift uneasily on the steps, immediately seething at this news. This is the second time I've heard of a *gaijin* expatriate living openly with two wives. In the first case, I met the older American wife at my friend's house. It was whispered that she was quite content with the situation. But I can't believe either woman really likes it. These men seem to feel free to live outside both American and Japanese rules, as if mimicking their image of a Heian-era Japanese society of polygamous noblemen.

I glance at Steven, but his face is a mask. I want him to be as furious as I am, or at least to show some emotion. Do he and Toru accept this triangle because it reflects their own fantasies?

The three of us enter the rambling two-story wooden house built in the traditional style, with several porches and lots of rooms opening off long hallways. The dark curtained living room is crowded with people, threadbare overstuffed chairs and couches, a beat-up piano, and a chipped coffee table. At one end of the room sits Knutsen in a massive chair with gaudy floral upholstery, his hands resting on the wooden arms, his head flung back on the wooden headrest. He is a large man, tall and wide. Not handsome, not ugly, rather ordinary, with a short haircut. But he fills up the chair with a presence that spills over into the room all around him.

At his feet, about a dozen men, both Japanese and *gaijin*, of various ages, but mostly younger than his fifty-odd years, sprawl on large flat pillows scattered across the rug. Toru and Steven push their way forward to join the circle of men and reach for beer and chips, while I choose a cushion near the back wall, the rough rug scratching my ankles. Glasses clink as more beer is poured, and peanuts and potato chips crunch in open mouths.

Toru didn't tell me I'd be the only woman at this party. This is exactly like most Japanese parties I've attended—all men, with me as the token professor's wife, expected to be silent. The wives tend to meet separately for their own occasions.

Knutsen's deep commanding voice booms as he tells story after story in English with broad gestures. It's not the content of the stories that I notice, but the tone. I recognize the smooth patter, boastful exploits, and polished meanderings of oft-told, well-worn tales that change and grow each time they're related. I'm reminded of my first husband, Tim, who told such stories with the same exaggerated charm, the same broad gestures. However, with Tim, I always knew when a detail went astray, when it wandered too far from the truth.

The men sit enthralled, laughing at every joke, slurping beer, clapping each other's backs. I can't see the charisma that attracts them. Perhaps it's that Knutsen lives other men's dreams—with women, money, drugs, and freedom from rules. Steven's face is alive and shining, caught up in the enthusiasm.

Finally, Toru introduces Steven to Knutsen.

"Oh, yeah, glad to meet ya. Toru told me about you." Knutsen extends his fleshy hand and flashes a wide grin. "Gotta good lawyer?"

"Yeah, Fukuda," Steven replies.

"Great. He's the best. He'll get you off."

Steven sits back, relieved, his faith in Fukuda confirmed. He twists his shoulder around to raise an eyebrow at me, and our eyes meet briefly. I, too, feel reassured about the lawyer—but not completely. What about a place to live?

The room grows stuffy and overheated with men's bodies, sweat, and digested alcohol. I burrow into my corner, barely listening, irritated at Knutsen's arrogant chatter. I am never introduced or acknowledged by him or anyone. I feel invisible.

I first learned to be invisible when I was about four years old. One evening my family was sitting at the dining room table, which my mother had graced with the usual two lit candles, a low vase of geraniums, our own individual napkin rings with cloth napkins, and her best wedding silverware. This was not a special occasion. Mom rejoiced in using her finest things daily. She had grown up poor but always believed in making the dinner hour a special ritual with touches of beauty, even if only a sprig of pine and a few winter berries in the vase.

My father sat at the head of the table, my mother at the other end by the swinging kitchen door, my older brother and sister across from me, their faces backlit by the low slanting sun drifting through the shadows of the oak trees. As the baby of the family I sat alone facing them, yet close to my mother. White-crowned sparrows chittered and danced at the flat homemade feeder outside the open window.

My mother and sister were discussing the interminable details of how to make a satin costume for her upcoming gymnastics performance. Their voices rose to a high pitch of excitement.

My father paused in the middle of carving the roast chicken and set the bone-handled carving knife and fork down on the table. "Virginia," he said to my mother, "please be quiet for a while. Speak only when you have something important to say." His baritone voice reverberated across the long table.

The room fell silent as he resumed the carving, slipping one slice onto each plate and passing it around to the next person. I shrank farther into the corners of my chair. How could I tell what was important or not? Better not to speak at all.

The meal continued in silence, as we chewed our peas and clinked our spoons and forks against the plates. The Steller's Jays swooped and shouted at the feeder, as I watched the flash of blue feathers glide through the sunlit trees.

At Knutsen's house, I quietly inch forward on my knees, Japanese-style, to help myself to beer and nuts. Retreating again to my cushion, I nurse the cool tangy beer, resigned to be a spectator at this spectacle, wondering why we have come.

As I peer down the long dark hallway that stretches off the living room, a flowing silk skirt swishes by. A glimpse of long black hair, and a beautiful slim bare-footed Japanese woman in her early thirties. Her narrow Western skirt of subtle gray-green and mauve vanishes behind a closed door. Two young laughing children, half-Japanese and half-American, leap into the living room and clamber up into Knutsen's chair. He pauses to hug them, then shoos them away as he turns back to his audience.

An American teenage girl appears at the door to gather them up and disappears with them behind another door.

Stretching out my cramped legs and crunching my teeth on the sharp nuts, I fume at the situation of these two women. I never see the older wife. She's probably my age, in her early fifties. How can she bear it? Even though they aren't divorced, I imagine her as the discarded wife, despite Toru's claim that she's happy with their arrangement. I imagine sneaking down that hall to chat with the two women, uncover their curious story, and to tell them mine.

The discarded wife. As I watch Knutsen hold forth, I feel inundated by the din of male laughter. The stuffy room closes in around me, like in the keypunch room where I worked thirty years ago at Scripps Institution of Oceanography. That was when I was discarded by my first husband Tim for a younger, more beautiful, dark-haired woman. I was thirty—she was twenty. Thirty seems young to me now, but at that point I'd already been married for eleven years and was the mother of a ten-year-old and an eight-year-old.

I remember that morning at Scripps, the deafening clack of my fellow keypunch operators next to me, the repeated clang of the shrill telephone. Each time it was for me, Tim calling. I stepped out to the balcony so I could talk, the surf of the Pacific crashing below me.

"Patty, Patty. You mustn't talk to her. Please, I beg of you."

"I'm sorry, Tim. I've already made a lunch date with Cindy. I'm meeting her today in Solana Beach."

I hung up, but immediately the phone jangled again.

"No, please, no. I don't want you to meet each other. This is terrible," he said, his usual low voice rising high and plaintive.

"I'm sorry," I repeated. "I have to do this. What are you afraid of? Please don't call again. I'm going to hang up now."

He must have called five more times that morning, trying to convince me to cancel. I held firm and then finally stopped answering. I don't know where I had found the courage to call her. It wasn't my usual style. I had never stood up to him before. But finally I was fed up with his stream of lovers, one after another, he brazenly telling me about each one or leaving out hotel receipts where I would find them.

I was young and naive for a thirty-year-old. I didn't understand how to handle his infidelities. I didn't know who to ask for help. I thought I was to blame, that I was supposed to put up with it. For the sake of the marriage, for the sake of the children. I strongly remembered the one set of divorced parents from my childhood in the fifties, bitterly condemned by my mother. Divorce was still rare in the early seventies in California. I knew no one who had chosen that route.

I had called Cindy, Tim's mistress of six months, a few days earlier, saying I'd like to meet her. To my surprise, she said yes, not asking why. Even I didn't know why; some inner voice compelled me to meet my competition, to try to do something to save my faltering marriage.

Now I left my office early for my lunch break and drove north along the coast to Solana Beach. I walked up the steps of the shoddy lunchroom in a strip mall. The café was empty at eleven thirty; the walls were barren, and the windows overlooked the hot asphalt parking lot. The greasy smell of grilled cheese and fried donuts greeted me as I opened the door.

A beautiful curvaceous young woman with long dark brown hair and wide dark eyes stood inside. We were the only two there. We walked toward each other like magnets, smiling and reaching out simultaneously to encircle each other's shoulders.

"I'm Pat."

"I'm Cindy."

In that brief embrace I felt an instant woman-to-woman bond. We were in this together. Us against Tim. I was surprised at my calm, suddenly feeling wise and mature. She looked nervous, licking her lips and fiddling with a strand of her hair.

I guided her to a corner table and ordered a tuna sandwich for myself, saying lunch was my treat.

"Thanks. I can only handle a Coke right now," she said, laying one hand on her tummy. I couldn't tell if she meant nerves or diet.

Looking her straight in the eye, surprised at my boldness, I said, "We both love the same man, don't we?"

She laughed, a little more at ease, her shoulders beginning to relax. "Yeah. I guess so." She touched the gold band on the finger of my left hand. "You still wear this?"

"Yes," I said with emphasis. "I'm still married to him."

Her face collapsed. "Oh. He said you were separated and had filed for divorce."

"We still live together." I picked at my sandwich. "With our two children."

"I didn't know that." She drew in a long sip of her Coke. "How old are you, anyway?"

"I'm thirty, and Tim is thirty-seven."

"He told me he was twenty-eight." She sipped more Coke. "I'm only twenty."

We sat in silence. I tried to draw her out, asking about her college classes, trying to find something in common with this young woman, remembering when I was her age with a new baby son. She replied with subdued yes-or-no answers.

As we walked down the steps of the café, she a half step behind me, I twisted back to give her a crooked hug goodbye. "I'm truly happy we met."

"Me, too," she mumbled.

I strolled to my car, admiring the fine blue line of the horizon, feeling elated. I didn't know what I had accomplished, but at least I'd shaken up Tim and given Cindy something to think about. It was the beginning of the end. He did move out to live with her, but he said she was never the same after meeting me. They broke up a few months later, and he begged me to let him return. But by then I had discovered feminism and its new freedoms. My answer was no.

At Knutsen's house, I glance up at Steven. He, too, discarded an older wife for a younger one. I know his history, but I trust him regarding other women, more than any man I've ever known. I never thought about other trust issues.

The men's voices rise and fall, competing with each other. Their glasses clang with toasts as they become drunker and drunker and lounge back on the rug against pillows. When will we ever leave? My impatience and irritation are growing. I want Steven to ask Knutsen about a place to live, or at least to find a way to talk with him. I suppose he sees this evening as an introduction, hoping for more conversations later. I want instant action. Sometimes my way works; sometimes Steven's does. Sometimes neither one.

At last, Toru and Steven rise and bow goodbyes to Knutsen and the roomful of his admirers. Knutsen raises his glass, grins, and waves absentmindedly. "We'll talk about making that film, right?" he calls out to Steven as we leave. What film? I ask myself, both puzzled and annoyed.

Steven and Toru swagger as they weave down the lane ahead of me, giggling about one of Knutsen's stories. Poking Steven in the back, I say, "Did you ask about housing?" Perhaps I missed it in the chaos of the party.

"There was never a chance."

So he didn't even try. How could he forget about that? Where does he think we're going to live? I wrap my coat tighter against the midnight cold, put my head down, and say no more as I trudge behind them.

After we drop Toru off at his house, Steven wraps his arms around my shoulders and snuggles his nose into my hair. "Wasn't he great?! Didn't you love him!?"

I pull away. "No, I didn't." My voice is as chilled as the night. "And we got no advice about housing or your legal case. I thought that's why we went."

"He said Fukuda was good."

"Why do you like Knutsen so much?"

"I'm not sure. He's done such interesting stuff. He knows everything. And everybody." Steven stumbles on the rough road with his unsteady feet. "I'd like to work on one of his films. He promised me a part in the next one."

"What films?" I demand. He explains that Knutsen makes films about Japan for some American company, which intrigues Steven because he once taught film at his university in Los Angeles.

I whip around and stomp my foot on the pavement. "Damn it. I don't care about his stupid films. How dare you think about such frivolous things when we've got no home?"

I stride far ahead, pounding the deserted sidewalk with my boots, and retreat back into silence. Steven doesn't seem to realize that he won't be here for that film. He'll either be in prison or safely home in America. The mystery man has been no help after all. All three men have let me down: Steven, Toru, Knutsen.

The next morning I clutch the folded newspaper with the marked ad and my scribbled directions to the vacant rental house. We're on the bus to southwest Kyoto for the appointment I made two days ago. I worry we won't be able to find it and worry about the man's surliness on the phone; I purposely didn't tell Steven about him.

This neighborhood is a side of the city I've never seen: a commercial district, new but already rundown, oppressive. No high-rise office buildings and apartment houses, no sprawling old wooden farm houses, no well-kept traditional shops with their large wooden signs hanging out front carved with intricate calligraphy. No trees or the usual hidden nooks of beauty with a special sculpted rock statue tucked in a corner. There are only low boxed-in stores and a few bungalows, small, square, and flimsy.

We stop in front of one of them. The landlord meets us at the door. He is shifty-eyed, with a day's growth of beard. He looks like a sleazy used-car salesman, wearing shiny dark gabardine pants and a limp white shirt with a frayed collar, his greasy hair slicked back. As we inspect the two rooms, he shuffles close behind, almost stepping on our heels, his eyes boring into our backs.

The house is clean, but shabby, dank, and bone-chilling. There is no heater. The kitchen alcove has no stove, no fridge. A steady drip falls into the orange-stained sink. I peer out the dusty rain-streaked window at an identical house only one foot away.

Steven joins me at the window. I whisper, "We can't furnish this. We'd need a futon, stove, and fridge. And what about a heater, a lamp, a telephone?"

Steven huddles by the window, his arms wrapped around himself for warmth. "It's impossible."

I pace the empty squares of the two barren rooms, measuring them in my head with yard-long strides. We're spoiled by the university apartment and by Takeda's, where everything was provided. "This is our only option so far," I say. "Maybe we could camp out here."

Steven says nothing, merely follows me around.

"Are we being too choosy?" I keep trying to move away from the landlord, pulling my coat tighter around me. "I don't think he likes us."

The landlord sidles up to us, wringing his hands. "What number months you here? What your occupation?" He seems to be trying to size us up and fit us into some category, wondering who we are and why we need housing. We certainly aren't the usual young *gaijin* couple.

Steven makes up something vague about research, but we both realize the Japanese want affiliations, group identity.

I ask, "Can we rent it one month at a time?" Though I've heard this is never done.

He squints at us, shifting nervously from foot to foot. "*Hai.*" His word says yes, but his face says no. He closes up and turns away.

Steven and I quickly back out the door, wanting to reject him before he rejects us. "We'll call you," I say, knowing we won't, so relieved to be out of there.

On the jarring bus ride back to Takeda's, we sit far apart in the narrow seat, both of our chests caved-in. Steven's eyes rove restlessly, refusing to meet mine. I stare out the bleak window, reconsidering. I'm sure that Steven doesn't want to live there, but this is all we've found. Maybe I need more imagination. My mom loves fixing up houses. What would she do? With great energy and enthusiasm, she would paint all the walls, sew curtains, buy used furniture. No, we're too far down for that. Scrubbing, and then searching, deciding, and buying are not the forte of either one of us, even when we're in good moods. And we don't know how long we'll be staying. I can't picture us there. My imagination is scorched as dry as a summer streamed.

THE SEARCH
Mildewed Tatami

Like river grasses
wandering currents, rootlessly
drifting, I'm driven
by someone else's whims,
propelled by his storms, his winds.

— MIBU NO TADAMINE (tr. Sam Hamill)

Walking through the dry stubbly field from the bus stop to Takeda's house, Steven says, "We've got to leave Takeda's. I can't stay there anymore. Too much anger, too many ghosts." It's been only three days since he told us to leave, but Takeda's stony silence each evening has made it feel a lot longer.

My toes kick at the dead weeds. "Where'll we go?"

"Misono. I can't do any more searching. We'll be comfortable there, taken care of. It'll be just us, you and me." We've stayed many times at this traditional *ryokan*, or inn, ever since Steven's son Robert booked it for us six years ago, for our first trip to Kyoto.

"But the police said we're not allowed to stay at an inn or hotel. We can't be transient."

Steven scoffs. "I know, I know. They make it all impossible."

I hesitate in my walking, my mind and emotions always working slower than his, torn by my usual ambivalence. "It's too expensive. And there's no way to cook."

"Shoot the expense. We'll eat in the neighborhood—that open market, the café, picnics at the river, like we used to in '87."

"Okay," I sigh. "But we can't stay there too long. We've got to keep looking. Will you call?"

Steven puts the key in the lock and pushes open Takeda's door. "Yes. I want to move there tonight." He hurries to the phone and dials.

"They have room! I'm calling a cab."

Steven writes Takeda a note while I straighten up our bedroom, replacing the knick-knacks and piles of kids' stuff as best I can remember.

After a fifteen-minute ride from Takeda's, the cab pulls up to Misono Ryokan, our Japanese inn near the center of Kyoto and near the edge of the Kamogawa, the slow wide river that intersects the city. The innkeeper rushes out to greet us, helping us carry our bags into the lobby where rows of slippers, each pointed out toward the door, are lined up for the guests. She is a busy doctor in her forties, dressed in a sleek Western skirt, her black hair pulled into a neat low bun at her neck. With deep bows and perfect English she welcomes us.

She smiles at Steven. "Remember the time when you lost that bracelet, the heavy one with coils of silver going round and round?"

"*Hai. Dōmo arigatō gozaimasu.* Thank you very much," Steven bows deeper. "I was certain I would never see it again."

"Months later the maid found it in the back of that futon closet."

"You were so very kind to mail it to me."

Steven treasures that antique bracelet that his spiritual teacher gave him when he studied animist rituals in his Northern Thai village. He often loses it. It always comes back to him.

More welcomes and bows, as she ushers us to one of our favorite rooms downstairs. It is peaceful and spare, with fragrant tatami mats covering the whole floor. On the wooden walls the grain swirls in meditative patterns like the flickering flame of a campfire. The window opens on to a garden with its small koi pond, stone bench and lantern, and one arching tree. We've stayed in this *ryokan* so often over the years that it feels like a homecoming.

In the middle of the room on a low table, the old woman has laid out a thermos of hot water, a packet of *sencha* leaves, and tea cookies. She's the innkeeper's mother, gray and stooped in layers of long faded aprons. The whoosh of the odor-free kerosene heater warms the air quickly. Thick robes, padded for winter, hang on a hook for us.

After tea, I slip into a robe and walk to the traditional deep bathtub that all the guests share. I swish and soak in the scalding hot water, relishing the silence.

When the old woman rolls out our double futon later tonight on the tatami floor, there will only be space for the futon itself. I shove our two backpacks in the corners of the room, and the bag of picnic food that I brought from Takeda's, into the low crawl-in futon closet.

That night we sleep in the same bed for the first time since leaving our apartment weeks ago. Sinking into the soft thick futon with the lush quilt on top, I feel wrapped in a cloud. Our arms and legs intertwined, we nestle like spoons all night. Worn out, but safe together. Now I am taken care of, no longer without a home. The delicate evening rain brushes against the *shōji* screen at the window.

The next morning, after sipping hot *sencha* in our room, we rediscover our *ryokan* neighborhood. First, coffee for Steven at "Brazil man," our nickname for the café down the street. Like many Kyoto cafés, it has a unique theme: mellow rhythmic Brazilian music, colorful posters of Rio on the walls, a proprietor who has lived in Brazil, and high-quality Brazilian coffee. Next, *tamago* for me at the bustling open produce market. At one of the stalls, I watch "*tamago* man" deftly cook a flat rectangular omelette in a closed cast-iron mold, like a cheese grill, and then flip the steamy golden egg onto my waiting square of brown paper. As we stroll the market together, I munch on the *tamago*'s fluffy smoothness. The heady fragrance of hot egg, raw fish, grilled tofu, sour pickle, and sweet cut-up orange greets us on all sides. The shopkeepers joke with each other and shout for us to buy their wares, pointing to piles of shiny purple eggplant and rust-orange sweet potato. For our picnic at the river, I choose apples, cucumbers, carrots. Steven chooses tofu, translucent red and yellow pickles, and tiny grilled silver fish shaped like oval leaves.

We stroll to the grassy sloping banks of the river. With a grin and a mock formality, Steven billows the cloth of his *phakama* up and down like the wings of a bird, then allows it to drift down to the grass. A *phakama* is a long rectangle of cotton fabric, with a checkerboard-and-stripe pattern, that is used in Thailand for everything from sarong to turban to baby sling. He smooths out the four corners with his palms. Standing up, he bows low to me as he sweeps his arm toward the cloth with a courtly flourish. "*Dōzo.*"

I sit down on one side of the *phakama*, stretch my bare toes in the grass, and spread out our tofu and pickles between us. I'm amused by Steven's attentions and lulled by the beauty of the river, almost able to forget our troubles.

After lunch, we saunter arm in arm along the Kamogawa in the early March sunshine, the smooth water lapping at the green shoreline. At the edge of the river an elderly man practices his trumpet. His posture is erect and still, his horn faces the water, the sun glinting off the brass. The melody drifts over the ripples as if he were playing his song to the Kamogawa.

On our way back to Misono, we meander the paths of the Kyoto Botanical Gardens. We admire the very first plum blossoms, not as frothy, translucent, or ephemeral as the cherry. To my surprise, the cherry will not bloom until April, and only for a few days. The plum marks the beginning of spring with its sturdy flush of shining pink that will linger on each tree for more than a week. A warm breeze with only a slight chill at the edges leftover from winter, the laughter of children playing, and the orchestra of melodies from the invisible birds follow us back to the inn.

Petals drifting off
as a bush warbler comes down
to some plum blossoms.

— EDITH SHIFFERT

In the afternoon I stand at the clunky pink pay phone in the Misono lobby, juggling coins, pen, and notebook, as I resume our search for housing. The thick square phone is on a pedestal by the front door, near the rows of slippers. Fortunately, this time we are able to receive calls. Each time, the old woman or her daughter comes to our room and taps her fingers as light as a whisper on our sliding door. If we're not there, the young woman takes a message. Her mother speaks no English.

First, I call Margaret, the leader of my Kyoto women's group for *gaijin*. It took me five months to find the courage to call her newspaper ad. Finally I attended the first meeting in January, only a few days before our crisis began. When I walked into Margaret's living room on a stormy evening and shook out my wet umbrella and soaked raincoat, I was instantly immersed in a circle of twelve lively, interesting women of all ages. They came from various Western countries and backgrounds, in Kyoto short-term or long-term, and for a variety of reasons and pursuits. We shared food, laughter, tears, and discussed our expat experiences—what was working and what was not. I was reminded of my first consciousness-raising groups in California in the early seventies, when I discovered the value and bond of intense friendships between women.

Surely among these Kyoto women, someone will know of a place for us to live. How did they find their own housing? On the phone Margaret is concerned and sympathetic but knows of none. She suggests I bring my request to the next meeting—in late March. But I can't wait that long. It's only March 4. I don't think to ask for all the women's phone numbers so I can call them one by one.

Next, I return Fumiko Suzuki's call from earlier this morning. I haven't spoken to her since our dinner at her home. Steven's been going by every few days to deliver and pick up new translations of the Letters of Recommendation, so she knows we've left Takeda's, but she doesn't know where we've gone. Once again she's been hunting for us.

"I very sorry. I not able find you housing. I call all my friends. No one know anything. I wish I can help."

"Thank you very much." I pause, pressing the cool pink receiver to my throbbing forehead.

Fumiko continues, "Liz want you to come for dinner." She's the receptionist and wife of the director at our language school, where Fumiko teaches. Liz is Japanese-American from Oakland, and she married a Japanese man soon after she moved here. She and I often chatted before and after class. She seemed happy to meet a more mature fellow American, compared to the young *gaijin* students who frequent the school. With friendly enthusiasm she helped me look for *shakuhachi* and *shodō* teachers. "Call her right away," Fumiko adds.

But when I reach Liz, she seems cold and unfriendly. She denies she wanted us over for dinner. She doesn't even want to meet for tea. I feel awkward and pushy, and I back off. I suspect that her first impulse, as a Japanese-American, was to invite a fellow American in trouble. But maybe her Japanese husband has intervened because he doesn't want to taint their school's fragile reputation: they can't be known as a place that harbors drug users. Later Fumiko will confirm my suspicions.

I hang up the phone and, once again in tears, slink back to our room. I'm grateful that Fumiko, by contrast, doesn't fear marijuana. She doesn't fear the director of her school, or the loss of her job, or her husband's. She acts from her heart. And from her experience in the West.

I slump on the tatami next to the blazing kerosene heater, trying to warm my chilled back, while I report my conversations to Steven.

"Who's left?" he says.

Flipping through my address book, I say, "I can't call Yoshiko." We became friends after that summer hike in the mountains with Takeda. But her husband is one of Steven's former colleagues at the university. "I've been afraid to call her ever since the police came. I've no idea what she knows or is thinking about us. And we can't compromise her husband." I bite into a tea cookie. "I can't ask any of my students, either."

I run through the list in my head. "There's no one left safe to call."

⺆⺁⺉

The next morning, Friday, I pick at my breakfast of wilted lettuce, gooey Thousand Island dressing, and cold hard-boiled egg—the only fare at the restaurant around the corner from Misono, and the usual "morning set" breakfast offered at many such places. Steven sips a cup of weak Western coffee and pokes at the "elevator" toast I've given him from my plate. This is our nickname for this white squishy bread, sliced about two inches thick and served lightly toasted and smothered in butter. No time for Brazil man or *tamago* man today.

I flip through the pages of the *Lonely Planet* guide until I find the section on guesthouses and circle all the potential ones.

All our friends' advice points to these temporary student lodgings. We've resisted them so far because we don't fit that category. But we are temporary. Or are we? We certainly are not poor young students used to crowded noisy dorms. Yet it may be our only choice.

After breakfast, we trudge from one stuffy phone booth to the next all over town, from the far south to the far west. Either the phone rings endlessly with no answer and no machine, or the language barrier prevents any communication. After we finally collect a few places that have space, I mark them on our map and plot our route. We circle round and round, trying to decipher our scribbled directions to the obscure addresses. Each one is worse than the last, dirty, crowded, and dilapidated with sleazy landlords gouging the naive young foreigners. Once we finally find a suitable guesthouse, they don't have room for us. Probably it's our looks, obvious misfits, the professor and his wife, clearly able to afford more, clearly not naive. Or do they really fill up that fast in March? I don't think so.

As we leave one clammy phone booth and head for the last guesthouse on our crumpled list, I recognize the neighborhood. "Steven, this is Margaret's street, where I go for my women's group. She's right next door to the Y. Maybe they'll have a room."

The YWCA is a square concrete Western-style building in a residential neighborhood. Inside, a young Japanese woman taps at an electric typewriter, and an older American woman reaches for the ringing phone. They both look up at us and flash welcoming smiles. The reception room is toasty, with carpeted floors, a few black Naugahyde easy chairs, and travel posters of the Grand Canyon and Golden Gate Bridge on the walls. It feels like a piece of home. A murmur of women's voices with American accents drifts toward us from a closed room.

With a lurch of homesickness, I listen with longing. Maybe I can join the Y, take a class, and find a sense of community among fellow American women. If only I could be instantly home in America right now, walking the cliffs below the Golden Gate. Or instantly back in my hometown, with my circle of close friends. Where I understood how things worked, what was expected, and what people meant with their innuendos and implications. Where I knew the rules of the game, how to read the street signs, how to find my way. And how to search for a house to rent.

I approach the polished counter that almost hides the two women from view.

The American woman smiles again. "Hello, I'm Jane. May I help you?"

I ask about lodging.

She shakes her head. "Oh, I'm so sorry, dear. We have none here. Only meeting rooms—for clubs and classes and parties. You might look at that bulletin board over there."

Steven scouts around, peeking in various rooms, and then eases into a chair and crosses one ankle over his knee. He flips through a stack of *Time*, *Newsweek*, and *Sunset*.

On the bulletin board I find one ad and pull out the pin to study it.

> In Fushimi. Beautiful large traditional Japanese house to
> share. On the shrine grounds. Available now. Call Chris at
> 713-4122.

I wave it at Steven. "Look! It's dated a few weeks ago. Maybe it's still available."

Steven finishes reading his sentence, then looks up from his magazine listlessly, one finger marking his place. "Where?"

"Fushimi. Some city to the south of Kyoto."

"Too far. Let's go home to Misono."

I copy down the number anyway and return to the desk. "Do you know of any place we might stay for a month?" Tears catch at my throat.

"No, I'm very sorry, dear. Here's our brochure of classes—you might like one."

Walking out the door, I stow the phone number in my back pocket and skim the class list. Bridge, rummage sales, and hot lunches. Not my kind of Western world after all.

We drag ourselves up the street toward the last guesthouse. Steven stops short at the corner, as if stuck to the sidewalk cement. "There's no point in even looking at this one. They're all dismal." His mouth turns down in a tight upside-down U.

I halt three feet away and look back, fists clenched at my sides. "Steven, we have to live somewhere."

"Misono—"

"How can you even say that?" My words sputter with annoyance. "You know we can't afford it. We've no idea how many months we'll be here." I resume walking and shout over my shoulder, "Besides, the police won't let us."

He answers with a grunt and plods on behind me.

The March clouds have turned heavy, the air nippy again as if winter has dipped back in, the promise of spring hidden away. I stare at the guesthouse, a large rambling two-story building, neither Japanese nor Western. Charmless, dilapidated add-ons have been tacked on here and there at somebody's whim. The paint is peeling in strips, the doors sagging. A porch clings to the front of the second floor, and young *gaijin* run up and down the stairs yelling to each other. We've stayed together at youth hostels in Spain and seedy pensions in Thailand. But that was years ago, usually for only one night at a time. Now we both crave comfort. But I know we can no longer be choosy.

When we enter the building, the landlord stands there with his arms crossed, gaping at us with a sullen face. Like the rental house landlord, he seems surprised to see a respectable middle-aged couple. Steven is professorial in his neatly trimmed salt-and-pepper beard, with a fringe of close-cut hair around his balding head. I look like an English grammar teacher with my straight gray-blonde hair pulled back into a soft bun and my thin severe face with its high cheekbones.

The landlord appears as shabby as his house, with a loose, dark shirt and stained, torn pants. Maybe he's only the manager doing repairs. His shaggy hair slops over his collar.

"What do you want?" he snarls in excellent English.

"Please. We need a place to stay," I say.

"How long?"

I hesitate, glancing at Steven who stands silent and stiff, his face emotionless. I want him to engage this man in friendly conversation, to win him over, so we'll have a place to live. I'm not sure who is interviewing whom.

I touch Steven's shoulder with my fingertips. He perks up and steps forward. "One month," he says decisively.

"Follow me," the man mutters.

We climb the rickety stairs, avoiding the sticky banister, and pick our way along the open balcony, cluttered with broken furniture and half-open boxes. At the end of the balcony, he slides open the door. There's no way to lock it. A dank moldy smell hits me. The room is even smaller than the one at Misono, barely big enough for a futon to be rolled out, with not an inch left over. I take two long strides to the window at one end, where a bit of faded light drifts in from the narrow porch, which faces an interior wall. Inside the room, the edges of the tatami are worn and frayed, with ink spots here and there; dust balls drift in the corners, and blue-green mold crawls up the water-stained walls. It feels like a prison cell.

The landlord leans on the railing outside, impatiently tapping his foot and craning his neck at us to see our reactions. I whisper to Steven in rapid English, "It *is* a room. We could sleep here." I stoop to open the empty futon closet, built low in one corner to store it at night. If only we hadn't been forced to ship our beautiful futon home.

Stumbling out of the room onto the balcony, I gasp for fresh air. The stench of rancid cooking oil and boiled pork stings my nostrils and turns my stomach.

"Telephone," yells a voice up the stairs, followed by feet pounding down.

"How many phones?" I ask.

"One for each section, about a dozen people," the landlord answers.

"And the kitchen?"

"This way."

We follow him back downstairs. I peer into the communal kitchen, with its one sink piled high with dirty dishes and its two hot plates, crowded fridge, overflowing garbage can, and one small counter. But we could make it work: cluttered, counters a bit gooey, but clean enough, and room to prepare a meal. I hold my nose as I poke into the toilet room. Smelly, with a running toilet, but not dirty. The shower stall looks usable, a steady drip pounding the floor. Maybe there's even hot water.

Steven is barely taking this all in. "Excuse me, we have to confer," I say to the landlord, and I usher Steven outside.

The landlord's grating voice calls after me, "Hurry up. Can't wait all day."

"What do you think?" I ask Steven.

Shaking his head slowly, with long gaps and sighs between each word, he says, "What do *you* think?"

"We have to take it. We can scrub the tatami and the walls, light some incense. Borrow a futon from Tom, and keep our stuff at Takeda's." In spite of Takeda's anger, he's allowed us to store our belongings in his upstairs spare room for as long as we want.

"What about that kitchen and toilet?"

I look at him intently, my arms crossed tight across my chest. "We'll have to manage. We've seen a lot worse. There are cheap places nearby to eat out."

He looks down at the unwashed sidewalk, his mouth still in that same upside-down ∪.

I put my hands on my hips. "Steven. We can't live on the streets. We can't stay at Misono." My voice rises in exasperation. "I hate it too. But at least here we can give the police a real address and phone number."

Steven stands completely still, with his head down, eyes closed.

"Will you go deal with the money part?" I ask. "On the phone he said thirteen thousand yen a night for two, and reductions for a month."

Steven yanks out his wallet, stepping back inside. "We'll take it for a month."

The landlord's shifty eyes dart around the entryway. "That'll be fifty thousand yen."

That's more than ten thousand yen over what he'd quoted me. Usually one of us would try to negotiate. Clearly, he's taking advantage of our status and potential wealth. And he must sense our desperation. Why else would we want to stay here?

But I'm too beaten down to argue. I fear antagonizing this landlord. I want Steven to handle things for a change. In Japan, this is men's work. Women don't interfere with men's conversation. But is that really the Japanese custom I am following, or is it my upbringing in America in the fifties?

Without a word, Steven counts out enough yen for the month and offers his hand to shake, Western style. "It's a deal," he says, with quiet resignation.

The man gives Steven's hand a limp shake.

"We'll move in tomorrow," Steven adds. The landlord shrugs and disappears inside.

Steven holds my elbow, guiding me away. Halfway down the block, I stop. "We should've gotten a receipt. The guidebook said we must—for this place especially."

"It'll be okay," Steven answers and trudges on.

We plod down the street to the subway, pulling apart in our unhappiness. Once aboard, he sits down first. I choose the seat behind, too angry to sit next to him, and blaming him for every-thing—the filth and mold of the guesthouse, that we didn't get a receipt, that the man gouged us. But I tell him none of this.

Without turning around, Steven mumbles, "Maybe we should move in day after tomorrow instead—it'll give us one last day at Misono." He pauses. "Or maybe something else'll turn up."

I bend forward. "We should've only given him a deposit to hold it, instead of the whole month."

Still facing forward, he answers in a hollow voice, "It's done."

I close my eyes and sit back, the stations whirling past me in the black subway tunnel as we hurtle back to the inn.

In the Misono lobby, Steven stoops to slip out of his shoes and into slippers, then picks up the pink phone, jingling coins in his pocket. "I'll tell the lawyer our new address and number."

I shuffle to our room in my slippers.

Moments later, Steven bursts in, his face gray with defeat. "Fukuda says we can't stay there. We have to have a private phone. We aren't allowed to share a phone with a dozen people. A guesthouse is for transients."

I gape at him in disbelief. Once again the police have foiled us. We never can figure out their rules. They seem vague and capricious on purpose. And what if we can't get our money back? I can't bear losing a whole month's rent. On the other hand, I'm relieved we won't have to stay there. I can't really imagine fixing up that place and living with all that mold and noise. And no place for solitude.

He sags against the wall, his eyes closed. "The police must be able to reach us at a moment's notice."

"That horrid man better give us our money back," I say.

I shove my hand into my back pocket, grab the Fushimi ad from the Y, the edges tearing as I unfold it, smooth out the wrinkles, and rush to the pink phone, the heels of my slippers flapping behind me. I had put off calling the number because it was too far away. I jam a handful of coins in the slot and dial the number. It rings and rings. No answer. All day long I call, pacing back and forth between our room and the phone, both anxious and determined. It never occurs to me that she might never answer, that the room might not be available.

Finally that evening a woman's voice answers the phone. "*Moshi moshi*," she says in a friendly voice with a California "non-accent" that matches mine.

"Hello. Is this Chris?"

"Yes," she says.

"My husband and I are looking for a place. Maybe a few weeks, maybe longer. Is yours still available?"

"Sure. C'mon over tomorrow. That's my day off. I'll meet you at the train station. You can't find my place without a guide."

"How 'bout around ten?"

"I'll be here all day. Just call me from Fushimi Station. I'm only five minutes away, and there's a phone booth right there when you get off the train."

I scurry back to our room. "Steven, I have an appointment! It's available, and she sounds really nice!" I plop down on the *zabuton* cushion. "It's right on the shrine grounds, a big traditional house, with our own room and bathroom, and a shared kitchen and living room. It sounds beautiful."

The next morning our train speeds toward Fushimi. "Listen, Steven." I read from our *Old Kyoto* book, "'Located where the Yodo River meets the Takase River . . . a rest stop for boatmen traveling between Kyoto and Osaka . . . Fushimi Inari is the old shrine to the god of the harvest . . . Some of the old shops still exist from the Edo period . . .'" I skim down the text. "Look, here's a famous sake brewery for you—we can take a tour. And it claims it's only twenty minutes from central Kyoto."

Steven holds my hand snug in both his palms, and I nestle in close, touching hip to hip, my head on his shoulder. The train flies south, leaving behind the houses and shops of the city, gliding past the patchwork of small farms, and entering the beginning of statuesque bamboo forests.

PART III

Chris's House: Fushimi Inari Shrine

SHIMMERING BAMBOO
AND STONE FOXES

Foxes playing
among the narcissus flowers
a bright moonlit night.

— BUSON (tr. R. H. Blyth)

A flock of small bright birds?
No, bamboo branches suddenly
freed by the south wind.

— EDITH SHIFFERT

As the train pulls into Fushimi, the bright vermillion of the station building beams at us as if in welcome. This is unlike any other station I've ever seen in Japan, painted the same color as the soaring *torii* gates at the entrance of every Shinto shrine. The train lumbers away, leaving us in a pocket of spring sunshine. The vivid orange and sudden silence of the tiny platform envelop us, while across the tracks, tall stands of bamboo shimmer.

I call Chris, and within five minutes, she's approaching us, the only *gaijin* in sight. Her stride is long and springy, an athlete's. She is pencil-thin with dark brown hair that coils in masses of tight curls pulled back in a low ponytail. She seems to be in her forties. Breaking into a toothy smile, she gives Steven and me firm handshakes. "Let's go. I'll show you my town."

Hurrying to keep up with her, we pass rows of small souvenir shops, selling live sparrows in cages and gaudy smiling dolls, and then one small grocery, a café, and a couple of greasy-spoon-style restaurants. We glide under a vermillion wooden *torii* gate that looms high and rectangular above our heads, and then we march up some wide steps to enter the main shrine. An expansive stone plaza stretches between the two-story wooden buildings with carved roofs that curve up toward the sky. In the center stands a raised covered platform for ceremonies and rituals. It's one of the biggest and grandest shrines I have seen. I'm already enchanted.

Up a series of stone steps we tramp, past an oval pond and a plum tree with sturdy blossoms. Chris stops at a stone fox, as large as a person, perched high on a pedestal. "*Inari*," she explains, "the animal spirit of this shrine. See that stalk of grain in his mouth? That means plentiful harvest." I've also read that *inari* has many meanings. It can also be a playful trickster. I pray our luck is changing—no tricksters here.

Finally, Chris veers left into a winding alley, bordered with chest-high mossy stone walls. As we rush past a series of small sub-shrines on both sides of the path, shiny orange trim glistens in the cool sunshine, ritual fires blaze in huge black metal cauldrons, incense wafts out, candles flicker, bells and gongs ring repeatedly, and the low chanting of male priests reverberates from behind the colorful screens placed in front of the altars.

Right past the last sub-shrine, she jogs left and steps up to her front door.

Her house is a two-story traditional one, made of dark wood inside and out, with spongy tatami, as fragrant as sun-dried summer grass, on the living room floor, paper-thin *shōji* on the inside of the sliding doors and windows, and long wooden porches along one side of each level.

Over tea at her kitchen table, Steven and I learn that Chris has been renting the house from the shrine for the last several years. She's an entrenched expatriate from Walnut Creek who teaches English at a nearby high school, speaks fluent Japanese, and signs up for every tennis tournament she can find, from Sapporo in Hokkaido in the far North to Kagoshima in Kyushu in the far South.

While Steven cracks jokes for Chris and she responds with boisterous laughter, I survey the kitchen. It's spotless and tidy, and more Western than the usual galley-sized Japanese ones: a full fridge and gas stove with an oven, wide sink, long counters, cupboards and drawers everywhere. Two velvety cats scamper in and out from kitchen to porch through the open back door. And right behind Chris's shoulders sits an apartment-size washer, with a dryer stacked on top. A dryer! I haven't seen one since we landed in Japan. I can't wait to have fluffy clothes again, instead of stiff wrinkled ones.

She leaps up and leads us upstairs. "My area," she says as she sweeps her arm toward the huge second floor: her neat bedroom, with plenty of empty space on the tatami floor, and large windows on three sides; a long wide hall, lined with bookshelves; and a sparkling toilet room, with a separate room for the shower.

"My porch. But you may hang your clothes here." I peer out at the shady porch. A clothesline is laden with her wet clothes. "You must never use the dryer downstairs," she adds.

"Here's my bathtub. You may use it whenever you want." She pauses. "When I'm not home." A deep traditional tub is set into a modern tiled bathroom. Sunshine pours through the windows that cover three sides of the room. Outside, the leaves of the bamboo forest flutter in the spring breeze, as the trees climb up Fushimi Mountain.

Chris steers us back downstairs. "Here's the living room; you may use it any time." A low coffee table with a portable CD player and a black phone. A few *zabuton*, square flat cushions used for sitting on the floor, and nothing else but wide tatami flowing toward the *shōji* windows at one end of the room. Steven ambles toward them, admiring the sunlight that glows through, subtle and translucent onto the golden floor.

"And your room." She slides open the door. Steven squints over my shoulder. The tiniest room in the house. Very dark and very cold. I step in, ducking my head under the low doorjamb. It's a four-and-a-half-mat room, a bit bigger than that three-mat one at the guesthouse. This one is immaculate. But there are no windows, and the low ceiling hits the top of my head when I stand up straight. At night, the futon will almost fill the entire room, with just enough space for the tiny rickety bamboo nightstand and the low square *kotatsu* table, with its cotton print skirt tacked around the edges and a single electric bulb underneath to warm our toes. In the old days, a charcoal hibachi stove was placed underneath the *kotatsu* for heat.

I swing back to Chris standing at the doorway. "Do you have a futon we can use?"

"No, I don't do that." She hesitates and looks away. "I could loan you a few old blankets."

Steven sits on the floor against the futon closet, his arms folded across his chest, his face serious, eyes down. He seems to be lost in thought, leaving the house details to me, as usual. I can tell he wants to take the room, no matter what.

"Tom said we can borrow two of his single futons," I say to Steven.

"Here's the store room." Chris pushes past us, pulls open a waist-high door in the back wall, and crawls in, like a samurai entering a teahouse. Steven and I stoop to peer around her. "All my stuff," she says, and she thrusts her wrist toward rows of floor-to-ceiling shelves, overflowing with boxes and clothing. "Don't touch or move any of my things. But you can use this." She points to three small metal shelves by the door. "You'll have to clear it off yourself."

"Thank you," I say in a quiet voice, as I back out of the doorway, bumping into Steven. I feel grateful for finding this rental but am stunned that she will be able to walk through our private bedroom any time she pleases.

While I linger at the doorway to scan the room one more time, Steven accompanies Chris back into the kitchen. Their voices rise and fall, laughing together as they discuss her tournaments. Steven neither cares nor knows anything about sports but can always draw someone out about her or his passion.

When I join them at the kitchen table, Steven raises an eyebrow at me, and we exchange a quick nod to indicate we'll take the room. Relieved he's taking charge, I let him negotiate the price, dates, and utilities. Their conversation swirls around me, while Steven tells her his marijuana story and then with expert polish steers the topic toward her life in Japan. As usual, the lively conversation is waking him from his earlier passivity.

I lift one of the cats up onto my lap and stroke its silky gray fur. I can tell that Steven is taken in by Chris's sunny charm and sympathy, but she puzzles me. She seems to flash hot and cold from moment to moment. I love this beautiful old house with its dark wood and its spacious graceful style. I love the gorgeous bamboo groves that surround us. But I feel uneasy with this woman and her rules.

The gongs and chants from the sub-shrine next door drift in through the window. Of course we'll take it. It's the best thing, the only possible thing, we've found in over a week of intense searching. We're lucky. And it's only a half-hour train ride back north to my *shakuhachi* teacher and my students.

As I reenter the conversation, Steven and Chris have returned to his legal troubles. She is saying, "I don't care about the police, the marijuana. Lots of people stay here who are in trouble. I like helping out. I'm not gonna lose my job."

I'm impressed with how secure and free she feels. Like Knutsen, she talks as if she enjoys flouting the rigid rules of Japanese society. I suspect she likes living at the edge of risk, secretly enjoying the intrigue and the danger of other people's secrets.

Steven slides a month's rent from his wallet. I watch him count out the huge stack of yen bills onto the table.

We all stand up and shake hands. We'll move in day after tomorrow.

The smoky incense and sonorous chants linger as Steven and I stroll back down the path. Hand in hand, lighthearted and light-stepped, we stop to admire the orange koi drifting in the pond and to greet the huge stone fox. We bow and clap our hands three times at the altar next to him, to give our thanks to the Shinto spirits.

At the top of the stone steps, I stop at the flowering plum and give Steven's shoulders a quick sidewise squeeze. "We've done it! We have a home again."

Steven grins and pulls me close for a moment. We descend the steps and float under the soaring orange *torii* gate.

The train clatters back to Kyoto, the stations flashing by in a blur, hurtling us past the run-down bungalows at the southern edge of the crowded city. "Steven, we've got to get that money back from the man at the guesthouse."

Steven squinches his mouth to one side and frowns. "Let's forget it. I don't like him. I don't want to go back."

"We must—fifty thousand yen's a lot of money. And besides, we can't hold the room when some young student might need it."

Steven snickers. "I doubt he'll hold it long in spite of all the money I gave him."

At the guesthouse, I push Steven ahead of me into the man's grimy office. I'm determined he has to handle this one. With a grim face and stiff back, he enters. I stand back at the doorway, watching.

"Absolutely not!!" the man shouts at Steven. "I never give refunds. Your problem."

"But, Sir—"

"No! No!" he shouts again. He disappears into a back room.

I want Steven to try harder, to argue, to threaten. But that's never his style, or mine.

As we trudge back to the train station, Steven says, "I'll pay for it. It's all my fault." He returns to his shoulder slump and down-turned mouth. "Money doesn't matter anymore." Then he adds in a barely audible voice, "Nothing does."

I fume all the way to the station. Yes, Steven tried. Yes, he's able to let go of both the money and the man. But I can't. I'm too distraught at the loss of all those yen to appreciate his efforts. It doesn't occur to me that this isn't just about the money. I'm grasping for some control in a hopeless situation.

Two days later, on Monday, March 8, we begin our new life in Fushimi. We arrive at Chris's by cab with our two backpacks and a few plastic bags stuffed with our picnic supplies of braised tofu and pickles. It has been thirty-eight days since the police knocked on our apartment door, and I feel like a homeless fugitive.

Steven and Toru move the rest of our belongings from Takeda's, making numerous trips together in Toru's tiny clown car again. I never return to Takeda's house. As before, Toru and Steven's friendship strengthens, while they haul heavy boxes, suitcases, and messy bags of food, joking and telling stories during the half-hour drive back and forth. Each time they arrive at Chris's, they are even more giddy. Steven looks carefree and silly as he bounces up the long narrow path from the car to the house, perching a precarious cardboard box high on his shoulder, and calling out another joke to Toru below. I smile at their camaraderie and at Steven's temporary joy but am also dampened by a lonely envy.

Chris greets us at the front door. "I'm very happy you're here," she says, with a friendly smile. "Once you're settled, let's have a meal together." She pauses. "Maybe Sunday." She retreats upstairs to her room while I tackle the unpacking.

In the kitchen, as I bend over the first box, the bells and chants start their song next door. I unwrap our gray-brown ceramic teapot from its layers of newspaper and place it on the table with its two matching cups, the only ceramics we've saved out from our collection. I love being in a real home. And I'm trying hard to like Chris. I want to make this work. As if in a silent swordfight with Steven, I argue with myself. It's true, she *is* open and friendly—at least on the surface. But I remain troubled by her underlying bitterness. I don't quite trust her yet.

After studying the crowded cupboards through their glass doors, I yank open the stuffed drawers, looking for space. We've brought along our grains and flours from the old apartment, and our bottles of Japanese sauces, both of us hoping to cook now that we have a real kitchen. When I open a food cupboard, her sacks of beans fall out. When I open a dish cupboard, the stacked plates teeter and almost fall and shatter. In the fridge, Chris has not emptied a shelf for us. But by nudging her stuff aside, I manage to squeeze our things in here and there.

Next, I deal with our four-and-a-half-mat room. I stack my clothes and my teaching notebooks in the futon closet. As I did at Takeda's, I arrange my alarm clock, flashlight, journal, *Genji*, miniature Buddha, and family photos on the bamboo night-stand. I shove the small *kotatsu* to the corner by the door, deciding to leave it uncluttered, as a place to write or drink a private cup of tea.

In the storeroom, I clear her things off of the small metal shelves as directed, and I organize my *shakuhachi* music, ikebana shears, calligraphy brushes, and Japanese poetry books and novels.

Once we're unpacked, Chris conducts Steven and me on a second tour of the house. She jokes with Steven and asks me with apparent sincere interest how I like my *shakuhachi* teacher and how long before I could blow my first note. But for each rule, she switches to a closed-up brusqueness. First, the kitchen.

"You must leave the door ajar just so, so the cats can get in and out. You must dry each dish—even when I'm out of town. Never leave them in the dish drainer." She flips her hand toward a set of dishes in one of the glass cupboards. "You mustn't ever touch these dishes." She says that first thing each morning, we must light the kitchen kerosene heater. "And, oh, you're responsible for buying more kerosene and filling up the tanks, here and in the living room. I'll take care of mine upstairs."

Guiding us into the living room, she jerks her thumb toward the phone. "You may use it whenever you want. But if I'm home, I must answer, not you." She strides to the heater by the windows. "This one heats the living room. You can roll it over to your bedroom door at night, but you must absolutely roll it back out here first thing, and light it so the living room warms up." Her voice heats up and rises in pitch, as if her former housemates have not complied. "Do you understand?" she asks with a fierce edge in her voice.

"Yes," Steven and I both answer at the same time, with matching calm voices.

Chris jabs her elbow toward a closed door down the hall from our room. "My other housemate's room." That's funny, I think, on our first visit, I didn't notice that door. She pushes it open a crack. "For now, it's only us three. She's gone for a month, home to the States." Chris never mentioned a housemate on the phone, or on the day we signed up. "She's never lived here yet. You'll like her. She'll fix up her room when she returns." I stand on tiptoes to snatch a glimpse over her shoulder. A medium-size room stacked with boxes high up to the ceiling, three feet above my head. Light floods in one large window, with glimpses of bamboo and *torii* gates beyond. If only we could have this room instead, I think, but of course that's impossible.

A new safe house. A new haven, a new place to wait. Steven has done all he can: cooperated with the Interrogation of the Customs Police, gathered and delivered all the translated Letters of Recommendation, visited the lawyer for weekly updates. The police have compiled and submitted their report. The newspapers have revealed the secret. Steven's case still sits in the hands of the prosecutor to make his own deliberation.

Steven and I both work hard to fit into Chris's household routine. Each night we roll the living room kerosene heater into our bedroom, the gassy smell choking us as we light it, and leave our sliding door open a crack, exactly enough so we will not be asphyxiated from the fumes, yet will not freeze from the damp air creeping in. Each morning one of us jumps out of bed the minute the alarm rings, drags the heater back to the living room, and lights it to heat up the room, to make it all ready for Chris. Every night we prop the kitchen door open two inches, as she has shown us, so the two cats can go in for food and out for the litter box. Somehow we never get it right, and there is often pee on the kitchen floor in the morning, which we hurry to mop up. Or the cat yowls at midnight to be let in and Chris pounds down the stairs in a fury, one of us trying to beat her to it. In the morning we rush to make sure the cats are in, close the kitchen door, and light the kitchen heater. It's true our room is closer, and it must be nice for her to descend the stairs into a toasty house. However, it seems to me that mostly Chris wants to be taken care of by her tenants.

But I'm too exhausted to care for anybody, not even Steven. And I'm not a servant. Yes, she's the landlady, but I expect respectful equality, if not friendship. As we had at Takeda's. Maybe she doesn't see it as a business deal at all, but instead as an exchange of favors: she provides a home for us during a desperate time, and we reciprocate by making her home life more comfortable. But I suspect Chris is probably not as strong as she appears; she puts up a fierce front to protect a fragile, lonely inside. I forget about my French housemates, back when I was single and working long difficult hours at a job I disliked. Every so often when I pushed open the front door, I was greeted by the delicate fragrance of French cooking and an extra place set for me at the table. I don't recognize that I could do the same for Chris, finding ways to ease her life. Her demanding manner pushes me away, and I'm not able to be generous.

Steven and I wash and dry every dish after each meal, never leaving anything on the dish rack, counter, or kitchen table. When the phone rings, I wait, counting the rings and my breaths, letting her run downstairs to answer. If she's out, I take a message and leave her a detailed note, propped next to the phone on the coffee table.

After washing my clothes in the washing machine, I make sure to avoid the dryer, lugging my wet clothes upstairs to her porch, always choosing a time she isn't home. The line drips with her clothes, but with some hesitation, I move them closer together and squeeze mine in, hoping she won't notice, and that they will dry on the shady porch.

Each morning, the minute she leaves for work, I run my bath water upstairs, because her hours are so erratic I never know when she will return. I soak deep and long, enveloped in steamy water and nourished by the fluttering bamboo, the song of the warbler, the fragrant blossoms of the plum tree outside the window, and the ever-present bells and chants from next door.

The early spring temperature drops steeply every evening, the house holding in the frigid cold all night and far into the next morning, the wind whistling through the cracks of the thin doors and windows, and even through the noninsulated wooden walls. We're lucky our room has no windows or outside doors;

it makes it a bit warmer. These traditional houses were not built for cold weather. In the old days, the Japanese would soak in scalding baths, wear thick quilted robes, huddle under the padded blanket of the communal *kotatsu*, or cluster by fires sunk in pits in the living room. But we have none of that.

We roll the smelly kerosene heater next to our two thin futons, pressing them close together, pull on our long underwear and layers of sweaters, and huddle together under the flimsy blankets Chris has loaned us. We're never warm enough.

Tall slender bamboo trees tower twenty feet above me on both sides, a thick forest stretching up as far as I can see. Each bamboo swishes and creaks in the light breeze, sprinkling slender boat-shaped pale green and yellow leaves on the path. It's my first week at Chris's, and I'm exploring Fushimi Mountain by following the narrow paved path that leads up the steep hill behind her house. I enter a long series of vermillion *torii* gates, each one about twelve feet tall and six feet wide. They create an almost solid tunnel of bright orange, slivers of light flitting in from the sides and top as I glide through. The bamboo on each side bends above me in a flexible arch like two tai chi dancers. It feels like a hidden passage to a secret garden.

After I emerge from the *torii* tunnel, the path becomes smooth raked dirt, strewn with newly fallen rustling leaves, and neat piles of more leaves mounded along each side. As the path loops and curves through the forest, I slip past tiny altars hidden here and there among the hovering bamboo. The altars are created on the forest floor, with often no more than a sculptured rock, and in front of it a vase of flowers, a miniature saucer with offerings of rice grains, an orange, a cup of sake for the spirits, and a bowl of sand with two or three incense sticks. Bells and incense swirl around me. Gray stone foxes, from miniature to bigger than life-size, pop out at me, tucked among lacy ferns, or nestled in green moss, or leaning against the wrinkled kneelike node of a bright green stalk of bamboo. The foxes seem to be guarding the path, the altar, the bamboo itself. This magic forest enchants me.

Kneeling on the moss, which is as velvety as a fox's paw, I choose a smooth red-brown pebble from those scattered about and perch it on the shoulder of the fox, along with many other well-placed stones by previous visitors. The mischievous spirit of the *inari* fox fascinates me, and I want to learn more about its symbolism. The Shinto animist worship of nature and the spirits that reside within each object, whether animate or inanimate, resonates with my childhood. My parents raised me in pine forests, instead of churches; they found their religion among the flowers, the birds, and the trees.

At a small teashop next to one of the sub-shrines, I sip *sencha* and contemplate the view back down the mountain, with its swirls of orange *torii* amidst the alternating shades of green and yellow leaves. Before leaving the shop, I buy a stylized watercolor map of the mountain, with sketches of fox, shrine, altar, and tree scattered at random all over it.

I find that the map's circular paths are realistic enough to follow, and I discover a sub-shrine with a square courtyard. Around all four edges are dollhouse-sized altars on stilts. Chanting and gongs echo out from the small shrine building, and in front of it, a brazier of fire crackles and smokes, shooting heat and light up toward the sky. As I circle the altars, I notice again some rice, sake, an orange, laid out on each one. I make an offering by arranging two round pebbles next to the orange, adding a silent prayer, thanking the spirits for guiding me to this mountain.

Sitting down by a small circular pond next to the building, I sift silky bamboo leaves through my fingers and watch the koi

Inariyama — Inari Mountain

meander in the dark green water, the design on their curved bodies of black, white, and orange as delicate as the glaze on a fine teacup. Sunbeams filter through the bamboo clusters above and slant into the depths of the water, illuminating the ebony black of a stone, the gold of a leaf, the russet of the sand. Yellow leaves float on top of the pond in wide circles, creating an ever-changing pattern of shadows underneath.

While eating my peanut butter sandwich, I mull over these first days at Chris's. This time at Fushimi seems to be a lull, and a chance to begin to heal. The beauty of the house, the shrine, these woods all nourish me. We're secure for another month. Surely it will be our last one. My fears have decreased. I no longer jump every time the phone rings. But I can't forget that Steven could still go to prison, be fined a huge sum, or be detained indefinitely under "house arrest." And yet each day is now a day of hope: that today will be the last in Japan, that we will be one day closer to home, to fleeing this country that has imprisoned both of us.

This is a new kind of waiting, more moment by moment, like Kuroda sensei waiting to begin his concert. But not waiting. Instead, gazing out the window in meditation. Or like in *zazen*, wholly on the cushion, in the body and breath, letting go of the thoughts as they flow through, not waiting for the bell.

A series of rapidly repeated gongs resounds from the sub-shrine, and the modulations of chanting rise up and down again. Maybe it's merely spring that lightens my mood: the plum blossoms, the melody of the warbler, and the steadfast bamboo of the forest, swaying and bending in the breeze.

Wandering on up the mountain, I explore each side path, the gentle upturned edges of each one beckoning me like a friend's open welcoming palm. The path, the forest, and the mountain climb almost forever, up and up toward the silvery blue sky.

I never reach the top that day. But I vow to return again and again, to venture on new paths, each time striving toward the top and what I may find there.

On our sixth night at Chris's, she and Steven and I gather in the kitchen. She chops and stirs at the stove. The fragrance of garlic, onion, and tomato and the bubbling heat from the sauce animate the room. This morning before she dashed out the door to teach, she called over her shoulder, "I leave tomorrow for a week for my tennis tournament. I'm having a few friends over tonight for spaghetti—won't you join us?" To my surprise, she's kept her vague promise from moving day, which now pulls me tentatively into her circle of friendship.

She refuses our help with the cooking but is eager to chat about her high school students, her admiration of her father, and her passion for tennis.

One by one, several of her friends join us, men and women expats, all about her age, all fellow teachers and tennis champions. The kitchen grows crowded with tall athletic bodies. Trying to mask my shyness and appear helpful, I fill up the bowl of chips as it empties and offer beer from the fridge to each guest. We all crunch on the chips and slurp beer, while they discuss various winning strategies for tennis. The room reverberates with their laughter.

These *gaijin* engage in a type of expat talk that I find typical in certain circles. Expats seem to fall into two types. One embraces the culture with its traditional arts and customs, becoming more and more "Japanese" in their thinking and conduct. The other type remains at the edges, criticizing the Japanese with their hierarchical rules and rigid behavior and delighting in observing and flouting at a distance. Perhaps it makes them feel more secure, more unique, to be separate from the dominant culture.

Chris and her friends are of the second type. I squirm in my chair as they mimic the vague language and impassive faces of their Japanese coworkers. These *gaijin* banter around the usual litany of complaints: you never know the rules of the game or what to expect; they say one thing and mean another; you're supposed to blindly follow authority, whether school principal, doctor, lawyer, or judge; you're under strict obligation to your boss; you must conform to the group. But I don't want to hear these complaints.

On the other hand, I don't know their private stories. Maybe they also were in trouble when Chris befriended them. I don't know what it's like to live long term in an alien culture. Maybe they're homesick for America. But they're mouthing blind stereotypes. Although I'm doing the same, lumping *gaijin* into two groups, not reaching out to get to know them as individuals.

Their Japan-bashing alienates me. I want to love Japan in spite of all it has put me through. I maintain a strange loyalty. I don't want to let go of the resonance I feel with their values of respecting silence, revering nature, and accepting impermanence. Maybe I've learned to distinguish between the public legal face of Japan and the private artistic face. I can resent the one and love the other.

In the crowded noisy kitchen, Steven has joined in their conversation, ever the anthropologist, subtly eliciting their opinions, as if in agreement, without ever really stating his own ideas. Sometimes I wish I knew how to play his game. But soon I retreat into my usual silent corner. Growing light-headed and irritable with hunger, for a moment I wish I had made myself an early dinner and escaped to my room to read the next chapter in *Genji*. I decide to use Steven as my role model. So I rouse myself and offer to set the table. While I lay out plates, forks, and spoons, I turn to the woman next to me and ask her to tell me about her Japanese students at the local college.

When the spaghetti is finally served, I bend over my plate and inhale the steam and a whiff of oregano. Pouring thick red sauce over the pasta, I dig in. The spaghetti is overdone and a bit soggy, but I'm so famished I don't care. Smiling over at Chris at the head of the table, I say, "Thanks, this is really delicious," and I manage to sound sincere. With some hilarity, all of us, even me, suck in long strings of spaghetti through our teeth with loud slurps, exactly as our Japanese friends have taught us, as the proper way to show polite appreciation.

TWO MENDED RICE BOWLS

A dozen broken shards
blue and white diamonds
one by one, we mend.

— Patricia Dove Miller

The day Chris leaves, we are jubilant. At last we have the house
to ourselves. For a whole week, it will be only the two of us once
again.

But before we can celebrate, we must first check in at the
local police station. Steven suggests we stop for lunch at the local
donburi restaurant on our way. We walk past the sub-shrines that
fall silent at lunchtime, trudge through the huge orange *torii*
gate as we leave the main shrine, and avoid looking at the caged
sparrows for sale in the tourist shops.

Steven has just returned from his weekly trip to the lawyer's
office. I ask how it went.

He shrugs and shoves his hands into his pockets. "Maybe I'll
tell you at the restaurant."

I chew the corner of my lip. I hate it when he does this. If I
push, he'll clam up. If I wait, he usually will open up. But I don't
want to wait. If he won't tell me, I can only fear the worst.

We both order *oyakodon*, a type of *donburi* which means
"mother and child," a deep bowl of rice mixed with egg, chicken,
and a strong, slightly sweet sauce. "So, what'd he say?" I prod. It's
my life in Japan that's at stake, not only his.

"His secretary brings a cup of *sencha*, I bow and say one of
those elaborate polite greetings in Japanese, he says good morning in English. And then we sit there for a while drinking tea in
silence."

"Then what?" I nudge. The waitress slides two big steaming bowls of *donburi* onto the table in front of us.

"He launches into a long, disjointed explanation of something. His English is so bad I only get a few words."

"I wish you'd taken Tom along to translate."

Steven leans back in his chair. "It doesn't really matter. I don't want to talk about it." He stares at his *donburi*, which is growing cold.

I jab a piece of rubbery chicken out of the rice with my chopsticks. I realize my questions are premature. He, who is usually so quick to think and act, is slow to process his own emotions.

Steven reaches for his chopsticks, studies the bowl of food, chooses a piece of chicken, and pops it in his mouth. After several more bites, he volunteers, "He says we must keep waiting. There's nothing he can do."

I whip the sauce into my rice with agitated circles. I chose to stay home alone to meditate, practice my *shakuhachi*, and walk in the forest. Instead of avoiding the lawyer and insisting Steven handle this himself, I should have gone with him. Yes, I probably would have been frustrated by the lawyer and the lack of information, but at least I would have seen it firsthand and been able to plan some action. Or at least to better accept the fact of more waiting, more nonaction. But I didn't go, so I feel as powerless as I did at Knutsen's house. Or at my father's dinner table. Next week I'll go, and I'll make sure Tom goes with us.

We eat the rest of the meal in silence. Steven seems resigned. Or else maybe he's practicing complete acceptance.

After lunch, we walk the two blocks to the police station. Every time we move we have to register with the local police, so they'll know where we are. We now walk hand in hand, cheered by the warmth and protein of the big bowls of *donburi*.

But as we approach the building, I clutch Steven's arm, remembering that the Osaka Customs Police, who interrogated him for all those weeks, still have his passport.

"They'll ask for your passport. What'll we do?"

"Whatever we're told. Don't ask questions. Don't volunteer anything." He pauses, his mouth a grim half-smile. "And pretend to be invisible."

In silence, we stand at the counter, filling out all the forms. My white knuckles grip the pen. When it clatters to the floor, the acid taste of the chicken from lunch rises into my throat. I stoop to retrieve the pen, avoiding the sharp looks of the uniformed men behind their desks. After finishing the forms, I glance at Steven's impassive face and calm hands. Why isn't he anxious? Perhaps he's pretending to play the role of submissive "prisoner," not doing anything to upset the "guards." Perhaps he's learned this stance during those long days of enforced politeness during the Police Investigation at the Osaka Customs Office. Still silent, we hand the forms to the officer at the window and are told to sit down and wait.

I try to count my breaths from one to ten and back down to one. But I never get past one. My thoughts bang up against the low ceiling and buzz off the four bare walls like a wasp in a closed-up room. I try to concentrate on each part of my body, as I've been taught, to breathe into my constricted chest, to lower my raised shoulders, to relax my stiff neck, and to unclench my toes inside my shoes. But I cannot. I've never been in a police station before—in America or Japan. What if they snatch him away again? What if they snatch me, too?

After what feels like an hour but is probably much less than that, they call out both our names.

"You may go. Everything is in order." The clerk bows behind his counter as he adds, "Thank you very much."

As soon as Steven has shut the door as silently as possible behind us, we grab each other's hands and squeeze hard, giggling and giddy with relief. Yet a chill still follows me up the street. They never asked for his passport, only mine. I don't realize that of course they'd know of Steven's detention—the police would coordinate such things. Yet it feels as if we're still being followed and watched. And perhaps we are.

Steven touches my shoulder to distract me and gestures with the open palm of his other hand across the busy street. "Look, a canal for us."

I smile up at him. "Let's follow it. Maybe it'll take us home."

The plum trees along the edges of the canal are beginning to bloom. The early spring sun warms our backs, and the white puffy clouds float in a soft blue sky, the color of my mother's Haviland china. With Steven's arm around my shoulder, I snuggle against him, pressing hip to hip. "Let's bring our bikes back here and explore," I say. We don't say much as we walk, both enjoying this rare togetherness, neither of us yet ready to discuss the big issues of betrayal and secrets, needing instead to first rediscover what we love about each other. We saunter toward Chris's house, discovering a Black-crowned Night Heron with its sloping black shoulders and down-turned head as if pensive or shy, and a Little Egret with its long curved white neck, graceful and strong as if doing a *kinhin*, a slow focused walking meditation, searching in the water for shadows.

With Chris gone, I rebel. Now I soak in the bathtub any time of day, with the sunshine pouring in the open window and the calls of the warbler, bell, and gong weaving their own melody. At night I slide open our bedroom door to allow the kerosene fumes to escape, no longer having to close it for privacy.

In order to heat up my chilled body, the kerosene blasts in all rooms, night and day, whenever I wish. After all, we're the ones paying for the kerosene. Without having to tiptoe around her, I expand my life into the living room, sitting on the sweet supple tatami, listening to our own Gregorian chants and Bach cello sonatas on her CD player.

Steven and I cook together, clattering and chattering in the kitchen while I chop onions and he sautés garlic, making a rich *nabe* with tofu, shiitake mushrooms, and *tai*, a kind of red snapper. I clear off her piles of notebooks and old bills from the kitchen table, shoving them temporarily into a box on the porch. I spread out the two bowls and two cups that we saved out from our Japanese ceramic collection. After dinner we let each dish drip-dry in the drainer. I make peace with the cats, working out my own system of doors ajar. With glee, I gather the soggy clothes off the line and toss them into the dryer. It hums and spins as it tosses my nightgown, underwear, and shirts, exuding welcome heat into the kitchen. Steven mirrors my rebellions without comment. He's less annoyed and more accepting than I, but clearly he too basks in this freedom.

I make Chris's house my own home for a precious week, luxuriating in the perfect balance between solitude and relaxed times with Steven. Finally we have enough peace and space to appreciate each other. It's unlike those first seven months in Kyoto before the crisis, those hazy somewhat estranged months, when Steven was so unavailable and we were both too preoccupied with our own pursuits. And it is unlike the previous forty-five days of unbearable tension.

Now we spend long playdates together. We explore the tea-growing town of Uji with its golden temple laden with Buddhist art and its rushing river made famous by the *The Tale of Genji*. I lead Steven up my mountain, and we prance through my vermillion *torii* tunnel arm in arm. We stroll the circular paths that wind up to the sky. We picnic and linger by my illuminated pond. And we lay pebble offerings on the fox's shoulder and next to the orange on the dollhouse altar. We stand next to each other, bow our heads, clap our hands three times, and thank the spirits for these days together. We're on a private retreat, immersed in this sacred mountain of bamboo, bells, and magical spirits.

One evening that same week at about five thirty, I'm sitting alone, writing in my journal at a window table in a quiet café. The type of café that serves barely recognizable Japanese versions of American dishes, such as curry, spaghetti, or omelette (which of course are themselves unrecognizable versions of the original Indian, Italian, or French). I've ordered *omuraisu*, a light omelette stuffed with white rice and covered with tomato sauce. Outside on the busy downtown Kyoto street, the streams of shoppers and businessmen are hurrying home or rushing out to dinner.

This morning Steven and I decided to attend an evening *shakuhachi* concert given by my teacher, Kuroda sensei, a rare chance to hear him perform. We traveled to town separately, each with our own errands, agreeing to meet at the downtown concert hall five minutes before the six thirty p.m. curtain time. I lingered at several stores, searching for a thank-you gift for Takeda. At the pillow store, I inhaled the musky fragrance of the intense blue-black indigo cloth, reminiscent of the hand-dyed cloth in our Thai village. I chose a *zabuton*, like the kind we use for meditating at home and at the Zen center. The one for Takeda has a simple repetitive Escher-like design of semicircles, like ocean waves or setting suns.

When I finished my shopping early, I decided to find something to eat, glad for a bit more time alone before the concert.

Noticing a row of cafés near the concert hall, I ducked into the first one.

When my omelette is served, I pull the wooden chopsticks out of their paper wrapper. Just as I'm lifting my first bite of hot egg into my mouth, I glance out the window. There is Steven strolling by, only a few inches away through the glass. We spot each other at exactly the same moment. My heart dances like a butterfly on a new spring lupine blossom, happy to have my precious solitude broken.

At the concert, we join the all-Japanese crowd, kneeling *seiza* as they are, on the wooden floor in the long narrow concert hall. We are crammed together, with no rows, only clusters of people, with their coats and packages gathered around them.

Kuroda sensei strides out to the front of the hall, in his splendor of black kimono and black *hakama*, the traditional formal wide-legged trousers. He stands tall, closes his eyes, and plays, swaying with the music. "Tsuru no Sugomori," "Nesting of the Cranes," one of my favorite pieces, with its mimicking of the trills of the birds. The rich resonant tones drift through the hall, the breathy and silvery sounds transporting me far away, as they did during my first lesson. The notes soar high and powerful like a mountain peak, then dip low and mournful like a river valley. They have a mysterious edge that wakens my soul. As always, Sensei becomes the flute, the music, the breath, the meditation. And so do I.

Several other musicians play solos, duets, and trios with *shakuhachi*, *koto*, and *shamisen*, and then Sensei invites everyone to come forward to try to play an instrument, with the help of the performers. He wants to introduce these traditional instruments to the many young Japanese who aren't familiar with them. An unexpected treat for us all.

I walk forward to pay my respects to my Sensei and to introduce Steven to him. I'm happy they're finally meeting each other, especially after Steven has heard so many of my stories about him and has endured the shrill shrieks and empty no-sounds as I learned to play.

Sensei responds with a slight formal bow and a big smile. "I am pleased to meet you."

Steven matches Kuroda sensei's bow, but bends slightly lower, and answers in Japanese. "*Hajimemashite. Dōzo yoroshiku.*" He pauses and then bows again. "Excuse me, Sensei, may I please try the *shakuhachi*?" he asks, in English this time.

"Of course." Kuroda sensei nods.

I wander off, circulating and listening. Over the heads of the others, I glance back at Steven and Sensei, their heads bent in concentration, as Sensei patiently guides Steven's lips, breathing, and fingers. A faint rough breathy sound emerges! Steven's first note, after months of sporadically trying my flute, and of my ineffective attempts to guide him. His grin is wide, thin, and illuminated, like a new crescent moon. Kuroda sensei smiles back, and so do I from across the room. Sensei offers his hand in congratulations, and Steven grasps it firmly. Then he bows again and again while backing away, offering repeated *arigatō gozaimasu.*

Steven and I glide out of the concert hall. He pulls me to him for a quick bear hug, forgetting for a moment the Japanese streaming around us. "Thank you for that," he murmurs in my ear. Hand in hand, we dance down the street toward home, under a pearly gray sky sprinkled with emerging stars.

During the week Chris is gone, Steven's world gradually opens up, one crack at a time, like a bird pecking at its shell. When I walk into the house after my weekly *shakuhachi* lesson, I'm greeted by the succulent aroma of a fish-and-sweet-potato *nabe.* The kitchen bubbles with steam, Puccini's *La bohème* cascades up and down from the living room, and Steven is puttering at the stove. Much to my surprise, he has cooked us lunch. So like his old self. His face looks clear and serene, his whole body relaxed. Hiroki, his Buddhist friend, and our first visitor to the Fushimi house, has just left. Steven looks as if he's been on a Buddhist retreat, as if Hiroki were a priest to whom he has bared his soul.

Steven sets a steaming bowl of the thick stew down in front of me and joins me at the table. "Hiroki understands me."

I pick out a succulent pink shrimp from the broth with my chopsticks and hold it in the air. "How's his girlfriend?"

"He now lives with her in another town—but the husband still refuses divorce." Steven lays down his ceramic spoon. "He seems resigned—no—he seems to really accept the situation, more than I ever could."

"Did you talk about your case?"

He bends his head to slurp up mouthfuls of broth with his spoon. "He sees our old colleagues. They ask about me."

"I wonder if they're still not allowed to see you."

"I didn't ask."

I choose not to probe more, wanting to respect the privacy of their friendship. I'm reassured by the calm glow on his face and relieved he has someone to talk to besides me.

A few days after Hiroki's visit, two of Steven's university colleagues call him, for the first time since the crisis. One of them, Fujimoto, makes the long trek south to Fushimi to pay his respects. Fujimoto had been Steven's young assistant. He's in his late twenties and eager to learn Western ways.

When Fujimoto arrives, I've already left for the day, on an outing with Fumiko Suzuki to the Urasenke Tea School, for a lecture, an exhibit of tea bowls, and a formal tea ceremony.

When I return, Steven and I sit on the tatami in the living room, the late afternoon sun streaming through the *shōji*, and sip our own cups of tea.

He blurts out, "Fujimoto really likes me. He traveled so far to come here. All these weeks he's been worried but was too afraid to call." He wipes his eyes, blows his nose with his handkerchief. "Takeda told him not to call or visit or even ask him questions about me."

I reach across the table to hold his hand with both of mine.

"He finally got the nerve to ask Takeda once more, for news of me, and if he could visit. This time Takeda said yes."

"Why?"

"I don't know. Nothing's changed. Nothing's decided." Steven fills up my cup, the stream of tea resonant in the quiet room, like a thin mountain waterfall pouring over a rocky cliff.

I drink my tea, inhaling its fresh green aroma, and watch the cats scramble in and out of the crack of open door to the porch. Does this mean Takeda has forgiven us? Will we ever see him again? Maybe we'll have a chance to give him his gift after all.

"Maybe Hiroki's visit helped," I say.

"Fujimoto didn't seem to care about what I've done. He doesn't agree with all the fuss they've made."

"He idolizes you, Steven. He probably misses all those hours you spent together."

For eight months, they worked closely, setting up Steven's complex computer system, devising research methods, and debating research ideas. They developed the same type of interdependent Japanese loyalty and hierarchy that Toru has with his boss, Knutsen.

Steven breathes a drawn-out sigh. "Those days are gone, I guess."

As I wash our teacups and let them drip-dry in the rack, I wonder if they ever smoked together. That is, of course, what the university and the police fear the most, that he was corrupting the young people here. As usual, I never ask. I'm still avoiding any confrontation with him. Ever since our bike ride to that bare deserted Shinto shrine, when I successfully interrogated him, I've backed off. Yet there's so much more to understand.

However, I'm not ready to grill him. I realize he can't yet handle it, and a part of me doesn't want to learn every detail. Maybe I'm still struggling to reconcile the parts of Steven I love with the parts I dislike or blame. I don't want to face the fact that the police may be right. I won't be able to accept that in Steven. I want marijuana to be his solitary recreation, not an addiction. And the fear still lingers in both of us that the less I know the better; the police could call me in for questioning at any time. But most of all, during this week alone in Fushimi with Chris gone, I know it's a time for "healing," not confronting. That can come later.

The second colleague to call is Murata. He's a senior professor in the department and a sponsor of Steven's first two business trips to Japan in the eighties. Unlike Hiroki, Murata isn't a soul mate, but rather a drinking buddy, a peer, and an esteemed colleague. His calling Steven is a major step forward in the attitude of the professors at the university.

Steven and Murata meet for lunch in town, at a noodle shop far from the university. But Steven doesn't look very cheery when I return home from my late-afternoon walk in the Fushimi forest. Once again, we sit at the kitchen table, this time with lacquer bowls brimming with homemade miso soup as a first course to our dinner. I sip mine with a ceramic spoon. He slurps his straight from the bowl.

"Murata seemed stiff and awkward, like he didn't know what to say. It wasn't like the old days."

"What'd you talk about?"

"His research, department politics." He clunks his bowl down on the table. "He did most of the talking. About what all our friends at the university are doing."

"Did you feel left out?"

"I wish I hadn't gone."

"Will you see him again?"

"He said we'll all meet for a drink in town soon, a bunch of them from the department. And me."

"You'll like that—if you force yourself to go."

I stir my soup with my chopsticks, mixing the suspended murky miso into the clear broth. I want him to have friends and things to do. I want his network to keep widening. These calls and visits help me as much as him. But I understand how hard it'll be to face his colleagues again, and how demoralizing it was to see Murata. They used to have such fun together—all that summer of '89, long days editing their book and long nights drinking sake at the local *izakaya*. I think the reality of seeing Murata face-to-face again makes him realize all he's lost, and how serious his crime is regarded, here in Japan.

Steven leaves the kitchen, his bowl of soup half empty.

But Steven no longer sits all day in a darkened room as he did at Takeda's. Now he's often away from the house. He does meet Murata and the others for a drink, even though it doesn't go that well. He joins Toru in town for a beer, a coffee, or dinner at their favorite *yakitoriya*. And he resumes his pottery lessons at Sato sensei's house in a new committed way, returning home one day with a passionate glow on his face and a new piece of pottery to show me, a long slender porcelain curl of olive green that becomes our new chopstick holder.

My life also opens up in Fushimi, unfolding like a delicate Japanese fan. With Steven often gone and Chris still on her tournament, I recapture a bit of myself. With mornings of solitude,

I have the time and space to wander the house and flow with my own schedule, while the sunlight plays on the lustrous tatami, the sounds of chanting and gongs float up from next door, and the dark green trees nestle against the downstairs porch. Time to meditate. Time to practice "Daiwagaku," which my *shakuhachi* teacher translates as "big peace and harmony," for my next lesson. To cook again—broccoli soup, zucchini quiche, banana bread.

With the house to myself, I can call my Kyoto friends to give them my new phone number, chat a bit, make a date. And have long talks with my son and daughter, finally able to catch up on the details of their thirty-year-old lives, the latest job, the latest girlfriend or boyfriend. Now that we're no longer searching for housing and are finally settled, I can resume my weekly lessons in town: cooking class to learn a new baked tofu dish; *shodō* calligraphy class to learn a new *kanji*, *haru*, for spring. And it's now a short, easy ride to my *shakuhachi* teacher, since he lives in the south of Kyoto, quite near Fushimi.

One morning, lying in Chris's upstairs tub, I am steeping in the water that I've made Japanese style, so extremely hot that you can barely enter or submerge, but strangely refreshing once you're in. I'm surrounded by forest, the tall bamboo swaying outside the open windows, as if I'm in a tree house. An olive-brown *uguisu*, the Bush Warbler, flutters onto a plum branch and whistles its poetry, "*hot-ket-kyot . . . kyot-kyot-kyot.*" Fumiko has told me this bird is the first sign of spring and quoted me the haiku that accompanies it.

> The bush warbler
> flings his body upside down
> with his first song of spring.
>
> — NATSUME SŌSEKI (tr. Meredith McKinney)

I'm filled with hope that we will leave Japan soon. Each day feels like my last in Kyoto. Each lesson, each forest walk, each friend, my last one to be treasured. And yet a part of me wants to stay here forever. I want to pack in as much as possible, to see every museum and shrine, attend every festival and concert. At last my life in Kyoto is all coming together, like a loosely woven tapestry of varied colors, threads, and textures. I like my life here. I can use my meager Japanese to order a meal, buy the correct size of tennis shoe, find my lost hat on the bus, ask for directions. I love working with my four students. I love creating my ikebana flowers, my calligraphy *kanji*, and my *shakuhachi* songs. And finally I have a network of friends. Thanks to Steven and the crisis, I've reached out for help. That's made these friendships blossom and grow.

But, in spite of all this, I can't wait to leave. I want to be free. I want to be home.

When I nudge the window wide open to hear the *uguisu* song more clearly, the dusky incense drifts up from below, intertwining with the sweet fragrance of the plum blossom and the white smoke from the fires in the cauldrons.

After my bath I pause at Chris's bedroom door before going downstairs. I peek into her spacious room, the sunbeams slanting in through a full bank of windows that open onto the porch, with the bamboo beckoning beyond. Like the bathtub room, it feels like an aerie on a mountaintop, full of light and air and tree. I imagine lying on her thick, billowy futon, so much like our blue one with its heron-wing design. I would be surrounded by pillows, listening to the chanting and watching the light play on the golden-green dancing leaves.

I step inside her room. Even though Chris isn't home, my heart thumps like a rabbit in a forbidden vegetable garden waiting for the farmer's footstep. As I slowly circle the wide expanse of floor, with its scattered plush cushions, my heart is in my mouth, my breath rapid and shallow. In my whole life I've never done anything like this. What compels me? I stoop to pick up the book by her bed and thumb through it, a sports biography of a woman I've never heard of. I yank open her dresser drawers and peer in at her clothes. I feel like a thief. I'm invading her private space. What's wrong with me? What am I looking for? I push open her closet and finger the heavy wool of her cardigans and the slick cotton of her solid-color shirtwaist dresses. Usually she wears jeans; these must be her schoolteacher clothes. I crouch in front of her low table, snatching up each item, studying it, replacing it exactly where it had been: a turquoise bowl, clumsy and factory-made, overflowing with earrings for pierced ears; a stack of letters bound together with a rubber band; a framed photo of an older man in a uniform.

I swallow hard, trying to make saliva in my parched mouth. Sitting down in the middle of the room, I study the complicated weave of the tatami. I don't understand why I feel so anxious and afraid. Who is this woman who's taken us in? Chris reminds me of a type of woman I tend to have trouble with. They all have a hard-edged, nervous energy and a needy hunger lurking beneath a smooth, confident, bossy surface. With a start, I realize Chris reminds me of Denise, Steven's drug dealer.

But there's something more. Maybe this isn't about her. It's about me. This snooping is my secret—I won't tell even Steven about it. I'm ashamed of myself and yet feel driven to do something wrong. I've been overly nice my whole life, always following the rules, trying to please. I want to rebel, but I don't know how.

As I come out of my foggy reverie, I'm horrified to find myself still sitting in the middle of Chris's room, clutching a CD of hers. I shove it in its slot and rifle through the rest of the CD stack, searching for more clues to this woman. I survey the room again. It's uncluttered, almost barren in the Japanese style, but lacking the intimacy of a Japanese home. I should be grateful that we aren't in that filthy guesthouse. Why can't I look for Chris's uniqueness and not judge her so harshly?

I must accept it's her house and not mine. I don't seem to do well sharing my home with other women, whether as tenant or owner. I suspect my young boarders resented me as much as I resented them. Like Chris, I'm a fierce guardian of my privacy and space. I always feel invaded, never learning how to protect my inner self and still remain sociable.

I don't recognize that by this absurd snooping, I'm transferring my anger to Chris, as I did with Takeda: my anger at Steven, Denise, Japanese culture, and the police who fingered my underwear. I'm unable to direct the anger onto either Steven or Japan because I still love them both too much. I haven't yet reconciled my love-hate toward Japan. And I have to stay aligned with Steven in order to survive. I haven't yet learned to be directly angry at my mate and then move on, within the larger context of love. I still think it's all or nothing.

I shove a CD of Latin jazz in its correct slot on the shelf. Trying to shake my mood, I stretch forward into a yoga pose, bending over my knees, sliding my palms down to my ankles. Rolling myself up to standing, I stare out Chris's window at the empty clothesline and leafy forest. Out on the porch, I sit in her wicker chair and bask in the sunshine. I want to live here on the second floor with Steven, not crammed into that closet room downstairs. No, I don't want to live here at all. I want to be home.

I ease up out of the chair, glance one last time at the burning flames and gleaming bells below me, and walk back inside to her large upstairs hallway. After studying her collection of Japanese and American literature, I choose a book to borrow, *The Pillow Book of Sei Shonagon*, the journal of a tenth-century lady of the court that I've been wanting to read. I feel guilty doing this without asking, but I promise myself to read as much as I can and then slip it back into its proper place before she returns.

Hugging the borrowed book tight to my chest like a secret treasure, I descend the stairs one by one, still uneasy and ashamed. I creep back to my closet room and sit down at the *kotatsu*, warming my hands and toes by the heat of its lightbulb. Pulling a blanket from the futon cupboard, I wrap it around me, huddle into its coziness, and open to the first page of *The Pillow Book*.

> "In spring it is the dawn that is most beautiful. As the light creeps over the hills, their outlines are dyed a faint red and wisps of purplish cloud trail over them."
>
> — SEI SHŌNAGON (tr. Ivan Morris)

The diverse corners of my Kyoto friendships are folding together, like a silk *furoshiki*, the square cloth used to wrap gifts, the edges gathered up into a soft knot protecting the special contents. I'm learning how to build a safety net of friends: Fumiko Suzuki, my Japanese language teacher and Steven's translator; Makiko, my student with the two little girls, who's gradually become a friend; Clover, the American artist, my confidante from my women's group; and Yamaguchi san, a new friend, the Japanese-American from the local elementary school. They all come together for me as I sit surrounded by the four at a lecture at the Women's International Club.

One morning a few days before Chris returns, I climb into the backseat of Clover's car and am surprised to find Yamaguchi san in the front seat.

"I'm so happy to see you again," I say. "I've wanted to call, but I didn't have your number, and I've been so busy . . ." My voice trails off as I glance at Clover, who knows my secret of course, and I realize I don't want to tell Yamaguchi about it. I rush to add, "I didn't realize you two knew each other."

We're on our way to the lecture. I've avoided these Women's Club meetings because I assumed they were attended only by Americans, but Clover has told me the group is a lovely mixture of *gaijin* from all over the world, including both newcomers and expats, and also many "returnees," Japanese women who've lived abroad and want to maintain their foreign connection and their English-language skills.

My student Makiko is a "returnee," so I've invited her to meet me at the lecture. I've also called Fumiko, who will join us there and has suggested that afterward, we meet our husbands for an afternoon outing of antiquing in Osaka.

Clover offered to pick me up at Demachiyanagi train station when I came in from Fushimi. I didn't need the ride but wanted the extra time with her.

Now as we drive along, Clover explains that she knows Betty, the lecturer. She's here on an arts grant too and is studying the kimono as both art and culture. "But I merely snip old ones to pieces to make clothes and collages," she says with self-deprecating good humor. I envy her easy style with friendships, always quick to know everyone in the community.

As she maneuvers through Kyoto traffic and chats with Yamaguchi, I fall silent, half listening, half watching the streets flash by with their mixture of high-rise modern office buildings and ancient wooden temples and shops. I've met Yamaguchi san only once before, weeks ago when I was observing classes at Shūgakuin Elementary School. After we were introduced, we ended up walking home together. Yamaguchi is a Japanese-American married to a Japanese. She only recently arrived and was finding it hard to adjust. She is from California like me and has family in San Diego, where I lived for many years.

When Yamaguchi and I came to my corner where the opulent piles of oranges and purple eggplants practically spilled over the counters onto the sidewalk, I longed to invite her for tea. But I didn't understand how or where or what the rules were here. Even though she was an American, she already seemed like a native Japanese to me. Maybe I didn't know her well enough yet. Was it okay to ask for her phone number? If only I had a *meishi* to give her. Clover had a beautiful set of *meishi*, those calling cards with English on one side, Japanese on the other. As it was, I didn't know whether to play by American or Japanese rules. I figured Yamaguchi was another "green tea" friend. We chatted, we connected, and she disappeared around her own corner down the street.

Now here she is again in the front seat of Clover's car. After Clover drives into the Community Center parking lot, Yamaguchi strides ahead to greet some Japanese friends. I linger with Clover and whisper, "How do you make so many friends here so easily? I'm shy—I don't know the proper way in Japan."

She stops, laughs, gives me a big hug. "I don't worry about that. I just bluster forward in my direct American way, give out my *meishi*, ask for a phone number, and make a date." Her enthusiasm bubbles all over her face and down to her round pregnant belly. "I met Yamaguchi in my kimono-dressing class. We're learning how to put on all those endless layers and sashes. She needs to master the proper way, now that she's a Japanese wife."

I return Clover's hug. "I'll try your way."

In the lecture hall, I find Fumiko, invite her to sit with us, and introduce her to the other two women. I'm sure they'll like each other. Makiko arrives late. I wave, gesturing her to join us, but she sits shyly in the back. I want her to meet my friends and draw her into my group, but she slips out at the end before I can. Even so, I still feel nourished by her presence.

I scribble notes, inspired by the lecturer's wealth of information about the kimono as both a work of art and an integral part of the culture. I'm reminded of my textile research in our Thai village, when I apprenticed myself to the master weaver, an eighty-year-old woman who spoke no English. She was the first real mentor I ever had, at the age of forty-five, and back then I didn't even know the word. I will ask Clover to introduce me to the lecturer, and we can compare notes about the two cultures. I want her to mentor me. Until I too can lecture like this, an expert giving a gift to a rapt audience, about an art form she is passionate about. I don't know yet what my art form might be. I'm still searching.

Sitting in this auditorium surrounded by my four diverse friends, and a larger circle of potential ones, I'm comforted as if we were all sitting under the quilted skirt of a *kotatsu* charcoal heater. I vow to myself that I'll now go to every International Club meeting. I'll ask for phone numbers and make dates for tea, as Clover does. Ever since the police knocked, I've felt burdened and closed down, with so much cancelled, and so much fear, unable to make an appointment or to make a friend. Shall I give up even trying because we may leave Japan any minute? Or shall I reach out to grab every last moment, every connection, every opportunity? I decide to choose the latter.

When the lecture ends, Fumiko and I rush through the several city blocks to Shijo Station. She grabs my arm, and we run like two Japanese schoolgirls, giggling and chattering about our favorite parts of the lecture. We find the men standing at the top of the escalator, engrossed in their own conversation. They hurry us down the stairs and onto the subway to Kyoto *eki*, where we transfer to the train for Osaka.

Breathless, we all sink into our seats and form a companionable circle of silence as we gaze out the window, each of us lost in thought, we women on one side facing forward, the two men facing us, riding backward. Out the window, it's a shiny pearl of a day, clear and promising. This is our first excursion with another couple since last fall. Our crisis seems to have caused Fumiko to reach out to us even more. She presumes and hopes we'll be leaving soon, so she wants to see us as often as possible.

The men resume their conversation about the influence of early Korean ceramics on the Japanese aesthetic. Fumiko turns to me. "Your time in Thailand, that elderly woman teach you weaving. Please tell me."

Once in Osaka, Fumiko and Hideo lead us to one of their favorite antique shops.

"*Irashaii!*" the proprietor sings out, the usual welcome. He seems well acquainted with the Suzukis.

He ushers us into his exclusive back room, settles us into comfortable antique chairs, and out of thin-shelled antique cups serves *gyokuro*. The only other time I've experienced such elegant and personal service was when shopping for a wedding gown with my first mother-in-law at her Saks Fifth Avenue shop in San Francisco. Now, one at a time, the proprietor brings out a series of well-wrapped antique dishes, lovingly unwraps them, and sets them out on the glass counter for us to contemplate and hold. A bowl, a vase, a plate, to be admired in hushed tones and then returned to its place and its wrapping.

Steven and I treat the shop like an art gallery. We sit back, sip our tea, marvel at each piece as it is presented with appropriate oohs and aahs. We're trying to learn this cultural ritual from Fumiko and Hideo by observing their polite interactions with the shopkeeper. They buy nothing at this shop but part from the shopkeeper with profound bows and thank-yous and promises to return. They repeat this ritual at a series of antique shops around the neighborhood, sometimes buying, sometimes only looking and admiring.

Finally, in one shop, Steven succumbs. We're watching Fumiko and Hideo contemplate the purchase of a small white teapot, decorated with a triangular ikebana-style design of three peonies, red, white, and gold.

He nudges me with his elbow. "We must buy something," he whispers. "They've done so much for us. And the shopkeeper expects it."

With my hand over my mouth like a typical Japanese woman, I whisper back, "I don't think we have to."

"I want something beautiful to take home." He crosses one leg over his knee and leans forward. "Please. Help me choose."

I shrug my shoulders. "Okay." But I keep a distance, continuing to treat the shop like a unique museum.

The Suzukis line their four choices up on the counter, ready to pay, and turn to Steven. His eyes shining, he places a set of six antique blue-and-white covered rice bowls next to their dishes.

"They *are* beautiful," I murmur. I cradle one in my palms, feeling its paper-thin delicacy, and study its design of alternating blue and white diamonds, the inside of each diamond embellished with overlapping blue waves. Once I let go of my protective aloofness and fully enter the beauty of this shop, these people, and this bowl, I too can love this exquisite set of antiques. And can even accept the extravagant price. Steven the anthropologist is an expert at being both careful observer and full participant; I only know how to be one or the other. I think Steven *does* need this piece of beauty. And perhaps so do I.

"But what about breakage? They'll never make it home," I ask.

"Oh, no, Madam, we ship all over the world," the proprietor assures me in perfect English. "We never have any break. We wrap them very, very well."

Now starting to worry about the price, I look at Steven. "Why so many? Why not just two?"

He counts on the fingers of one hand, Thai-style, as he always does, the thumb tapping the three sections of each finger, up one finger and down the next. "Two for my sister and her husband, two for my son and his fiancée, two for us." He examines the underside of one of the lids, with its design of three tiny chrysanthemums inside a circle, like a family crest. "Martha's helping us so much here. And so's Robert. Without his friend Tom, we never would've made it this far."

I raise both palms toward him. "You're right. Let's do it."

On the shipment home to the States, one bowl will break. Working together, we'll mend it, gluing the pieces back together, shard by shard, like an intricate jigsaw puzzle, so it can sit with its mate on the Buddha shelf in our meditation room.

BLAZING FIRES

Flames in black cauldron
when will you leap your boundaries
and blaze into ash.

— Patricia Dove Miller

During the first week that Chris is back from her tournament, our idyllic forest retreat shatters as if struck with repeated crashes of lightning.

Chris returns on a Thursday, tanned and triumphant, with her many bronze medals.

Steven and I resume our careful household habits under her rules: the dishes, the cats, the kerosene, the bathtub, the doors. But I keep using the dryer, sneaking in a load when she's out. I can't stand returning to soggy clothes on the line, still damp and moldy after long days and nights outside.

On Friday afternoon Chris arrives home early from work. The dryer is spinning away in the kitchen. She yanks the door open, grabs the still-wet clothes, storms into my room, and hurls them at me with all the strength of her athlete's body. Sodden shirts and underwear slap my astonished face, drip down my chest, and scatter all over the tatami.

"How dare you!" she screams, shaking her fist, her face blazing red.

I step back, stunned. Stooping to gather the scattered clothes into a pile, I say, "I'm sorry, Chris. I know you said not to. I'll pay for the extra utilities."

"No." She stomps her foot. "You can't pay extra. There's no way to figure it out. Besides, I don't believe in dryers. They ruin the clothes." She stops to catch her breath, her body rigid. "You can use the line like everyone else. They dry just fine."

I know I've done wrong, but I can't understand the extent of her fury. I hold both palms out flat in a gesture of defeat. "Okay, I'm really very sorry. I'll use the line." I start for the door with the wet clothes in my arms.

She blocks my way, her arms stiff on each side of the door-jamb. "You'll only use it when my clothes aren't there. I don't want you hogging it. I've got to go to work each day and you don't."

"Fine, Chris," I say, keeping my voice steady, trying to calm her down even though I want to scream back at her. But I have to make this work—we can't move again.

She continues to stare at me, eyes bulging, breath heavy and ragged.

"It's okay now. I'll do as you say."

Gradually she drops her arms, turning away. Her feet pound up the stairs. Her door rattles closed.

I mound the clothes on a corner of the *kotatsu* tabletop, so they won't stain the tatami. They'll have to wait for the line, the next time she's out.

Saturday morning I climb the stairs with my wet bundle and walk out to the porch. Her clothes are spread along the whole line, in differing stages of dryness. I consolidate them, gingerly hanging them closer and more efficiently, hoping she won't notice, and squeeze my clothes in. When I check on Sunday, she's moved some of mine into the shade, piled up the rest in clumps, and kept hers in the scanty sun. Fighting back tears, I spread mine out a bit, hoping eventually they'll dry. At least she hasn't thrown them off the porch.

That night, Steven and I huddle close in our windowless room under the thin quilts, trying to keep warm. "I can't win. I can't use the line, I can't use the dryer," I wail.

He rubs my back, leisurely even strokes with his palms. "I know. She's terribleimpossibleunreasonable," his words running together on purpose. "I hate her too."

I sit up in bed sputtering. "But you're always extra nice to her. You let me fight all the battles." I blow my nose hard. "How can you be so two-faced?"

Steven sits up, his head in his hands. "It's the only way for me."

I roll over, my back to him. Who is this man I've married? I'm trying hard to find the positive in him, but his passive obedience shoves me away. I want him to stand up to Chris, to not let her push me around. But I can't expect him to solve my disputes. I have to defend myself.

For Steven, it seems easy. He's the adaptable anthropologist blending with his environment. He's also in survival mode. He bows to his "captor," as he did with his police interrogators, willing to do anything to please the one in charge. He happily accepts Chris's rules and idiosyncrasies, daily grateful that she's taken us in. He seeks out her company to charm and pacify her. At the kitchen table over breakfast, or in the hall as she comes and goes, he chats and lingers with her. On the other hand, the minute she enters the kitchen, I disappear, taking my cereal bowl to our room, muttering to myself. I do everything I can to avoid her, plan my routine in the house so I won't run into her. I'm not good at pretending to be friendly to someone I don't like. But I never even try.

I pull the blankets over my head, and I toss and turn, trying to rest. Steven, on his back, snores me awake every time I fall asleep. Maybe we two women are fighting over the man in the house in some subtle way. She never moves *his* clothes, when he does *his* laundry. But I'm sure she isn't attracted to him; she flirts with every male I see her with, including Steven. No, I don't think it's really about clothes or Steven. Chris and I both want control of the house, *her* house. It becomes a constant silent battle between us.

I too had silent battles with my boarders when I was a single mother. The macrobiotic woman who every morning at dawn took all the food out of the fridge because she thought it should be at room temperature. Each morning when I entered the kitchen for breakfast, I silently put it back. After weeks of this, I tried to reason with her, asking her kindly to stop, but she never would. For her, it was a philosophy of life, for me a matter of spoiled food and the health of my two young children.

Is this how Chris feels about me? Her house, her rules that I must follow. But I never think about the macrobiotic woman, or that our roles are reversed. I don't try to negotiate and say: You know, Chris, I don't believe in dryers either; back in California I prefer the natural way too, the golden fragrance of sunshine; but here it's so cold and wet and shady, and we're trying to share. I could bow graciously to Chris's rules and recognize this is the wrong time and wrong place to fight my loss of autonomy. Or I could say to myself: This is an unstable woman, no discussion will help; instead, how can I placate her, like Steven does, and not lose my soul?

That same Friday afternoon after Chris hurled sodden clothes in my face and stomped upstairs, I slide closed the door to my room. Pacing the squares of tatami, I feel restless and confined but don't want to venture into the rainstorm raging outside. Usually I love walking in the rain, the storm venting my mood. But now I want to hide. Pausing, I stare at the square cupboard door cut into the far corner. Maybe I'll look one more time in the storeroom for my missing daypack.

The day after Chris left for her tournament, when I went to my shelf in the storeroom to load my small brown daypack with *shakuhachi* and music, the daypack was gone. I searched and searched all over the storeroom, on her shelves and mine, and all over the house, in her room and ours. I told myself I was being paranoid, but I still suspected Chris had taken it. When she returned I never asked her. I merely kept brooding and searching.

Now I crawl through the low cupboard doorway. Standing up and stretching on the other side, I peer down the length of the murky, narrow storeroom. I clamber past Chris's clutter. Tall, rickety metal shelves loom on both sides several feet above my head, threatening to teeter on top of me. They're crammed full of boxes, spilling their contents onto the walkway—clothes, Christmas ornaments, tools.

At the far end on the right, a glimmer of light casts shadows on the top shelf. Where can it be coming from? Edging closer, past the last bookcase and around a corner, I follow the light. A window high up in a second story beams a patch of sun down onto my face. The rain has stopped, the sun breaking through a hole in the clouds. I've discovered a secret hideaway.

I climb up the wooden ladder, vertical and narrow like on a ship. At the top is a second storeroom, like a loft, stacked high with torn, stained futons and ragged blankets. When I sit down on the futons, small puffs of dust billow up around me, but they seem clean enough. Out the window the tile rooftops of town stretch out far below. It looks as if Chris never comes up here. Yet this must be where she found the blankets she loaned us. I wonder why she refused to loan us one of these futons.

I burrow into the wooly blankets, wondering at their warmth on this chilly day. The afternoon sunshine must warm them through the window. I'm happy no one knows where I am. It's the first time I've felt truly safe in this house.

I stretch out on my back, pondering Chris, and watching the clouds change shapes, now a prancing dragon, now a ruffled peony. I've never experienced such arbitrary and willful tirades. Once in a loop she can't seem to stop. I curl myself small and invisible, like a small child with a willful mother, and vow never to break another rule—and yet I'm worried that the rules might change at any moment.

I'm not used to anger. In my family it was hidden away. I didn't know it was there until years later, looking back. My father was quiet and reserved, my mother a cheerful chatterer. Never any shouting or screaming. Only my father's occasional sharp quiet reprimand. Or my mother's shattered glass jar, thrown into the trashcan late at night, in a silent anger against my father.

Now the clouds begin to bloom with puffs of gold tinged with gray, and the light fades. Steven will be home soon, and Chris will descend to the kitchen to cook dinner. If she finds me here, she'll be furious; if he doesn't find me in our room, he'll be worried, searching everywhere, calling out my name. Reluctantly, I push myself up from my nest. Rung by rung, I climb back down the ladder, descending into reality.

On Monday at lunchtime, Steven removes a small china plate decorated with tiny pink rosebuds from the forbidden cupboard. He spreads his bread and cheese on it and sits down at the table. He's often admired these fine dishes, has used them before, always quickly drying and replacing them before Chris returns. His one act of rebellion.

Chris walks in, unexpectedly home from school in the middle of the day. She freezes in the middle of the kitchen, staring first at the plate, then up at him, then back to the plate, with wild, wide eyes. "How dare you!" she screams. She grabs the plate, dumps the bread and cheese onto the bare table, stalks to the sink, and scrubs the plate furiously, her shoulders heaving.

When she turns to glare at him, her face is that same blazing red. She grasps the plate so tightly I fear it'll break. I'm cowering at the doorway, afraid but fascinated. What's he going to do?

She stamps her foot at Steven, her voice rising higher and higher as if it will burst. "I told you these're special. They were my mother's. You're not allowed to use them."

Steven reaches out his hand, as if to touch her and calm her, but she jerks away.

"Put this back right now!" she yells.

With a calm, silent deliberation, Steven rises and gently extracts the plate from her grip. He nests it in the cupboard on top of its matching mates and returns to his chair. Placing his palms flat down on the table, he looks up at her with a steady, soft gaze. "I am sorry, Chris. Never will I use those dishes again." His words are measured as if speaking to a child or a foreigner. I can see his own breath rising evenly and slowly, trying to cause hers to match his. "These dishes are beautiful. They must be very special to you. Tell me about them. Tell me about her."

Her breath steadies, her fists unclench, her face loses its flush. Sitting down across from him, she spills out stories about her mother.

I tiptoe into the next room, grab my purse, and let myself out the front door. I don't know where he's learned to do that— maybe from all those years of meditation or from his therapy training. Or maybe from his mother. He's used to this type of random anger from his young widowed mother, who never recovered from her husband's death. He learned how to soothe her, how to read her ever-changing moods. With Chris, he's able to sidestep the surface issue and probe for the emotion underneath. Whereas I tend to react in anger and stubbornness. I wanted to throw that pink plate at her but know that I never will. I only did that once—the night my first husband announced he was leaving me after twelve years of marriage and two children. I threw all the dirty dishes from the kitchen sink onto the floor and raged out of the house, leaving him to clean up the pieces.

Later that night, lying on my back, close to Steven on the lumpy futon, I say, "You were so good with Chris this afternoon. I don't know how you do it."

"Do what?"

"Dive below the surface and discover the real issue—her mother." I stare up at the low ceiling. "And you're so willing to be nice to someone even if you don't like her." Turning toward him, I dig my elbow into the futon and poke my fist into my cheek. "But aren't you angry at her?"

"Why should I be? It's her house. I tune out when someone screams at me. I'm used to it." He rolls over closer to face me. "Besides, I must work at keeping the peace. I can't ignore it." He strokes my hair. "Sure, she's scary, but I like her anyway. She intrigues me. A tough lady."

"I never learned how to do that. When I was little, my mother used to say to me in exasperation, you don't have to like the shoe salesman, just buy the shoes. But I always refused. I couldn't seem to separate the two." In Kyoto, I don't yet know that, like Steven, I can pretend to be friendly to someone I don't like, and that sometimes it leads to really connecting with that person.

I roll away to the far side of the futon. It's good he's keeping the peace. But I don't want him to like Chris. I want him to join forces with me and confront her. What do I expect him to do? Get us kicked out again? Clearly his way's working better than mine. But isn't there some other way to deal with her? Some middle ground. Not hidden fury, not hypocritical friendliness. I don't see that his is a survival strategy, that sometimes you have to be hypocritical to get by.

Here in Kyoto, we seem to have switched roles. I used to be the submissive good girl who never rebelled. He was always the "wild and crazy" guy—like Knutsen—the rebel who didn't care what others thought. Now he's the good guy, doing anything to maintain harmony. The traditional woman's role that I used to be so good at, with family, husbands, boyfriends, and with every feuding hospital doctor at work. Now I've broken loose to be the bad one who storms, snoops, breaks the rules. But when I rebel, I flail uselessly like a broken clothesline in the wind.

We both are afraid to confront her. Is that what bothers me so much, that he's acting as passive as I am? Why do I expect him to grapple with these conflicts? Because he's the man? Or perhaps because he's the one who got us into this mess?

I want us to work as a team. I want us to sit down, make a plan, and meet quietly with Chris to smooth things out. In spite of Steven's therapeutic skills, none of us knows how to talk to each other about these problems.

I turn back to Steven. I can never stay mad at him for long. Besides, my mother gave me three pieces of advice before my first marriage at age nineteen. The first was, never go to bed angry with your husband. Deal with it first—with him or by yourself. She and I usually chose the latter way. I slip my arm around his chest, nestle into his back, and drift off to sleep. Chris never screams at Steven again. They've turned a corner I can't find.

That same Monday afternoon after Chris ranted at Steven about the forbidden plates, I'm on the train speeding north to Kyoto, escaping. I've left the two of them at the kitchen table still talking about her mother. I'm eager to find refuge with Makiko and plunge into both my teaching and her friendship. I sink into the solitude of the train, trying to read some of *Genji* or plan the lesson, but mostly staring out the window at bamboo forests and rice fields that mingle with rambling old two-story farmhouses. The neat squares of farmland disappear, the clusters of small new houses of Kyoto's southern edges appearing. When I arrive at our old Shūgakuin neighborhood, I stroll through the familiar streets, passing the bakery with its long loaves of French bread in the window and nodding hello to the fishmonger.

Makiko greets me at her apartment door with a smile. "I'm so happy you're here," she says, in her careful, unaccented American English. Her dark eyes shine into mine, her shoulder-length pageboy swinging like a graceful bell, as she takes both my hands in hers and squeezes. "The girls are at school. We can talk in peace." She ushers me in, seats me at her formal dining room table, and serves us cups of hot *kōcha* with cream and a plate of homemade butter cookies. "My girls and I made these this morning—especially for you! A recipe I learned in America."

Makiko lived two years in New Jersey with her physician husband and two little girls. She still misses the freedom and independence of her life there, as an "American" woman. She doesn't really need a teacher except for a chance to practice her English and receive some fine-tuning. Her lessons consist of long meandering conversations, sometimes about American politics, or about feminism in Japan and the U.S., or about elementary schools in the two countries. Today I guide us toward the kimono lecture we both attended last week, listen to her stories of wearing kimonos at various occasions since the age of two, and tell her my story of learning to weave in the Thai village. Here and there, I delicately demonstrate a grammar point, encourage her to speak in long full sentences to stretch her knowledge of English, or have her practice short new colloquial phrases and idioms.

At the end of the lesson, she hands me the yen in a discreet envelope, as is the Japanese custom. I am so cheered by her companionship and the joy of the teaching interaction, I feel guilty accepting her money. Even though I can't tell her my secret, I feel a real bond between us. To my surprise, in my search for friends here, I've discovered a rich source right in front of me, in my women students of all ages. But even more than in the States, it's tricky here to break the strict boundaries of the formal hierarchy of teacher and student and build a friendship. With Makiko, I've managed to dissolve that barrier.

I've two hours to myself before Makiko's five-year-old daughter Miku arrives home from school for her lesson with me. I pull on my thick sweater and saunter in the cool spring air the few short blocks toward the Berg, my usual café. Crossing the river, I pause on the bridge, looking left up toward the wooded hills, the neat rows of vegetable gardens, the stream rushing down toward me, and the lanes winding up to our old walking haunts. To the right, the lane leads to Saginomori shrine with its green pine forest and roosting white egrets.

I detour up to the shrine, to pay my respects to the Shinto spirits, as I used to do every evening when Steven returned from the Police Investigation, once again safely home and not in prison. As usual, I bow my head at the main altar, clap my hands three times. This time I whisper thanks to the spirits of the forest for the Fushimi house, in spite of its difficulties. I ask for more strength and more courage in dealing with Chris. I'm not used to prayers and don't really believe in these foreign spirits, but this Shinto ritual performed among the towering fragrant pines comforts me, and strangely my whispered words give me some strength and renewal.

The spring breeze snaps into a chilly wind. Wishing I'd brought my coat, I head downhill toward the Berg. In the cozy café, I choose a cheese Danish and sit at my table by the window in back. Lingering over a hot cup of *kōcha*, I watch the leaves of the *hagi* bush rustle in the wind, listen to the modulations of a Mozart quartet, and plan my lesson for Makiko's daughter.

Back at Makiko's apartment, Miku hides from me, making squeaking noises. Pretending I don't see her under the dining room table, I search in the closet, under the sink, on the porch, asking Makiko repeatedly, where can Miku be? She jumps out giggling. I swoop her into my arms, twirl her around, and lead her to the dining room table, nudging my chair close to hers.

I ask her to read me the story she's written about a bunny. She uses a high squeaky voice, pretending to be the bunny, the first-person narrator of her story. On each page under her drawing, she's written two or three sentences. I'm amazed by her writing skills, much more advanced than my kindergarteners back home. We discuss the rabbit and its adventures, she sticking to her squeaky bunny voice and her role as the rabbit. I show her my favorite part about the bunny riding the airplane to America. I gently point out a few places where she might try a different word to make it better English, or where she might add a little more detail about what clothes the bunny wears. But the main point is less to insist on accurate English or effective writing style and more to encourage her to write, read, and speak in English instead of Japanese, and for her to mimic my native intonation and pronunciation.

"For next week, tell me what happens next to the bunny," I say.

Miku leads me to her bedroom, which she shares with her older sister. She snuggles next to me on the tatami, as if she were a favorite grandchild, while I read her two of my old favorites, *Are You My Mother?* and *Make Way for Ducklings.* When it's time to leave, I rise from the tatami reluctantly, gazing with fondness at Miku's glossy black hair as she buries her nose in the book, still caught up in examining each picture. At the front door I linger, chatting with Makiko. I take her hand in both of mine and thank her, fighting back the tears. I don't want to leave the snug cocoon we three have created here.

Shivering, I hurry to light the heater in our bedroom. It's early Tuesday morning, the fifth day of that first week after Chris returns from her tournament. I scratch the match, choking on the sulfurous fumes. A slow hiss. Then a loud silence. No flame. It's out of kerosene. Steven shoves the heater out to the living room where it belongs and tries the kitchen heater. Empty. Chris also uses the two downstairs heaters. But when we first moved in, she insisted it would be our job to buy and pay for the kerosene for them. At the time we didn't know what that would involve, but readily agreed, so anxious to do anything in order to live here.

Before Chris leaves for work, Steven asks her where to buy kerosene.

"Oh, it's down that street, then a left, a right, over by the post office, just ask as you go." She waves her hand vaguely toward the street that runs alongside the house toward town.

"Is it far?" I ask, thinking of the maze of alleys and the careful maps that the Japanese usually draw for us and for each other. I slide a piece of paper out from the stack on the kitchen table and with an uncertain half-smile begin to hold it out to her. "Would you mind drawing us a little map?"

She swats it away as if it were an angry hornet. "Not necessary," she snaps. "You'll find it. Here's the gas can and a cart to carry it home." From the kitchen porch, she lugs out a rusted metal shopping cart with lopsided wheels and hands Steven a bungee cord. "Strap the canister on here."

The cart looks rickety and dubious. How will the huge tank, once full, balance on this small cart? "How do you usually get it?" I ask.

She tosses her head. "I swing by in the car on my way home from work."

"Would you mind—" Steven begins.

"Absolutely not! I don't run errands for my tenants. I already told you it's your job." The red flush rises on her neck, spreading up to flame her cheeks. "It's only ten blocks for god's sake." She slams the kitchen door and tramps up the stairs.

But Steven follows her, calling to her from the base of the stairs, in his lowest, calmest voice. "Okay, thanks, we'll do it. But would you mind telling us, please, what's the word for *kerosene store*, so we can ask along the way?"

"*Tōyu*," she snarls over her shoulder, without breaking her stride. Steven and I look at each other in silent dismay, strap the empty canister on the cart, and trudge down the hill.

"Wow, she's tricky," I say, as I yank the cart over the rough cobblestones.

Steven grabs the handle to take a turn. "I see why you don't like her. But we have to keep on her good side. I don't want to be evicted again."

I snatch the handle back and stride on ahead.

After endless false turns and numerous halting requests to passersby, we locate the kerosene shop. It's nowhere near the post office.

Laboring back up the hill, Steven pulls and I push the cart. We grasp the heavy metal canister with all four of our hands interlocking, to keep it from slipping off.

But as we round the first corner, the can slides off the cart and rolls down the cobblestones. "Damn," I cry. Steven chases after it. "I bet she's never tried this," I say. "Why won't she give us a ride?"

He restraps it on, gasping for breath and fuming. "Or get it herself. What an asshole."

A block later, the left wheel snags on the cobbles and falls off. Steven kneels on the sharp cobblestones and jams it back on. "This is impossible. We'll never get it home."

We struggle on. The can slides off a second time and we strap it back on. Again and again. The right wheel snaps off, then the left. We're both furious and exhausted—at the canister, at the cart, at Chris. But for once I feel no anger toward Steven—the teamwork has united us. We're determined to make this work, to reach the top of the hill, to arrive home.

At the house, I droop on the front steps, my shoulders aching. Steven unstraps the can. Usually he's the first one to give up when physical tasks are too hard. Today I'm grateful for his strength. "I'm afraid to go inside," I say.

He bends down behind me, massaging my shoulders. "C'mon in. Her car's gone," he says. Hooking his elbows under my arms, he lifts me up and wraps his arms around me. "I'll make you a cuppa tea."

This time my afternoon escape is to my ikebana class. At the doorway to the studio, I bow low to my Sensei, then to each of my fellow students. Still bent over, I enter the flower-scented room and sit *seiza* on the tatami at the low table. I breathe and listen, drinking in this silent world of beauty and color, with the quiet murmurs and genuine smiles of my fellow students, and the kind, steady hands of my elderly Sensei. She inches around the table on her knees, guiding one student's hands to adjust a creamy white rose to the proper angle, and another's to trim a golden yellow acacia branch, so that it cascades like a waterfall over the pool in the vase below. When it's my turn, she sits back on her heels, studying my arrangement. A small clap of praise, a wise interior smile, and a gracious nod of her head. She reaches out to adjust only two stems to allow more space between them. Then, as usual, she motions for me to pull each flower out and begin again.

At the end of class, I bundle up my used flowers in a newspaper, carefully inserting them into my ikebana carrying case, a long conical sheath of lavender nylon that looks like a huge floppy ice cream cone. Unfolding my long legs from under the low table, I stand halfway up, in order to bow a circle of thanks to Sensei and the students, a ritual I've learned by watching the other students at the beginning and end of each lesson.

On the train, my nose nestles into the fragrance of rose and acacia as I cradle them on my lap, proud that everyone, because of the case, can recognize that they're for ikebana.

Back at Chris's, she and Steven are both out. I wander the house, searching for a vase, never finding one, and feeling uneasy with my flowers. I pace from room to room looking for a peaceful space where I can rearrange the flowers in a meditative way. I don't want to have to ask Chris for a vase or for permission to display them. Unlike for Takeda, I don't want to give her a gift. I fear her barked critique or that she'll toss the flowers out without comment.

After much deliberation, I stick them as one bulky bunch into an old jar and shove it to the back of the cluttered kitchen table. The next morning the flowers stare at me, begging me to arrange them. And the next morning, and the next. Soon, I'll find a vase, make an arrangement. I never do ask Chris nor does she comment. The flowers wilt in that glass jar, un-arranged and shriveled, until I throw them in the trash.

Each week I feast on the transient world of flowers at Sensei's house. When I leave, I wrap the flowers in a cone of newspaper and carry them with me, because she'll be insulted if I don't. Before returning to Chris's, I quietly balance them on the rim of the trash can at the train station, hoping someone will pick them up to create her own world of beauty.

BUBBLING FOUNTAINS

Round stone fountain
bubbling an endless circle
a perfect path.

— Patricia Dove Miller

We're still waiting. Like a becalmed ship in the middle of the Japan Sea, sails flapping in the wind, revolving in slow circles, without oars or engine. We're trying to make the best of it, as if learning complicated knots, studying the stars for navigation, identifying the passing birds, searching for the wandering albatross. Forty-eight days since the police knocked on our door, and twenty-nine days since the Customs Police Investigation ended.

Today I'm soaking in the tub upstairs. Chris has recently left for work. I hear Steven's footsteps running to answer the phone.

"*Moshi moshi*," he says. A lengthy silence. His voice drifts up the stairs, punctuated by throaty laughter and mumbles of conversation. More laughter. It must be his sister. Only she can make him laugh like that.

When I walk into the living room, Steven's still on the phone. I'm toasty and snug from my bath, wrapped in my cotton *yukata*, my wet hair rolled up in a towel high on my head, like a Shinto priest's tall conical hat. Steven calls it my candle. Now he smiles at it with his eyes. Raising his eyebrows at me, he tries to hand me the phone, mouthing, "It's Martha. She wants to say hi."

"Not now," I whisper. "I need to dry my hair. Give her my love."

I bend my head over the heater by the window, my hair cascading like a waterfall. The low morning light begins to slant through the *shōji*, drawing shadow patterns of squares and disjointed angles on the tatami. Martha's voice crackles over the line. That familiar voice and soul, the bond of their fifty years of siblinghood, all soothe Steven. She lifts his spirits, offering that rich connection with family and home that he craves, a poignant reminder that he needs to persevere and find a way out of this.

Martha and I are Steven's main support in Kyoto. I appreciate the way she bolsters him. But I don't yet recognize that I could've joined with her for a unified effort, instead of resisting her calls. I don't appreciate how hard it must be for her, thousands of miles away, frantic and terrified for her brother's safety, wanting to save him yet unable to.

I move to the kitchen heater to finish my hair and to give Steven privacy. Then after his call, I putter in the kitchen, recognizing he likes quiet space after the intensity of their talks, first digesting it, before reporting it to me. Opening the kitchen door a crack, I peek in.

"C'mon in," he says.

I join him on the large floor cushions by the window, the sun now streaming in through the *shōji*, turning the tatami golden. "I'd love to hear her news."

Steven pauses thoughtfully, his hand smoothing the front of his wool shirt in a repetitive circular pattern. "She's trying to use her connections to set me free. A friend of hers—a prominent San Francisco attorney—is going to contact Senator Barbara Boxer. Maybe she can call some key Japanese official or the American consul and put some pressure on." Steven's voice sounds optimistic. But for me, a senator feels remote, alien from our life here. How can she possibly help?

"I'm afraid it'll hurt; it'll make your case too special, too famous, so they'll have to prosecute to save face," I say.

"It's worth a try," Steven says.

To myself I think, we have no way of discovering if the senator will really call, what she'll say, how the Japanese will respond. But we can only cling to the glimmer of hope Martha offers.

"What'd she say about Robert?" I ask.

The hope drains from his face, leaving it pale and stiff.

"Did something happen?"

"No." Steven sits up straighter, stretching his spine tall. "It's happy news, but . . ." His eyes fill with tears as he buries his face in his hands. Shaking his head, he looks up. "Robert's getting married in July. I'm very, very happy for him." He wipes his eyes.

I wrap my arms around his shoulders.

He blows his nose. "I'll never get out of here by July. I can't bear to miss my son's wedding." His voice is choked with pain. He jumps up, pacing the tatami from wall to wall with quick short steps like a caged cougar.

Now tears spring to my eyes. "We have to proceed as if we'll be free by then," I say.

Steven gives me the details about the wedding: the live jazz quartet, the many family dinners, the rabbi from New York, the outdoor ceremony by the pond. Martha's told him the dates she'll arrive on Nantucket, the name of the cottages where we'll all stay, the car she'll rent for us. But we must immediately book our own flight to Boston and our own cottage.

Sitting back down, he says, "Maybe I'll talk to the prosecutor, convince him to let me go to the wedding. I could promise to come right back. They believe in family—the Japanese. And in weddings."

"You can try," I say, in a flat voice without conviction. "If you're allowed access to him." To me, it sounds like pure fantasy. But anything that gives him hope or a reason for action seems worthwhile.

In silence, I study the gray shadows of the bamboo leaves rustling against the *shōji* windows. This one's hitting him hard. Finally he's feeling the consequences. Nothing matters more to Steven than family. He's always been especially close to his three children, the same way he's close to his sister. Ever since his divorce from their mother, when they were three, five, and seven, he's worked hard to be an active father, not merely a Sunday father like many of his generation. He was the one to take them to the dentist appointments, the emergency room for stitches, horseback riding in the canyon, kite flying at the beach. He especially identifies with Robert, a graduate student, already a serious scholar, a future professor.

I look up at Steven. "Okay. Let's pretend. You're good at that. I'll call the airlines. You reserve the cottage." I hand him the calendar. "When should we fly? How long shall we stay?" I don't believe any of this. But it gives him confidence. And me, too. "I'll book a flight from L.A. Surely we'll be home by then."

He closes his eyes, a smile flickering over his face. I imagine he's dreaming of the wedding on the island. Watching his son and the bride standing under the huppah, beachcombing with his three children, cooking family brunch with his sister, and the whole family—nieces, nephews, cousins, in-laws—clustered around a huge picnic table overlooking the ocean.

We're bicycling toward Zuiko-ji, a nearby Buddhist temple, to see a calligraphy exhibit. The fresh spring air is laden with plum blossoms that pinken and whiten the shiny blue sky. Steven plunges into our excursion with exuberance, his black curls dancing, his eyes gleaming as he sings out hello to each new blossom. I'm surprised and delighted he's agreed to come along. It's the day after Martha's call.

We're both trying to forget our worries, about the senator and the wedding. And to escape a new worry that looms. The lawyer called this morning to say that any day now the prosecutor might call Steven in for the next step. But, as usual, the lawyer doesn't seem to know what that step might be. Or maybe Steven can't understand his English or is too spacey to take it in. It seems to be part of the legal strategy, to keep us in the dark. I could ask Tom or the consulate, or go to the lawyer with Steven. I hate not knowing.

But by now I've pulled away from the legal trouble, letting Steven handle his case on his own. I've been doing that ever since the week when Chris was gone, and I sat in the Kimono Lecture surrounded by my four dear friends. Ever since I recaptured my own life.

We glide through the city streets, Steven racing ahead and then hovering at a corner for me to catch up. "Stop," I say, "we're going in circles. We should be there by now." I consult my map and point us in a new direction. After more searching and wrong turns, we find the temple, like the inner square of a maze, much closer than I expected. It's tucked into a neighborhood, hidden by houses and tall pines.

Zuiko-ji is a small temple, consisting of several buildings, a garden, and a Buddha Hall. We stroll the garden, with its sprinkling of flowering plum trees, a pond shaped like a water lily, and two bridges. The long one curves up over the pond; the short low one rolls over a stream. A stone fountain bubbles in between the two bridges.

People from the neighborhood are pouring into the garden from the Buddha Hall, calling out greetings to each other or stopping in the sun in little clusters to chat. An elderly woman with her hair up in a knot walks toward us on bowed legs, a wide smile on her face, drying her hands on her apron.

"*Konnichiwa*," she says, with a slight bow. I glance at my watch; it's only eleven. She's used the afternoon greeting, but I guess it's too late for the early morning one. While rattling off an insistent stream of Japanese that we can't understand, she sweeps her arm toward the open door of a building to our left, where more neighbors are gathering at tables inside. Unsure of what is happening, we follow obediently, the only *gaijin* here.

She ushers us in, shows us where to hang our coats in the hall, and seats us in chairs next to the others at long, bare tables. We are immediately served a tray with two bowls: a small one of miso soup and a large one brimming with hot vegetable stew. Steam and the fragrance of simmering vegetables spill out of the narrow kitchen in back, along with the high-pitched chatter and laughter from the women cooking, probably neighborhood volunteers. It feels good to be cared for.

We eat in congenial silence, soothed by the parishioners' friendliness and the delicious hot food. We've learned from the Suzukis that many Japanese prefer to eat in silence, saving the talk for after. It reminds me of the meals at *sesshin*, Buddhist retreats, in the States. This must be their weekly luncheon after the morning Buddhist service. Neither of us are hungry yet, but we eat anyway because we want to be part of this community, even if only briefly.

Our companions smile and seem to accept us, as if we belong to their neighborhood, almost as if we are not foreigners. After the meal, they don't ask us the usual questions, which by now we've learned to understand and answer in Japanese: where are you from, how long will you stay, what is your profession. It's just as well. Ever since Steven's secret hit the newspapers weeks ago, he's preferred to remain anonymous, avoiding his usual friendly conversations. He wants to not stand out, to be merely one of them.

Watching the others to discover what to do next, we follow them to the racks outside the kitchen and slide our empty trays into the proper place. We walk back through the garden, crossing the curved bridge over the pond, to view the calligraphy exhibit. But all we find is a large, barren room, lined with musty pieces of rice paper, torn at the edges, swiped with awkward black brushstrokes. Probably they have some personal or historical significance to this congregation, but to us they look more like a beginner's work, a student's perhaps, like the ones we do in our class. I lean into Steven's ear, murmuring, "Remember our *shodō* teacher last fall, how she taught you to draw the *kanji* for sake? She slashed those huge orange corrections on yours with a wide brush?"

Steven chuckles. "I made you both laugh by pretending to be drunk." How much fun we had in the back of that class, helping each other with each new *kanji*.

We link arms, heading for our bikes at the gate, the soup still warming us. After crossing over the pond, we pause to admire the fountain. It's a mossy sculpture made of rough black-and-white stone, speckled like a bird's egg. Water gurgles up from the center and then curls back down around its edges. Plum blossoms drift down, sprinkling both water and stone.

A woman, dressed up in a black silk suit, stops us, mumbling something about *ocha, matcha, chadō*. She points across the low bridge on our left toward a wooden hut, about the size of a garden shed. The stone fountain must mark the path that leads to the entrance of this thatched-roof tea hut.

"Are *gaijin* welcome?" Steven mutters to me, stepping back a few paces.

"I'm not sure what type of tea ceremony," I say.

I've attended several classes in formal tea ceremony but still haven't learned all the rules for the behavior of each participant: host, first guest, or secondary guests. I know we'd be secondary, so could mimic the others. The rules take years to learn and practice: how and when to sit, bow, eat the candy, sip the tea, rotate and admire the tea bowl, say the ritual phrases. Each small step has a complex, ritualized procedure. The more I understand, the more I appreciate.

The woman urges us on, her whole face smiling as she stretches one arm toward us, the other toward the tea hut. "*Dōzo, dōzo,*" she says, "Please welcome, please go ahead."

We cross over the stream, tread on the stepping-stones of the garden path, glide open the door while holding our breaths, and peek in.

Inside sits a man wearing an elegant pale brown kimono, his sleek black hair thinning above an aristocratic face. From his position by the fire, I recognize him as the host, who will both prepare and serve the tea. His four guests kneel near him on the tatami, around a sunken, glowing charcoal fire over which hangs an iron teakettle. Next to him is a tray with all the proper tea utensils, made of bamboo and enameled lacquer. Since he's already begun the ceremony, we start to back out. He glances up. "*Chotto matte,*" he says, with enthusiasm in his hearty voice, indicating we should wait outside for a few minutes for the next round.

We return to the fountain and wait on a wooden bench.

"I don't want to wait," Steven says.

"He seems sincere about including us."

"I want to go home." He pops up, pacing back and forth on the curving, earthen path. "I don't want to be trapped in there."

I pat the bench. "C'mon, sit down. This looks like a simple ceremony. Probably only an hour, or less. Not like that all-day affair at your *Rōshi's* house on New Year's." I'm puzzled. This is not the old Steven, the anthropologist eager to plunge into any interaction with the exotic culture. "Steven, I want to do this."

We stay.

It's cool in the mossy garden. The stream under the bridge hums, an occasional bird chitters, and the distant sounds of subdued voices drift out from the calligraphy hall.

I imagine how it will be if we go inside. The brilliant colors of the red enamel tea caddy, powdered green tea, and lustrous tatami; the sounds of water poured, tea whisked, tea slurped in politeness; the communal silence, like *zazen* with the *sangha*, broken only by occasional, quiet ritual phrases between host and first guest; the grassy fragrance and soft texture of tatami; the bitter, foaming tea complemented by the overly sweet *okashi* candy; the rough texture and irregularities of the raku pottery tea bowl, about the size of a slightly lopsided cereal bowl, and the revelation of its beautiful design of glazed swirls at the bottom. Most of all, I yearn for the intense concentration, the complexity broken into tiny separate steps, and the meditation of it all, when I let myself sink in.

We sit in the garden, stroll, sit, wait, debate. The congregation of men and women leave the calligraphy hall, strolling the garden path home, bubbling with animated conversation.

Steven starts down the path toward our bicycles.

"You go on home. I'm staying," I call out. I'm firm and determined, happy by now to let him go. Steven turns back and settles down again next to me.

I'm about to give up when the door to the tea hut slides open, the four guests emerge smiling, two in kimonos, two in Western dress. They step down onto the large flat entry stone, cross the bridge, and pause at our bench, bowing. The host beckons to us from the door. I grasp Steven's hand and we walk the stone path toward the tea hut, one stepping-stone at a time.

"*Hai, hai*, yes, I understand," Steven repeats again and again, in between long silences, nodding his head, bowing into the phone. It's very early on the morning after the tea ceremony. Steven has run to answer the phone while I hasten to light the kerosene and put on water for tea. He stoops over the phone with its short cord, shivering in his pajamas. I wrap his thin *yukata* around his shoulders as he covers the receiver and whispers to me, "It's the lawyer."

"*Dōmo, dōmo arigatō gozaimasu*, thank you very much, goodbye."

Clutching the receiver, he begins to set it down, then clenches it with both hands as if to break it in two. He raises his head to look at me, fear and panic twisting his face. "The prosecutor."

"What, what?" I rush to him.

He glances at his watch. "I've got to catch the next train to Osaka."

He hurries to dress in his best suit and tie while I help him pack his briefcase. We've no idea what this summons means. As always, it could be freedom. It could be prison. It could be a huge fine. The lawyer has said there will be no trial; that isn't how the Japanese legal system works. Instead, these lengthy Police Interrogations, then a prosecutor, instead of a judge, makes the final decision. All we know is the Customs Police sent their report to the prosecutor and it's still in his hands. Fukuda, the lawyer, will go with him today, but we don't know if he will be allowed to plead Steven's case at all.

At the door, I wrap my arms around Steven's waist, pressing him to me, belly to belly. We linger, holding onto one another. Once again, I don't know if he will return. I've been lulled by these thirty-one days of waiting ever since the Interrogation ended, have forgotten that daily terror as he set out each morning for the Customs Police office. Now he pulls away, his face as gray and taut as a slab of granite. Straightening his shoulders, jutting out his jaw, he marches down the path. I understand how scared he is. This time he takes no toothbrush, no change of underwear, no plastic bag. Not like he used to do during the Interrogation, in case he was sent directly to prison.

It doesn't occur to me—or to him—to accompany him. Steven now prefers to handle his legal case by himself. Perhaps it's his penance. Perhaps he's protecting me. We're both caught in the web of Japanese rules, or at least in our perception of them. The wife does not go along; her job is to stay at home and wait. I wish I'd asked him if he wanted me to go with him. Or even insisted on it. Walking him to the train station, or sitting next to him on the train during the one-and-a-half-hour trip to Osaka, holding his hand. Or walking him to the prosecutor's door. I do none of this. I sense that Steven wants to be alone with his own thoughts on this next journey, probably to meditate on the long ride. Maybe this is best—I do not know for sure.

I close the door, walk to the phone, and call Clover. I can't stay home all day, roaming the house alone. I tell her I need to see her, but I don't say why. She suggests we meet for an origami demonstration in downtown Kyoto. I catch the next train out.

I rush up the elevator of the high-rise office building and search for the correct room. Finding Clover in the back row, I slip into the chair next to her. When I murmur to her where Steven is today, she folds both arms around me.

Up front, a young Japanese man is creating magic with paper, right in front of our eyes. With incredible ease and sleight of hand, he twists, folds, and bends colored papers of all shapes and sizes into a sculpture that grows and grows until it's taller than he is. The colors and folds are like those of a Heian kimono, the outer layer all lavender, with endless robes underneath, each one peeking out at neck and cuff and hem, glimpses of scarlet, mourning dove gray, and a touch of peach. The shape isn't realistic, not the usual origami crane or boat. To one person, it might be a huge cloud adrift at sunset, to another person a smooth river boulder, catching the glimmer of the water in its many curves.

He begins a new sculpture, and another and another: pieces of paper, big or small, smooth or rough, elaborate design or plain, layer on layer, each one ending up as a new spontaneous work of art. Colors flash, pliable papers wind inward and outward, every sculpture unique, with smooth graceful curves, soft and feminine. The papers crackle in the silence, and the audience breathes out oohs and aahs. Each creation is indescribable. They evoke emotions that soar, plummet, rise again, like when I listen to Bach or Debussy.

> Two hands bend papers
> mauve seashell curling inward
> when will I find my way?
>
> — PATRICIA DOVE MILLER

Drawn into this magnetic world with Clover next to me, I can forget Steven and the prosecutor for a moment. When the demonstration is over, we circulate the room, admiring each finished piece. The shadow of each sculpture dances against the room's plain white walls. It's a palace filled with glowing seashells, shimmering ocean waves, and the beckoning interiors of Georgia O'Keeffe flowers. I dream I can crawl inside, become one with the magic, and fly to faraway places, both safe and mysterious.

I hurry off alone to catch the bus to connect with the train to Fushimi. I'm not sure when Steven will arrive. But I want to be there. The views from the train window flash past like a silent movie on fast-forward, shapes and colors without sound. I can't absorb them. Will his news be good or bad? What if he never comes at all? But another part of me doesn't want to return to Fushimi and have to face the next step. I want to preserve the peace of the origami world. I wish I'd accepted Clover's invitation to wander the open produce market with her, to bask in her geniality and in the vibrant colors and tangy smells of the market stalls. But I must get home. To Steven.

When I enter the house, I smell the sweet tang of a tomato sauce, with sautéed garlic and onion permeating the air. Steven is cooking! A very good sign.

Flinging my arms around him from behind, as he keeps stirring, I ask, "How'd it go?" He lays down the wooden spoon and turns to face me. Rich bubbles of thick tomatoes pop and chortle in the pot.

"Great! Nothing happened."

"What do you mean?"

Before answering, he twists around to sprinkle in more oregano, more basil, crushing the leaves with his fingers to release the fragrance. "Fukuda and I stood there a while, a few feet in front of the prosecutor's big desk. Then he stepped forward to hand over that thick file of Letters of Recommendation, and then he rejoined me. The prosecutor peered at the Letters, rifled through them, and added them to a tall stack of papers on his desk, probably the police report about me. Then he looked up at me and mumbled something in Japanese. Fukuda translated: he will study all the papers, make a final decision, and then call Fukuda."

"Didn't he ask you any questions? Why in the world did he make you go all that way?" Why can't I just be thrilled he's home once again, instead of peppering him with anxious questions I realize he can't answer?

"The usual: where were you born, where did you go to grad school, what's your research. I think he wanted to see what I looked like. And what I sounded like." He pauses to taste his sauce. "Look, I bought this roast chicken on my way home."

I realize he means it as a celebration, as a gift, but I'm not there yet. I'm slow to catch up with his joy. "But when will he call?" The tension of the day whirls out in a burst of flames. "I feel all mixed up. All day I was afraid you'd go to prison. And all day I was sure you'd be free and we could finally go home." It seems we remain lurking in that gray ocean somewhere in between, revolving in slow circles.

"Pat. This *is* good news. I'm not in prison. Not yet. The longer the delay, the better my chances."

"But I can't stand it. It could still be days or weeks or months." Now it's me, not Chris, pacing her kitchen, stomping my feet. With my same old frustration—the not knowing, the lack of control. I'm being unreasonable. But I can't seem to stop myself.

Steven sits down, his palms flat on the table, letting me simmer until I sputter out. His belly rises and falls in deep breathing. I understand he's meditating, not allowing me to snatch away his joy. But he doesn't cast down his eyes. Instead his calm loving gaze follows my face. He reaches for my hand, drawing me down into the chair next to his.

"Come, sit down and eat. I cooked chicken cacciatore. Remember, like I made for your birthday surprise that time in Thailand? You'll love it."

He places a steaming plate in front of me. I look down at the breast of chicken bathed in a rich red sauce studded with shiitake mushrooms, eggplant, and zucchini. His distractions have worked, as usual. Picking up my knife and fork, I break into a grin. "Remember how it was almost impossible to find cheese and tomato in the village, and how you had to convince Pa Saeng to kill one of the ritual chickens for our dinner?"

I nudge open the low wooden gate to the house of Sato sensei, Steven's pottery teacher. Strolling down the path through the overgrown garden, I admire the loops of lacy vines that weave the trees together and the wild arms of the bushes that dance and beckon in the breeze. As my hair brushes against one of the flowering vines, a perfumed fragrance cascades down, much like the honeysuckle back home in my own garden that tangles in tousled profusion. As with the garden of Kuroda sensei, my flute teacher, this one contrasts with the neat squares of well-manicured grasses, bushes, and trees in the neighborhood. Those remind me of the temple gardens, as if groomed by an ikebana master, each plant complementing the next, unnecessary branches trimmed away to open up space, emphasize shape, and allow distant views. In Kyoto, I've come to love both types of garden.

I'm here at Sato sensei's house to meet Steven after his pottery lesson. This morning we returned together to this Shūgakuin neighborhood for the first time since our eviction. Today, as we hurried past the looming five-story apartment building, averting our eyes, we didn't speak, trying not to think about that day the police came knocking. Instead, I tried to remember the good times there—our little Christmas tree made of one curving branch that we decorated with colorful silk temple charms, or the Valentine's party itself when I played my *shakuhachi*.

Steven turned to the right up the hill toward Sato sensei's, while I turned to the left, crossing the bridge to Yuki's house, to teach her English lesson. As with Makiko and her two little girls, I treasure entering this world of Japanese women, even for a brief hour. With Yuki, it's the naive world of a twenty-year-old secretary, with her enthusiasm for tennis, her golden Labrador, and her dreams of travel to Italy and America.

Finished with my lesson, I tap on the front door of Sato sensei's house, a small one-story wooden cottage next to Tom's. I've never been here before and am not sure what to expect. I introduce myself to the woman who answers. She's in her sixties, wearing the ubiquitous apron. Her black hair is pulled back into a low bun, instead of the usual short perm common among women her age. Wrinkles from years of smiling crease her face. This must be Mrs. Sato. She bustles me inside, with many bows and smiles, apparently excited to meet Steven's wife. She hovers while I untie my shoes and slip into the guest slippers she's set out next to me. Then she leads me down a cool, clean hall with gleaming polished wooden floors. After perching me on a smooth handcrafted bench at the edge of the pottery studio, with a good view of the students at work, she serves me a cup of *sencha* and an *okashi*. I bow a silent thank-you, not wanting to disturb the students' concentration.

I've only seen *okashi* offered at formal tea ceremonies, never in a home. This is one of my favorites, covered with sugary green icing, decorated with a pink plum blossom design, and filled with a sticky, slightly sweet red bean paste. The *chawan* feels paper-thin and delicate in my palm as I cradle it, taking tiny sips. I feel as if I'm holding a large tulip blossom, the way the round cup curves up in overlapping subtle folds, softening the fluted edges. With its dark purple-chocolate color, it could be a piece of candy itself. It must be one of Sato san's porcelain cups that Steven has described to me with admiration.

As I drink my tea, I watch Steven and the other students in silence. The damp and dusty smells of clay, and the thwacking of the slabs as the students wedge it, saturate the air. Sensei gives me a silent bow, then circles slowly to help each student. He's the same age as his wife, his thin hair pulled back in a long, straight ponytail down his back. He wears an indigo work shirt and pants, baggy and loose with ties at the waist, the traditional garb for both workmen and artists.

The students sit or kneel on the bare floor, working with lumps of clay or half-finished pieces at small platforms in front of them. Steven sits among them, absorbed with forming a porcelain incense burner, his face glowing, the happiest I've seen him in almost two months. When I murmur an answer to Mrs. Sato's question about more tea, he glances up at the sound of my voice, for an instant raises an eyebrow, his whole body smiling, then quickly resumes his work, not losing his focus.

At last he's found his own haven, his hands immersed in clay, puttering and experimenting, among the camaraderie of his fellow students and the guidance of his Sensei. I've never before seen Steven as an artist. I remember him bent over his desk in his study in Topanga, pouring over his books and encyclopedias, fussing with his papers, pen in hand, writing his own books. Always the industrious professor. Like my father. Always an appreciator of the arts, a museum-goer, but never a doer with his hands like this, his imagination running free.

One of the students offers me a piece of clay and a place to work. I decline, feeling shy, though I'm enveloped by their hospitality. No paranoia here, no treating us like criminals, to be avoided or feared. I let the flow of mellow chatter and swish of working hands wash over me, partly wishing I could be part of their group, working with my hands, with Sensei guiding me. But, no, I have that already with ikebana. I prefer to sit back, relaxing into my tea and observations.

When Steven finishes for the day, Sato san rises also, beckoning for him to wait in the hall by my bench. He disappears into a back room, reappearing a few moments later. He holds a ceramic piece in both hands, lifting it up above his head toward Steven as he bows his head down, a traditional respectful way for gift giving, but unusual from teacher to student. It's an exquisite square box with a smooth opaque finish. The lid has notched edges that create a kind of crooked jack-o'-lantern grin, making a perfect fit. The glaze is the ocean at dusk, the fine blue-black line at the horizon, stretching toward home.

Before dawn Steven and Chris sneak off to a sumo match in Osaka, a major daylong event with all the big-name wrestlers. I can hear their giggles disappear down the path as they set out through the morning fog. I imagine their shadowy shapes loping past the dark closed-up shrines and altars, too early even for the priests to begin their morning fires and smoke. It's a Tuesday, March 23, only four days after Steven's visit to the prosecutor. We're still waiting.

Steven and Chris rose at this awful hour so they could take the long train ride to Osaka, then wait in endless lines for hours to buy tickets for the match. He would never do that with me. We would've talked each other out of it; he would've complained about the hassle, the discomfort, the lack of sleep—and the endless waiting. Steven hates waiting in lines of any shape or purpose. Why is this event so different for him?

I lounge in bed, cozy and alone. Thank god Steven has left the heater in our room for me. I was not invited to go to sumo. I don't want to go. I don't want Steven to go either.

Last night in bed, our only private place to talk, we waged yet another battle over Chris. Realizing how thin the walls were, I whispered to him, "How can you spend a whole day with her?"

"She's an expert on all their bios and wrestling records. I like having a native guide. She'll explain each move."

"I wasn't going to tell you—" I jerked up to a seated position. "When I told my women's group where we were staying, they all gasped, urging us to leave right away. Chris beat up one of her tenants—with her fists." I don't understand why I hadn't told him before. Maybe I was trying to adopt Steven's approach, ignoring the negative. Or trying to accept his tentative friendship with her. But ever since I heard this news a few days ago, it had been poking at me, not going away.

"But I'm intrigued with sumo. Anyway, I don't believe it. I'm not afraid of her."

I fell silent. For me, trapped with Chris all day would be far worse than trapped in a tea hut on my knees, not certain how long it will last. Maybe he didn't hate her as much as he said. Maybe it was the anthropologist once again, eager to study the culture and learn.

He curled his arm around me. "I want this as a special gift to myself."

"Okay," I mumbled. Right then, I decided to not fight him anymore—at least not about her. A long tiring day would take his mind off his troubles. Besides, I had my own special day planned.

I rouse myself from my snug bed—Steven and Chris have been gone for hours—and get dressed for my trip to Ellen's house. She's my ESL teaching buddy from the women's group. We like to compare notes about our teaching techniques, our students, our very different lives in Japan. We've seen each other often at the group, chatting afterward as we stroll toward Demachiyanagi station, before going our separate ways home. On one of these walks, I confided my secret—long before I told the group. But there's never been time for the whole story.

Gradually our friendship has grown, she quickly becoming much more than a "green tea" friend. We've spoken frequently by phone and have made several dates to meet for tea. But each time, as with so many of my friends here, I've had to cancel our dates at the last minute—to rush off to the lawyer's office with Steven, to xerox or deliver yet another Letter of Recommendation, to bolster his sagging spirits, or even to escape to Tsubaki by the sea. Now at last we'll have some real time together. This will be my first visit to her home.

Like the first trip to my flute teacher's house, this one is a long bus and train ride to an unknown part of town. As I watch out the window for the correct bus stop, I have much more confidence about finding my way or asking for directions than I did six months ago for Sensei's house.

As the bus glides and skims around corners, I think about Ellen's story. I've learned she escaped a dead-end blue-collar job at a print shop in New Haven to try this Japan adventure for a few years. A new life, like a pioneer woman fleeing to California by wagon train. Except at first there was no wagon train, no circle of support. She and her husband are barely scraping by, unlike the younger and single *gaijin* English teachers who are able to piece together several lucrative jobs, managing to live well and save for their return home. Ellen struggles with expensive day care for her five-year-old and with high rent in a good neighborhood in order to be close to both work and childcare. She supports her husband whose only job so far is playing the violin in the park, his hat out to collect yen coins.

I step off the bus and follow her detailed directions for the two blocks to her house. When I walk up her path, she flings open the door with a big smile, clasps both my arms, and pulls me to her. "You made it! Welcome! Come on in."

She guides me into her living room, nudges me toward a huge ragged, over-stuffed chair, with a pale pink chenille bedspread thrown over it. "Make yourself at home. I'll make us tea. Green or black?"

I huddle into the soft chair and glance around her living room, with its sleek wooden walls, plaid gingham curtains at the windows, and a ceiling held up by thick wooden beams. The house has a homey, lived-in quality, reminding me of my days as a single mom. The furniture is well-worn, flea-market style. Toys, dishes, and books are scattered all over the room. The kerosene heater radiates next to me, smoothing away the cold drafts and musty smells typical of these old Japanese houses. I feel safe and cared for.

Ellen returns, carrying a chipped orange enamel tea tray, with Western cups missing their handles—more flea-market items. She's in her mid-forties, her hair a short blonde cap with a few silver strands lacing through, her body tall and slender, with a strong, angular New England face and a no-nonsense attitude of stoic perseverance.

She fills my cup with *sencha*, then leans forward with her elbows on her knees. "What's happening with Steven's case?"

I spill out my story, from beginning to end, unburdening myself at last with its entire fullness, as I haven't with anyone else. The room stands silent, only the clock on the wall ticking, the ancient walls sighing, and the sound of our two voices ebbing and flowing. I shake with emotion as I speak, reliving each difficult scene. Pulling the chenille off the chair, I wrap myself in it. Ellen tucks an old knit shawl around my shoulders. I hadn't expected to tell her in such detail. At last I have the luxury of time and privacy.

She offers her full sympathy, listening intently, asking questions at key points, echoing back my feelings, and even suggesting gentle opinions. Ellen's close to my age, and she's been through hard times herself, unlike some of the other friends I've made here. Ellen's the only one who really understands where I've been. She's refused to discuss her past troubles, even when I try to draw her out, but I sense my story strikes a chord with her. In spite of our different backgrounds, I've finally found a real soul mate here.

We rouse ourselves out of the depths of the cozy chairs. I feel as if I've been here all day, not merely two hours. Ellen jumps to her feet. "Let's go out for lunch! I know a good fish fry place on the corner."

Outside, I blink into the bright sunlight and let the warmth of the air float me away from the burdens I've left at her house. The restaurant's a modest lunchroom, clean, airy, modern, and anonymous. I eat as if I haven't eaten for weeks—a huge platter of *kaki furai*, deep-fried oysters. She insists on paying. I'm sure she can't afford it and argue with her, but she holds firm. I sense it's her way of comforting me, a gift that's important to her to be able to give. I accept with gratitude, a bow, a laugh. "Okay. *Dōmo arigatō gozaimasu.*"

While we saunter back to her house, I urge her to tell me more about her life here. She anticipates finding a better teaching job, one with higher wages and fewer rules. Her current one, teaching English to preschoolers, feels like a straitjacket, with no freedom, no creativity. Like me, she's come to Japan to find herself, to find her true passion. Recently, she's finally discovered painting, and in her spare moments she's now taking lessons in watercolor with a Japanese artist, working toward her first show in the fall.

As we walk through her front door, she asks me about my teaching in the States. I mention that I've learned a new technique with my fifth graders, called Writer's Workshop, a method that allows writing freely within a simple structure. I explain that we taught the children to have a daily writing schedule—first thing in the morning, for half an hour. They could write whatever they wanted and never had to show it to anyone. We taught them about peer feedback; they could read a portion of their work to a small group of fellow students and receive respectful suggestions, about what worked well and what might be improved. But a student never had to read aloud. In 1990, these were brand-new ideas in Los Angeles private schools.

I tell Ellen that when I tried writing with them, it gave me the freedom I never had as a child, when struggling over rigid assignments, writing on topics that didn't interest me, with outlines that cornered me into a box, with excessive emphasis on grammar and punctuation that stifled me. The teacher never spoke of creativity or imagination. For a shy child like me, never having to show the work or read it aloud would have been an inspiration, a blessing.

"I've just the book for you," Ellen says. She leads me upstairs. My slippers pad on the well-worn boards of the winding, narrow staircase, and I dip my head to avoid bumping the slanted dormer ceilings of her bedroom, which is strewn with clothes and papers. Light peeks in from high windows laced with cobwebs. She seems comfortable with the chaos, not apologizing as many women would.

"Here," she says. "Borrow this. I bought it in New Haven, thinking I might try writing here in my new life, but I've found painting instead. Why don't you try it?"

Curious, I slip it in my pack, hug her goodbye in the downstairs hall, and start for the bus. As I settle into the seat for the long ride home, I open the book and begin to read. *Wild Mind: Living the Writer's Life*, by Natalie Goldberg. Immediately I plunge into a world of the imagination I didn't know existed. I absorb each page like a thirsty sailor at sea, trying not to race ahead with excitement, and barely noticing the bus stops or my transfer points.

With amazement I read that Goldberg's process is like the fifth graders' Writer's Workshop—the same freedom to write whatever I want, writing for a specific period of time, never reading aloud unless I want to. With one huge difference—no feedback from peers. And more structure.

To me, it seems like *zazen* or ikebana—a great freedom within a structure of simple guidelines. Freedom: to delve deep into my unconscious, follow my mind, free-associate, let go of it all onto the page, and move on to the next words. Structure: write in ten-minute segments; write from a prompt to inspire my spontaneous thoughts and run with them; once I begin, keep my hand moving, not pausing to think. And letting go: forget grammar, punctuation, logic; forget being nice or polite. Just write.

I almost forget to jump off the train at Fushimi Station. Arriving at Chris's house, I'm happy to find the house empty. Flinging off my jacket, I grab a fresh notebook and sit down at the low living room table. The clean house bursts with the fragrance of afternoon sunshine and the aged wood of the walls. The heater glows next to me, removing the edge off the chill of the house. The *uguisu* sings in the bamboo outside, and the bells chime from the nearby altar.

I breathe in the solitude and begin Natalie's first exercise: "I remember . . . Go for ten minutes." I write and write, page after page flowing. Her process is awakening in me something I didn't realize I possessed.

This is not like fearing my ninth-grade English teacher who held up the corner of my essay in front of the whole class, pinching it in his fingers as if it were dirty, and saying, "This stinks!" Not like fearing my college freshman English teacher who threatened to flunk me because I didn't know how to write. Not like feeling I never had anything to say. Suddenly I have everything to say, so much that I cannot stop. The words, thoughts, feelings flood onto the page.

I didn't understand writing is about playing with words, playing with images. Like playing with ikebana flowers, removing them from the vase again and again, trying each time a different way. Like playing with the musical notes of *shakuhachi*, feeling the music in my body intuitively—instead of slavishly scribbling notes in my notebook—becoming one with each phrase, then letting it go. Learning to focus on ikebana or *shakuhachi*—or writing—as a meditation, not on a later performance or display. I didn't know art is all about the process, the playing, the experimenting, the trying; it's not the end product that matters. I don't know where this process of "Writing Practice" will lead me, but I know I love it already.

The jangle of the phone on the table jolts me. Who can it be? I don't want to answer. Glancing out the window, I see the sun has left the *shōji*. Soon it will set. I've been writing for hours—way past the suggested ten minutes. The phone, for me, usually means bad news. During those long days when Steven was interrogated by the police, I startled with every ring of the phone. Would this be the one saying he'd been taken to prison? The phone screams at me, insisting, bouncing off the silent walls. Or it meant Takeda's wife evicting us, or Denise threatening me. I glare at the incessant black ringing. Probably it's for Chris. Or maybe it's her calling about Steven. Oh no, maybe something terrible has happened to him.

My fingers tremble as I place them on the black receiver and lift it toward my ear inch by inch. "Hello," I say, not "*moshi moshi*," as Steven does. I want the caller, whoever it is, to speak English to me.

"This is Fukuda." The lawyer. Speaking in better English than I've ever heard him use. My knees tremble. I can't catch my breath. All the blood and energy drain out of my body.

I tell him Steven is gone for the day.

"The prosecutor decided last Friday not to indict your husband." The monotone of his voice plods, dry and matter-of-fact.

This time my heart leaps to the top of my head, rolling with handsprings, with somersaults. I can't believe it. We're free!!

But then I protest silently to myself. Did he have to wait four whole days to tell us? Why do I always flash the negative side? Of course, Fukuda doesn't work on the weekend, maybe not even on Monday. He doesn't realize we've been waiting for this call since January 29, counting each day for fifty-four days.

"Madam?"

"Yes."

He continues, more friendly now, as if he knows me well, as if we've talked often. "There will be no indictment," he repeats. "Your husband must come to Osaka tomorrow, to retrieve his passport." He pauses. "He is required to leave Japan within two weeks."

I repeat it back to him, word by word, to make sure I've heard it right. My mind races with questions: Did our senator intervene after all? Did all those Letters help? Can Steven ever return to Japan? Instead, I only gasp, "I am so very happy. Thank you very much. I will tell Steven."

I lay the receiver down in its cradle. Bursts of bubbles flood my whole body, each one holding a rainbow, like when you blow them in the sun. I can't think where to run with my joy, who to tell. Steven needs to be the first to know, but when will he be home? Chris was vague. I want to call someone, to shout it from the porches, from the trees. I could call home, to Mom, to Martha, to our children. I could call Ellen or Clover. Or Tom, Takeda, Fumiko Suzuki. No. It has to be Steven first.

I shove my writing book, notebook, and pen into our room, slide the door shut tight, turn off the heater, and dash out the door, grabbing only my camera. There's exactly enough time for a walk before sunset.

I skip up the path into the forest shrine. We're going home! Steven has a passport! It's over! I thank every corner of my forest, circling all my favorite paths. Each gray stone fox grins, each resilient bamboo frond bends and caresses my arm, each pine showers its tangy resin into the dusky air, each orange *torii* gleams, blessing me as I pass under. At every miniature altar, I light shimmering candles, ring tawny bells, and press my palms together into a *gasshō* prayer. I click photos everywhere, trying to preserve it all. The green bamboo sways up toward the pure blue of the sky and sings in the wind to me, "You are free, you are free."

At sunset, I return from my jubilant walk and cook a zucchini quiche to celebrate. While it bakes I meander the house, step-by-step, breath by breath, playing "Kyorei," "Empty Bell," on my *shakuhachi*. The notes bubble up, overflowing the room. I hover on the joyous ones that sound like a waterfall. I blow strong and clear. As the last phrase of my song tapers to the end, the front door clicks open.

I race toward it. Steven stands there, all alone.

"Steven! Steven!" I grip both his shoulders, laughing and crying at the same time. "Fukuda called!"

He steps back, startled, uncertain how to interpret my tears.

"You're free! We can go home!"

He scoops me into his arms, and we waltz round and round on the sweet fragrant tatami, as the bells and gongs of the shrine ring out their evening song.

CODA
A Rainbow of Streamers

Nothing changes. Everything changes.

Steven and I still begin each day with our morning tea, sitting on top of our tufted blue futon, with the herons' wings soaring across the sky, and under our maroon quilt, with its profusion of meandering blue and white flowers. We fill the burnished-gray teapot three times and sip our *genmaicha* together while chatting about our feelings and thoughts for the day.

Kuroda sensei strides toward me across the wide expanse of plaza, grass, and trees on the University of Colorado campus. We look up at the same time and recognize each other. His face breaks into a wide smile. When he reaches me, he stops, bows from the waist. Then with that same sparkle in his eyes and with a new warmth, he clasps my hand in both of his.

"I so very to see you," he says. I almost don't notice the missing word in his greeting, since his voice resonates with joy.

It's been five years since Kyoto. I'm here for a weeklong international *shakuhachi* festival with teachers and students from all over the world, including all the great masters from Japan. I saw his name in the program but didn't expect to connect, still fearing his reaction to my letter.

"How are you *now*?" he asks, still holding my hand, his eyes searching mine. The unspoken questions: Have you recovered? Are you okay now? Is your husband okay?

When we left Kyoto, I couldn't say goodbye because he was still in Thailand on his trip with his family. Soon after I returned home I wrote him a detailed letter, telling him exactly what had happened, why we had to leave so suddenly, what Steven had done, and asking him to understand. I didn't know how he'd react, but I needed to unburden the secret, bring some closure for myself. He might accept us as part of the artists' world or the Western world. He might condemn us. He never answered.

Now here he is in front of me grinning, with that same thick black hair streaked with iron-gray, that same white smile. I have been forgiven.

We do not speak again in Boulder, but I attend all his performances and workshops, as well as those of the other teachers. A week of pure *shakuhachi*, pure music in the mountain air. We *shakuhachi* players are a rare breed, but as I sit playing and listening with three hundred fellow students and teachers, I'm inspired and comforted by this community.

Over the next several years, Kuroda sensei travels once a year to Berkeley to give a weeklong workshop. I attend every one. There, I meet a disciple of his, an American man who studied with him in Kyoto for many years, and I travel north from San Diego once a month to study with him.

Seventeen years after Kyoto, I still play the *shakuhachi* daily and take lessons every few months from my Berkeley teacher. Kuroda sensei no longer comes to California. Now he teaches a workshop every summer in the Rocky Mountains outside of Boulder. I haven't made it there yet. But I will.

Before we leave Kyoto, we do give Takeda his gift of the indigo pillow with its ocean-wave design. We invite him to Chris's house in Fushimi, on an evening when we know she'll be out. Steven cooks a feast of Thai specialties—the main dish is *geng khiaw wan*, green curry with chicken, the same dish he wanted to make for Kuroda sensei before he went to Thailand.

Takeda and Steven sit drinking sake, sitting around the low table on the tatami. I serve a steaming pot of fluffy jasmine rice and three serving bowls overflowing with the dishes Steven's prepared, then join them.

As they linger over the meal and resume their rounds of sake, I wash the dishes, listening to their laughter from the kitchen, peeking in now and then to watch. They sink lower and lower onto the tatami, their elbows propped up on cushions as they sprawl late into the night. Laughing, telling stories about living in Spain and Thailand, resuming their long-ago debate about Italian opera and Japanese kabuki. As if nothing ever happened. As if all is forgiven, their friendship restored. And perhaps it is. At least for this moment, this evening.

We never hear from Takeda again, nor do we try to contact him. We learn from a friend that he soon retired, moved to Spain to live once again with his wife and children.

As we stand on the dock of Kamijima Island watching Fumiko and Hideo Suzuki depart, the people in the stern toss out streamers of long multi-colored ribbons that unfurl and float out onto the water. An old custom, a way to say goodbye, to keep the connection until the very end, a way to let go. We watch the colors grow smaller and fainter in the distance. They seem to last forever. But suddenly they are gone.

The Suzukis have given us this goodbye gift of a trip with them to this tiny island off the Shima Peninsula, a few hours south of Kyoto. As usual, they arranged it all: the train, the meals, the boat to cross over, and the side trip to pay our respects to the eighth-century Ise Shrine, the mythical home of Amaterasu, the sun goddess who created Japan. The four of us climbed up and down the hills of the island, on meandering paths and vertical stone steps—there are no roads—visited all the many shrines, walked round and round the circumference at the shore to see endless ocean vistas, no land in sight. We spent the day together, and then before they left they arranged for us to stay overnight in a *minshuku* by the shore, ordering us special menus for dinner and breakfast. And then they were gone, back to their own lives, the streamers trailing behind.

As their colorful ribbons fade into the horizon like a sunset, I feel as if our positions are reversed. They return home while we stay on the island. But it's our time to return home, only two days from now.

Alone on the island, we say our own goodbyes to Japan, revisiting our favorite shrine atop the tallest hill to bow and clap our hands, strolling the paths once again, chatting with the fisherman about his views of the war as he mends his nets at the dock. As we sit on the beach gazing out to sea, collecting seashells to take home, our hands touch. Arms around each other, we spin our dreams for America and our new life there.

Then it's our turn to board the boat, toss our own rainbow of ribbons, watch them stream out far behind, slowly fading into the wake, as the island becomes one tiny blip on the horizon, like the green flash at sunset.

At first, our marriage struggles. Yet like the butterfly tree that fell almost to the ground in a storm, we begin to grow again. Month by month, year by year, new deep roots, long leafy branches, and tender blossoms.

We spend the first month in the States at Martha's, waiting for my tenants to leave my Del Mar house. I choose to stay with her so she can help me with Steven. I can no longer take care of him alone. Martha and her husband comfort us, feed us, give us wise counsel.

We live in a small wooden cabin in her backyard that's only slightly bigger than our four-and-a-half-mat room at Chris's house. Many nights at Martha's I bolt upright at two a.m. and flee to the spare room in the main house. I can't stand these four walls closing in, can't bear to be cooped up with Steven. I know they often lock the spare room door from the outside before they leave for work each morning, to keep the cat out. So I tack up a sign on the outside of the door: "Don't lock me in."

Steven and I are sitting on Martha's wooden deck when she calls out to us from the kitchen. Denise has left a message for him on her machine. Once again, she's tracked us down. As I argue with him, the hot sun broils my head, the wood burns the soles of my feet, and the dusty purplish-red bougainvillea leaves droop above me.

"You can't call her back," I scream at him. "You promised you'd never speak to her again."

"But, but," he sputters, pacing in front of me.

Martha stands at the door, watching us. Even though she's a professional therapist, she holds back, wanting to let us work this out ourselves. Finally, she steps forward, sits down next to me, lays her hand on my arm. "I think you need to let him make this one last call."

"No. I can't. She ruined our life. I don't want him in touch with her."

Martha persists gently. "I know, Pat, but it will bring closure for all three of you. He needs to tell her directly to never call him again. He has to be strong." She puts her arm around my shoulder. "And so do you."

Steven retreats inside to the far room to make the call in privacy. He returns quickly, with a determined stride, his face serious, yet light and clear. "I'm done with her." His arm slices through the air in a sharp downward stroke. "She didn't like it—argued with me—but I held firm and hung up on her."

I believe him. I'm not sure why. Perhaps I feel safe on American soil, safe in Martha's home. I believe our ordeal is finally over.

And it's true: He never hears from her again.

"Is the envelope ready?" Douglas asks Steven. He's the therapist Martha found for Steven the week after we arrived home.

Steven pulls an envelope from his pocket that contains his last stash of marijuana from Topanga. Even though it's small and white—not large and light brown—that familiar pain jabs my stomach like a jagged saw.

Martha, her husband, the therapist, Steven, and I are all gathered in our Del Mar living room for a ritual that Steven and Douglas have planned. With a serious intent face, Steven holds the envelope in both hands against his chest. He carries it to the brick fireplace, where he's already laid a small pyre of newspaper, kindling, branches, and logs. He props the envelope between two branches. It blares ghostly white against the blackened sooty cavern.

Steven turns to us, bows, gestures for us to stand and hold hands. He closes his eyes and takes three sturdy breaths, then passes out copies of the Heart Sutra, a Buddhist chant. His voice leads the way, rich and sonorous as usual. My voice rises steady to join him, the others softly following.

Kan ji zai bo sa gyo jin han nya ha ra mi ta ji
sho ken go on kai ku do issai ku yaku . . .

Steven moves to the fireplace, kneels, murmurs another prayer to himself, strikes a match, and touches it to the envelope. It bursts into flame, blazes sharp and uneven, lighting the kindling and releasing an acrid-sweet smell. The smell lingers in the air, then slowly fades up the chimney with the smoke and disappears. The envelope dissolves into loose gray ash as the fire glows and blazes light and clear.

Another bow and then he rejoins the circle. Douglas steps forward, presenting him with a small gift of congratulations, a finely turned wooden vase with a sprig of caspia, a dried purple flower that will last forever. He gathers Steven in a strong hug. Martha and her husband step forward to do the same. I am last, with a hug and a kiss.

Steven never smokes again.

Our life of adventures finally resumes.

We are speeding north up Interstate 5 to our temporary home for the summer in Santa Maria, a dusty farm town in Central California. The old black Volvo sedan is piled high with all we will need for three months there. An old brown futon is tied onto the roof of the car. Before we left, back in our Del Mar driveway, we stood on each side of the car on tiptoes, stretching to tie on the big double futon, wrapping the rope round and round to secure it. This is not our Kyoto futon with its heron-wing design. That one's too precious. Instead, this is an old foam hand-me-down from Steven's daughter.

Steven will spend the summer doing his first regional theater job, as Peter Quince in *A Midsummer Night's Dream*. I will work on my writing, then drive further north to my first conferences—at Squaw Valley and Napa—to begin my pursuit of the writing life. Then back to Santa Maria for more writing, more time with Steven.

Suddenly a gust of wind, a horrid flapping noise, a tearing sound, and out of the corner of my eye, I see the futon fly into a field at the side of the road. Steven screeches to a stop. We plunge down the grassy slope to rescue it, slipping and laughing at the absurdity of it all. How could we be so stupid to think our rope would hold the flapping wings of foam when we drove sixty-five miles an hour? Amidst more laughter, we wrestle it back up to the car, dust it off, and tie it on, more snugly, with more layers of rope. We continue up the highway, this time at forty, my hand out the window onto the roof, and stopping every few miles to check the futon.

This move has taken lots of planning, with numerous long strolls along the same Del Mar beach where we had courted, with sanderlings and godwits scurrying at our feet, and foamy ocean bubbles on the sand ebbing and flowing toward us and away. We hashed out how to make Santa Maria work for both of us, whether to do it or not, the pros and cons, the conflicting emotions, mine and his. He's been honing his craft in San Diego theatres for the past five years, and now it's time for him to move on to the next step in his new career.

It's the beginning of our new vagabond life together as we live all over California, following his regional theatre gigs—two or four months at a time—in Santa Maria, Walnut Creek, Lake Tahoe, Nevada City, San Francisco. Once home from Kyoto, he retired from the university, turned his back on academia, and soon launched a full-time second career as a professional stage actor, eventually winning the Bay Area Shelley Award for Best Supporting Actor.

Now on our way to Santa Maria, six years after Kyoto, we're recommitted at last, once again fully in tune, fully in trust. More so than ever before. A new strength, a new blossoming.

"Is this *the* Pat Dove?" Ann cries into the phone. "We lost you, we didn't know where you'd gone. All our letters were returned."

"I guess so." I've never been asked this before; nor do I usually expect people to remember me or my name. "This is the Pat Dove that used to come to retreats there. We've been in Japan."

I sign up immediately for two retreats in a row. The first one will be Ann's "Zen and Art." I will escape alone to Zen Mountain Center, where I first heard the *shakuhachi* played four long years ago.

When I arrive at the grounds of the Center the very next weekend, I'm immediately reimmersed into my Japanese world. The huge wooden sign with its bold embedded black calligraphy greets me at the entrance. Small carved stone Jizō statues dot the wooded paths.

Ann throws her arms around me. "We've missed you. Welcome back." She ushers me into the rock-lined tearoom where the host whisks *matcha* and passes around the ceramic communal tea bowl. A wooden gong calls us to meditation in the *zendō*, and a melodious brass bell begins and ends each sitting period. On the altar stands a simple ikebana of mountain lilac and pine branches, and the smoke of incense drifts around the room. Next we walk in silent meditation up and down the mountain trails. Laughing at myself, I realize for the first time how much of Japan is embodied in Zen practice. At night we gather around the campfire under the stars, listening to the *shakuhachi* player blow his songs. The same man who played years ago at four a.m. in the pine forest.

The next morning I play my own *shakuhachi* by the waterfall upstream. In the afternoon we spend a full hour rolling out long wide pieces of butcher paper onto the floor of the spacious *zendō*, taping them down securely, to cover every inch of the thin brown rug. The teacher carries in buckets of thick black paint and a few full-size white mops, with floppy white strings at the end, like a rag doll's hair. First she demonstrates, then tells us to do anything we want, as big as we want.

I pick up the mop, dip the dry white head into the thick paint, twirl it into a compact globe of black. Standing poised over the long white panel of paper, my mind is empty, my paper is empty, my brush is full. Leaning my whole body into the brush, I move my arms, my body in huge circles as I waltz down the aisle of white, playing with the ink. A swirl, a squiggle, a circle, a long heavy stroke, a short light one. I am becoming the brush, becoming the black curls on the white canvas.

Surrounded by mounds of quince, stock, and camellia spread out on the table, and in buckets on the floor, we sit around Mrs. Jones's dining room table, a group of women dedicated to ikebana, some American, some Japanese. We all work in quiet concentration, with an occasional murmur in a blend of the two languages. I've begun a new ikebana apprenticeship with Mrs. Jones, a woman in her sixties, born in Japan, married to an American sailor after the war, now a well-established master teacher of the Ōhara tradition, the same one I studied in Kyoto. I attend weekly lessons at her home. Her Japanese art collection of paintings, screens, scrolls, ceramics, dolls is arranged all over the walls and tables. She's much like my Kyoto Sensei, but her boisterous laughter alternates with a strict gruffness that hides her kindness. And instead of kimono, she wears Western gabardine slacks.

As she moves around the table, making slight alterations, improvements, suggestions, she peppers her fluent English with Japanese phrases.

"*Sensei, watashi mo mite kudasai.*" I'm asking her to come take a look at my ikebana.

"*Jōzu desu ne,*" she exclaims, applauding my language as well as my flowers.

Sensei doesn't treat me as a beginner. She gives me credit for all my lessons in Kyoto, copying down the dates from my calendar onto the Ōhara "attendance card." It seems to me you're ranked more for how many lessons you attend, and less for your abilities. Gradually I move up from rank to rank until I receive "Assistant Teacher" status. An artistic certificate hangs on my wall, drawn in curving black calligraphy. But I still feel like a beginner, even though the feel of the flowers now lives in my fingers.

A sweet roasting fragrance floats through the room from the kitchen. She has baked sweet potatoes. Often she cooks something for us to all eat together after we've finished our flowers—a simple lunch, Christmas cookies, *edamame*. But my favorite is these *yaki'imo*. Exactly like the ones we used to buy from the street vendor outside our Kyoto apartment as he drove slowly by, calling out "*Yaa kii mooo . . . yaa kii mooo . . .*" She serves them to us wrapped in a napkin to eat like an ice cream cone, the Japanese way.

I follow the path of Natalie Goldberg's *Wild Mind*. My first summer home I form a writing group based on her ideas, to build a new network of friends, and to learn how to write. We work through her prompts, her chapters, one by one. I follow

Natalie to Spirit Rock Meditation Center in Northern California to attend my first all-day retreat with her. Sitting in the *zendō*, surrounded by my fellow students, I scribble in my notebook from each of her prompts, feeling safe enough to read aloud to my partner in a whisper. She leads us in sitting meditation and on a long silent walking meditation up the wild oak-studded valley behind the center. Right then, I vow that this is what I want to do: lead workshops that combine my three favorite things: writing, meditation, and walking in nature. Two years later, I begin leading weekend retreats at Zen Mountain Center.

In Taos, I attend a weeklong conference with Natalie. She encourages us to read aloud from our notebooks. It will help us let go of our writing and move on. I can read in the small group of five writers but am nervous in the large group of fifty. Finally, toward the end of the week, I stand up and read to the whole group, my eyes on Natalie, her face giving me courage. I read about Japan, about Steven, the marijuana, the anger, the secrets. I break the silence. For the first time, I feel the power of words, the power of speaking them aloud.

When I receive my MFA in creative writing at the age of sixty-six, I write my final graduation lecture analyzing *The Pillow Book of Sei Shōnagon*, the book I first discovered on Chris's bookshelf in Fushimi.

I stand in front of a new audience, my *shakuhachi* held vertically in my hand, resting at my side. My first concert in America. I've been invited to the Fallbrook Haiku Society for their spring celebration to play my *shakuhachi* and join with the members as we read our haiku. A rose trellis blooms above my head. A soft breeze brushes my hair, my fingers.

I arrived early with a bundle of flowers and one of the numerous *suiban* that Steven has created for me at his pottery studio. He's become a ceramicist as well as an actor, creating whimsical garden sculptures, refined tea trays, rough raku tea bowls—all inspired by the Japanese aesthetic of understated simplicity and asymmetry. In the quiet of the rose garden, I arranged white cherry blossom, called *sakura*, yellow lily, and asparagus fern and placed the ikebana on a table near my music stand.

We each recited our haiku. Most of us had labored hours on them to make them sound spontaneous. While Steven listened to each of us read, he quickly jotted down his own, in his usual spur-of-the-moment way. At the end, he stood up to read his.

> Cold coast wind blows me
> to Fallbrook's white *sakura*
> miles are seasons here.
>
> — STEVEN SOLOMON

Now Steven sits in the audience, eyes intent on my face, silently cheering me on. I close my eyes, take three steady breaths. This time, will I manage to blow all the notes, to finish the song? I hold the *shakuhachi* horizontally in both hands, then raise it up a few inches above my eyes as I bow my head, in the traditional manner. I have chosen "Kyorei." I play it strong and clear, the notes breathy and soaring, melancholy whispers and warbling trills, the way Kuroda sensei taught me.

ACKNOWLEDGMENTS

So many people have helped, supported, and inspired me during the long process of making this book come to life. I offer my deepest gratitude to each of them.

Gratitude to my first two mentors. Natalie Goldberg, with her book *Wild Mind*, her Taos workshops, and her "Writing Practice" methods, first opened this world of writing to me. Sands Hall reached out to me when I was a fledgling writer and gave me continual guidance and nourishment, from beginning to end, as mentor, editor, teacher, and friend.

Thank you to my other teachers along the way: Karen Kenyon at Mira Costa College; Steven Kuusisto at Centrum, the Port Townsend Writer's Conference, who urged me to apply to graduate school; Sandra Scofield at the Community of Writers at Squaw Valley. And special thanks to all my mentors at Vermont College of Fine Arts: Laurie Alberts, Phillip Graham, David Jauss, Diane Lefer, Christopher Noël, and especially Sue Silverman, who taught me both the craft and the art of memoir.

I am grateful to my community of writing friends, who have read endless drafts and offered valuable critiques along with constant encouragement: Julie Barton, Betsy Blakeslee, Nichole Gavel, Shirley DicKard, Heather Donahue, and especially Barbara Newhall, my Squaw Valley writing buddy, who is a strong role model, always just one step ahead of me in this process. Thank you to my fellow students at Vermont College: Harrison Fletcher, Lois Grunwald, Dawn Haines, Marie Masters, and especially Patty Oliver-Smith and Janice Stridick. Thank you to my two writing groups: the Rosehip Writers in San Diego, especially Julia Alter Canvin, Liesel Eprile, Dietel Giloi, Irina Gronberg, and Barbara Takahashi, where very early drafts of this book began; and my Nevada City writing group, especially Lea

Barrow, Perissa Busick, Gail Entrekin, Ronnie Paul, Susan Solinsky, and Robin Wallace. And many thanks to other writers who have given me helpful suggestions and courage over the years: Kim Culbertson, Judy Crowe, Tony Eprile, Betsy Fasbinder, Laura Goldin, Donna Hanelin, and Bill Pieper.

I offer gratitude to Deanne Larsen, another Squaw Valley writing friend, who has been a steady advocate and early reader, and who presented me with the perfect book of haiku.

Thank you to my many students who all inspired me and taught me so very much: in San Diego, in Idyllwild at Zen Mountain Center, and in Nevada City. I especially thank Pamela Adams, Joan Griffin, and Barbara Lawrence, who gave me valuable encouragement and ideas during the book's final stages.

Special gratitude to Barrett Briske, my outstanding publishing assistant, who helped me in every way with her efficient, cheerful manner, including with research, permissions, endorsements, copyediting, and much more. And to my two superb, astute, and sensitive editors, Kirsten Painter and Ellen Lesser, whose strong and honest opinions I value. This book would not have been possible without the moral support, insight, and advice of these three women.

I am especially indebted to Joan Keyes at Dovetail Publishing Services for her meticulous work as she shepherded the book through the final stages, from design to printing. I value her calm expertise, artistic sensibility, and warm generosity; she is a treasure to work with.

I also thank Jim Shubin at Shubin Design for his careful and patient work on the cover design; Laurie King for marketing advice; Brad Bunin for legal consultation; Sam Barry, director of the Path to Publishing program at Book Passages Bookstore in Corte Madera, for his good counsel; and Mary Helen Fein at Parallax Design Group and Valerre Aquitaine for their computer expertise and technical assistance.

A special note of thanks to Takayo Harriman for carefully checking each Japanese word and each English translation for correctness and context. And to Christopher Blasdel and Nancy Beckman for crucial last-minute Japanese language suggestions. Many thanks for helpful research regarding Japanese culture, Japanese names, haiku, ikebana, and *shakuhachi*, provided by Nancy Beckman, D. Max Moerman, Eiko Stefanko, Kaoru Sugie, Katsuji Sugie, and Hiroko Tayama.

I appreciate the artistic eyes of friends and family who helped me choose the cover design: Nancy Beckman, Carin Berger, Christian Ford, Barbara Lawrence, D. Max Moerman, Michael Moerman, Kirsten Painter, Luka Painter, and Hiroko Tayama. I am especially grateful to Katsuji Sugie for finding the final cover image, *Bamboo and Plum*, and obtaining permission for its use from the Tokyo National Museum.

A huge thank-you to my steadfast friend, Karen Freeman, who was a welcome cheerleader with her weekly phone calls. She never doubted that this book would happen. And thank you to my loyal friends, Andrea Baruch de la Pardo and Marcelle Cecchin, also regular cheerleaders, who inspired me to keep working.

Heartfelt gratitude to Dr. Jim Stratigakes for giving my husband and me in-depth and invaluable guidance at the last minute when the publication of this book faltered.

I offer my deepest gratitude to my family. First, to my mother, Virginia Dove Miller Russell, for her quiet, loving support during the early stages of my writing this story. She always maintained pride and confidence in me and knew I would persevere and finish the book. During the last few months before she died, she asked me again and again to sit at her bedside and read to her from the manuscript. Second, to my two children, both of whom gave me devoted encouragement throughout the process. My son, Erik Painter, offered me important feedback on early drafts, aided by his thorough knowledge of Japanese culture; he was the first in our family to know and love Japan. My daughter, Kirsten Painter, worked with me on the book during its later stages as advisor and mentor. She was the first in our family to become a writer, and she served as a role model.

Finally, and most important, my immense gratitude and love to my husband, for his continual devotion, compassion, and unwavering support during the long years of my writing this memoir. I admire his courage for blessing its final publication. Even though the subject matter was painful and even though I never let him read the manuscript until it was finished, he respected my need for daily solitude in my studio, and every evening he welcomed me back with a home-cooked gourmet dinner.

CREDITS

ABOUT THE AUTHOR

Patricia Dove Miller is a third-generation Californian, born and raised in the Berkeley hills. She has lived in the mountains outside of Cali, Colombia, in a tiny rice-farming village in North Thailand, and also at the edge of the northeastern hills in Kyoto, Japan. She attended Stanford University and, much later, at the age of sixty-six, completed her MFA in creative writing at Vermont College of Fine Arts. She is also an alumna of the Squaw Valley Community of Writers. She now lives with her husband in the foothills of the Sierra Nevada in Northern California, where she teaches creative writing and practices ikebana, *shakuhachi*, and Zen meditation.

Joel Perlish Photography

CPSIA information can be obtained
at www.ICGtesting.com
Printed in the USA
LVOW12s1403310717
543261LV00003B/430/P

9 780997 253900